*The College History Series*

# Broward Community College

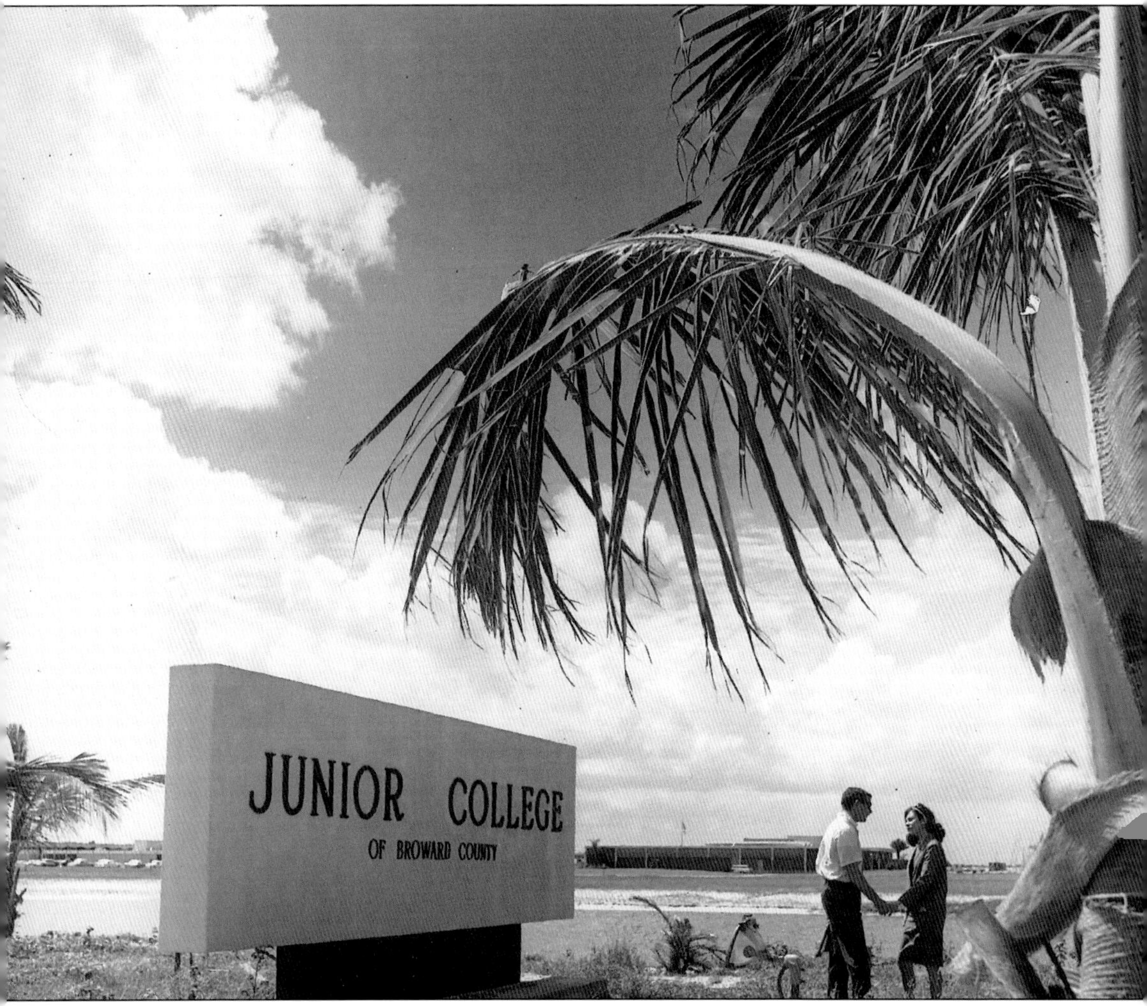


Two students enjoy a quiet conversation in 1963 on the Davie Campus.

*The College History Series*

# Broward Community College

Cynthia Thuma

Arcadia Publishing

ISBN 978-0-7385-1436-9

Published by Arcadia Publishing
Charleston SC, Chicago IL, Portsmouth NH, San Francisco CA

Printed in the United States of America

Library of Congress Catalog Card Number: 2002103386

For all general information contact Arcadia Publishing at:
Telephone 843-853-2070
Fax 843-853-0044
E-Mail sales@arcadiapublishing.com
For customer service and orders:
Toll-Free 1-888-313-2665

Visit us on the Internet at www.arcadiapublishing.com

*Though limited by modest physical stature, Dr. William Alfred Porterfield was nonetheless a giant of a man. As one of Broward Community College's early employees, he had a front-row seat to a considerable portion of college history and a facile mind that retained the play-by-play as well as many of the rich details. His recollections were invaluable in the compilation of this book and in turn, it is dedicated to his memory—he was a kind, patient, and generous educator and gentleman.*

# CONTENTS

# ACKNOWLEDGMENTS

Many people graciously and generously offered their support and reminiscences to assist in the creation of this pictorial history, among them: Judy Bowen, Bill Buckler, Lynn Buford, Gail DellaVolpe, Fran Fletcher, Dr. Bill Greene, Donna Henderson, Terri Justice, Sharon Kelly, Lydia LaCava, John Payne, Tracy Porter, Jillian Printz, Dr. Tom Ryan, Joyce Warden, Julia Wood, and Kay Wynne.

The biggest acknowledgment is reserved for Dr. Will Holcombe, who provided a trove of historically significant pictures, tapes, and other documents for the book. More valuable than the memorabilia, though, was his generous counsel, which was always readily available, and greatly appreciated.

# REFERENCES

Albertson, Harry and James Wattenbarger. "A Short History of Florida's Community Colleges." *Visions*, Spring 1998.

Grazier, Allen C., et. al., *The Community Junior College in Florida's Future: The Report to the State Board of Education by the Community College Council*. Tallahassee: 1994.

Rushing, Joe B. et. al., *This Is How We Started: The Junior College of Broward County*. unpublished manuscript, 1963.

Smith, Walter L., Jr., *The Magnificent Twelve: Florida's Black Junior Colleges*. Winter Park, Florida: FOUR-G Publishers Inc., 1994.

# Introduction

Broward Community College was created at the crest of Florida's wave of support for creating two-year colleges. The Junior College of Broward County (JCBC) was one of four Florida junior colleges to open its doors in 1960. By that time, 10 community colleges were already operating in the state and another 14 were to follow. The last, Pasco-Hernando Community College, opened in 1972.

JCBC welcomed its first class—701 students—in August 1960. Classes were offered in the former Naval Air Station Junior High buildings at what is now Fort Lauderdale/Hollywood International Airport. The facility was spartan, without air-conditioning and possessing only limited parking. Bells rang to signal the change of classes.The only things not in short supply were enthusiasm and sandspurs; the administration and faculty endured hardships just as the students did. The college's first president, a laconic Texan with a reputation as an innovator, had been hired only 90 days earlier.

The Junior College of Broward County was representative of the state's plan to make the first two years of college available and affordable to most Floridians and to offer it to them within 30 miles of their homes.

When the state released its plan in 1957 to create this network of junior colleges, Broward County was not among the original Priority One areas. Broward was relegated to Priority Two-A, which encouraged the county to work quickly toward achieving readiness. In 1959, Broward was ranked Priority One and JCBC was off and running. A group of influential and politically astute supporters lobbied Washington to provide land for the school and got the property they sought—a parcel of land formerly occupied by Forman Field, which was a training field for Naval aviators several miles west of Fort Lauderdale.

While students groused about the temporary facilities, work on the first campus west of Fort Lauderdale began in 1960. The first seven buildings on what is now Central Campus were ready to greet students at the start of fall classes in 1963. From there, the growth in programs, physical stature, and national prestige has been phenomenal.

In just over 40 years, the Junior College of Broward County has evolved into Broward Community College (BCC), an educational institution that draws on the vitality of Broward County and provides a technically proficient work force. The success of Broward Community College helps assure the stability of the community and maintains a high standard of living for its citizens.

From its first day, a heavy emphasis has been placed on quality. The graduates of the college and their achievements have made it evident that the goal of the college has been realized.

Broward Community College graduates serve their community, their state, and their nation in a variety of ways, from the automotive technicians who keep our cars running perfectly, to police officers who keep our streets safe, to attorneys, physicians, dentists, writers, actors, and community leaders.

Just beginning its fifth decade, Broward Community College is a proud and impressive member of the "Great 28" public community colleges in Florida. BCC is still a young institution of higher learning, but already has a wealth of notable achievements, an impressive number of accomplished graduates, and a legacy to be proud of.

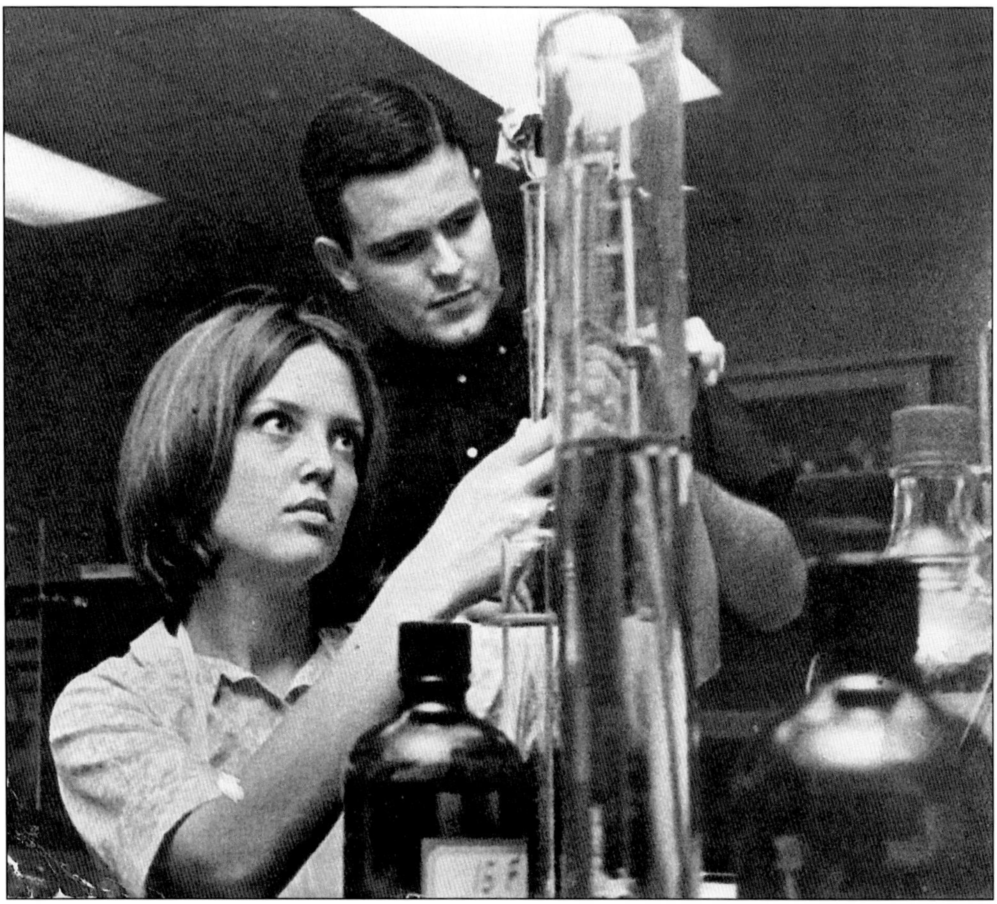

From the college's first day to the present, trustees, faculty, administration, and staff have kept an emphasis on excellence.

# *One*

# The Rushing Era

## A Foundation of Excellence

*A son of the Lone Star State, Joe B. Rushing found the opportunity to preside over the birth and early years of a college that strongly appealed to him. At the time he applied for the presidency of the Junior College of Broward County, Rushing was serving as vice president for administration at Howard Payne College in Brownwood, Texas, his alma mater.*

*Rushing, who earned his Master of Arts degree at East Texas State College and his doctorate at the University of Texas, had also served as director of adult education at Howard Payne and held the same position at Wharton Junior College in Wharton, Texas.*

*He and his wife, Elaine, came east to South Florida and helped coax the young college from the sandy earth where Navy aviators had earlier honed their skills, and before that, where dairy cattle roamed and grazed. His mission was to create a junior college of exceptional quality and he took his charge seriously.*

*Rushing was hired March 17, 1960 and reported to work on April 7. During his presidency, JCBC survived its growing pains and established itself as an educational asset for the community.*

*In 1965, Dr. Rushing announced his departure from Broward County for two reasons that very much pleased him—to return to Texas and to oversee the birth and early development of another community college as founding president of Tarrant County Community College in Fort Worth.*

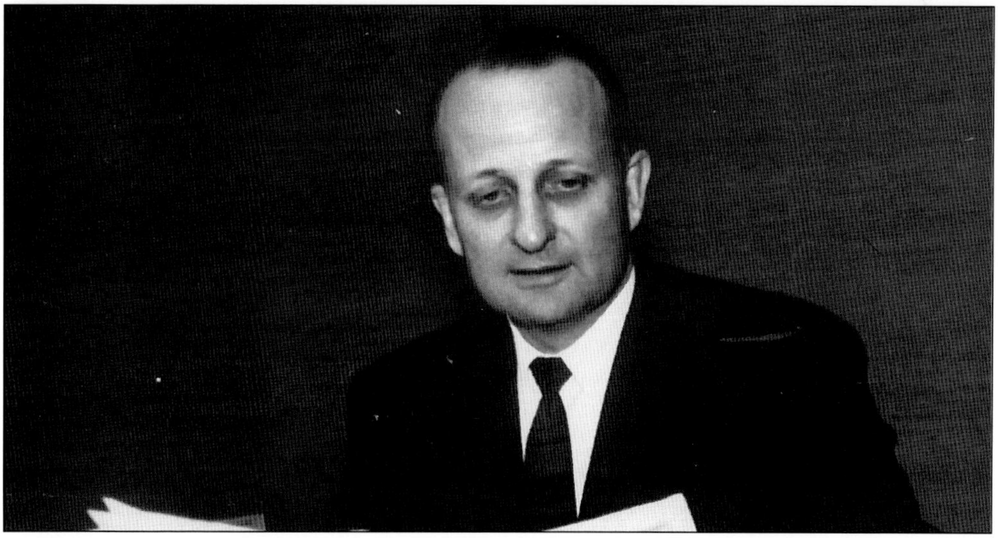

Dr. Joe B. Rushing served as the first president of the Junior College of Broward County.

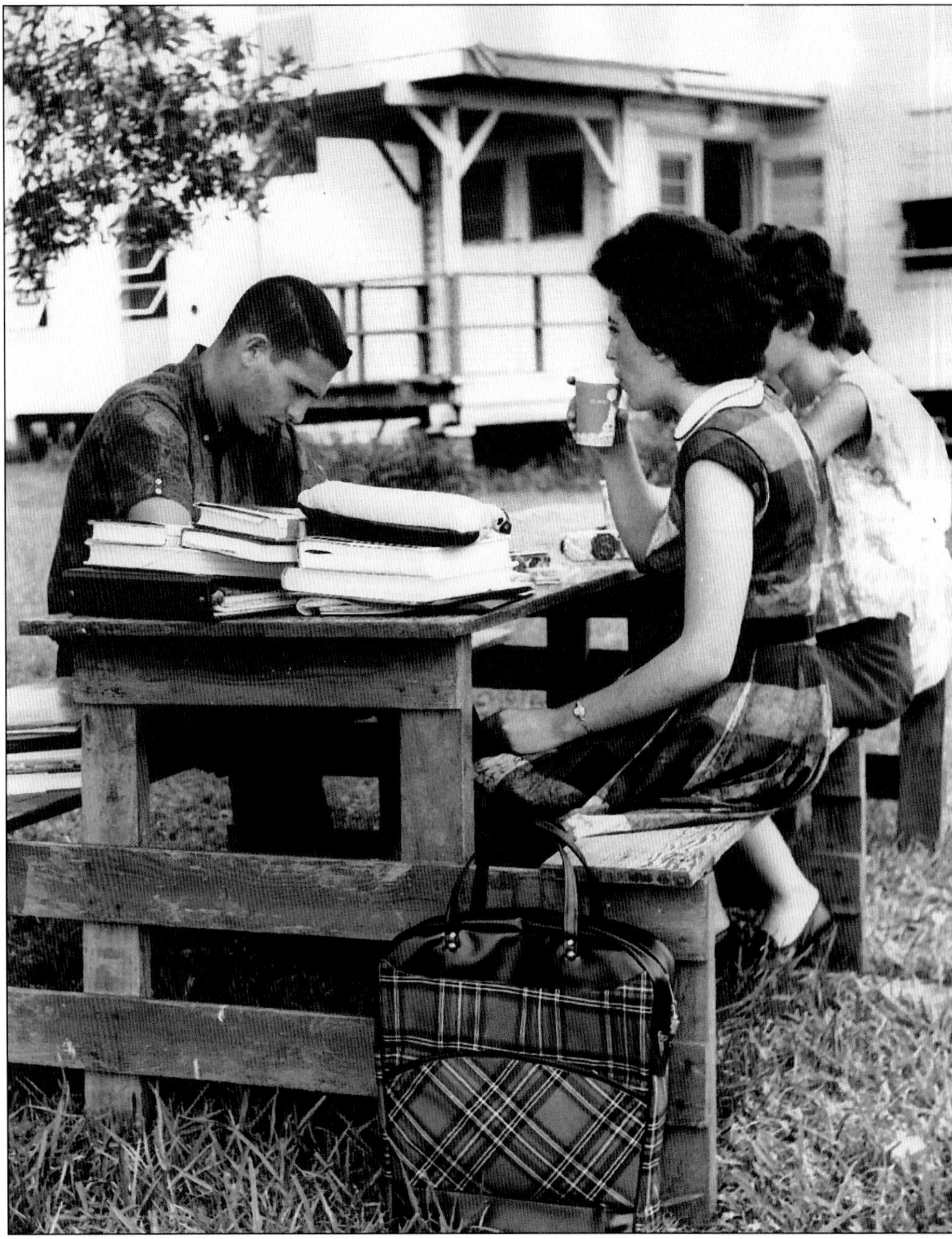

With 28 faculty members, the college opened to its first class of 701 students at the Naval Air Station Junior High buildings on the western edge of Fort Lauderdale-Hollywood International Airport. Classes were conducted there from 1960 to 1963.

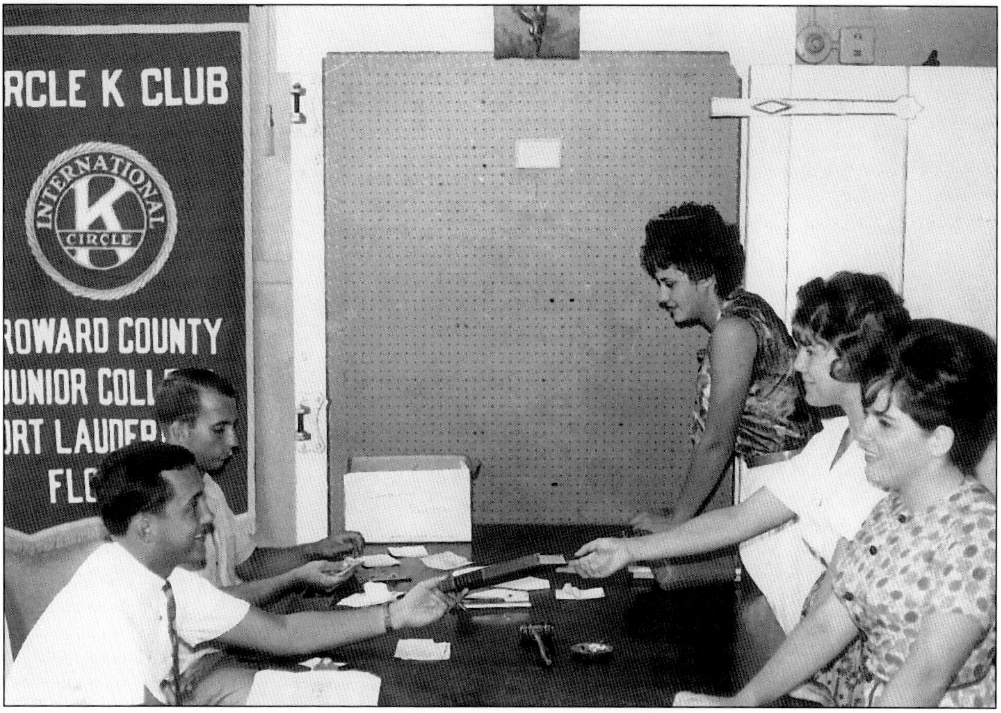


Amenities were few because of the space crunch, but the college offered a variety of student services, service clubs, publications, and interest clubs from the start.

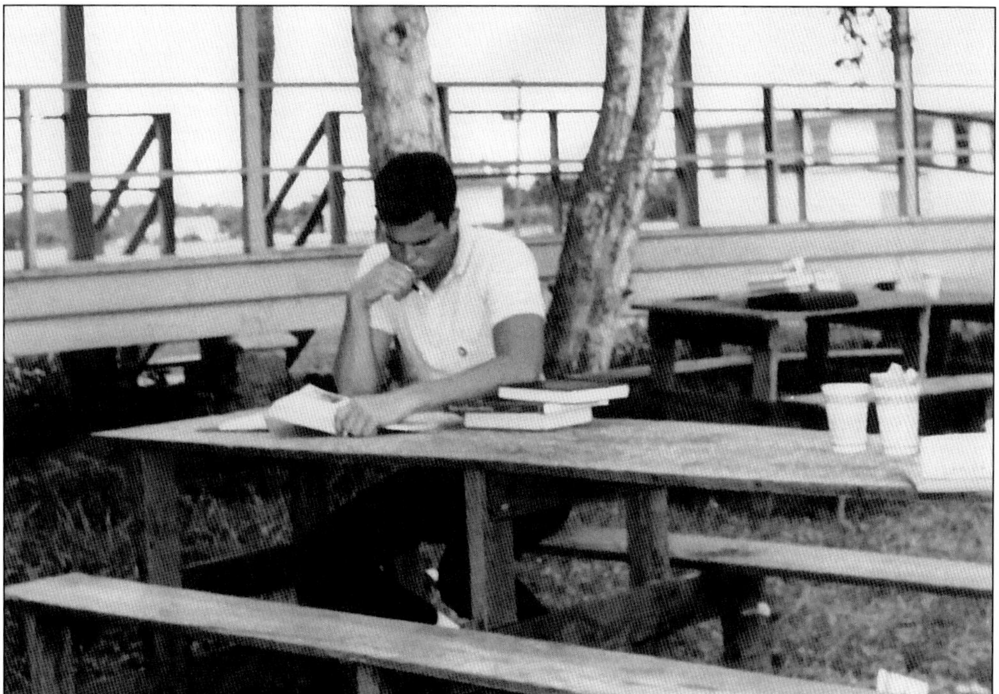

Accommodations were cramped at the temporary site and students had to do their eating and studying outside.

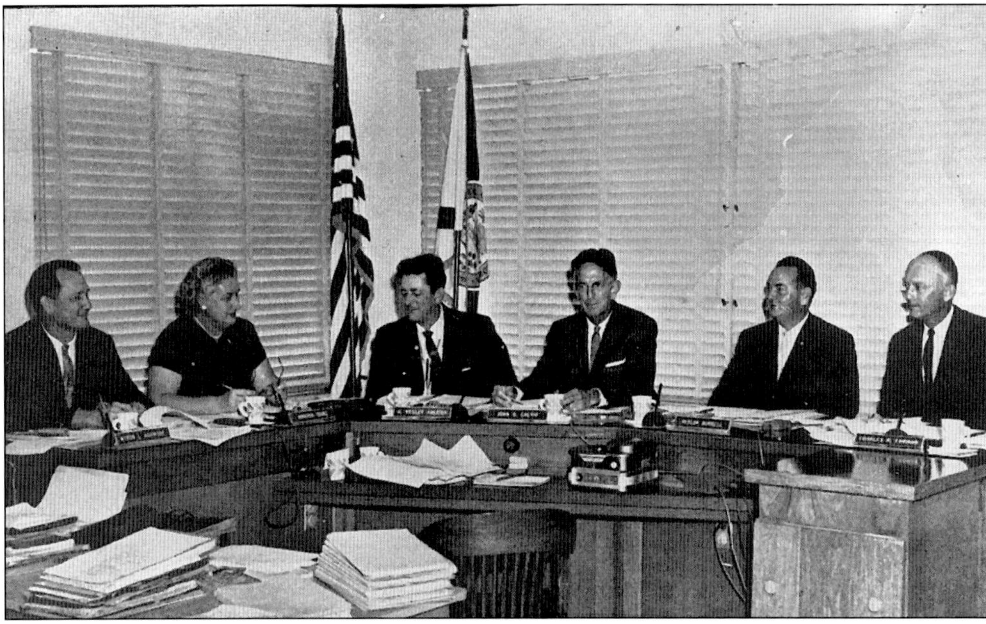

The Junior College of Broward County was first governed by the Broward County Board of Public Instruction with input from the Advisory Committee. Superintendent of the board was Dr. Myron Ashmore, at far left. From his left to right, the members are Virginia Young (the board chair), A. Wesley Parrish, John O. Calvin, Verlon Burrell, and Dr. Charles Forman.

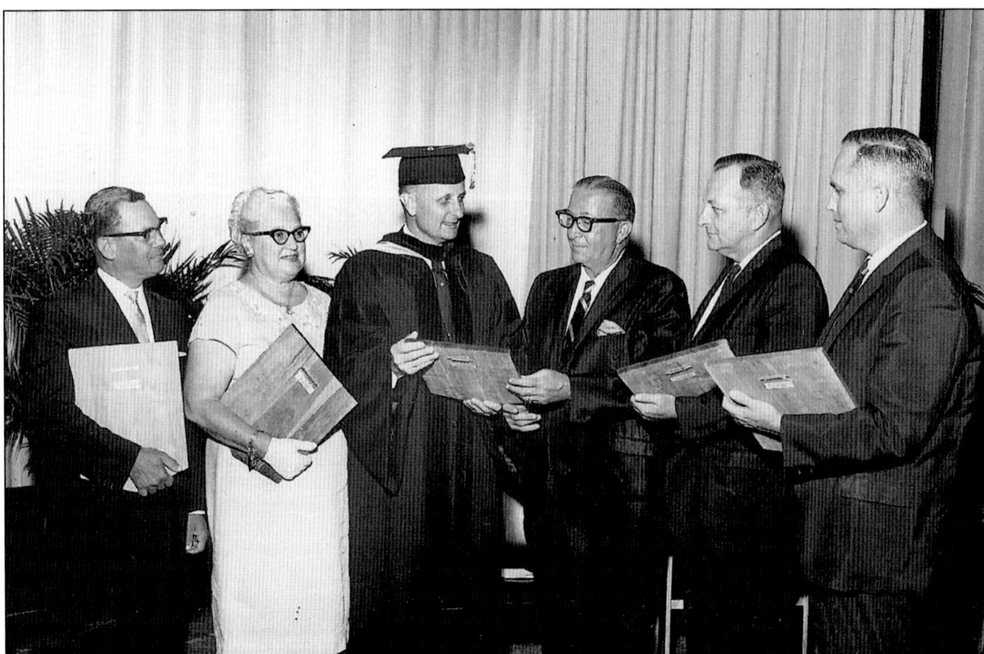

The Advisory Board brought together a diverse group of distinguished professionals and community leaders from throughout Broward County. Dr. Rushing provided the five members with service plaques at graduation ceremonies. From left to right, they are Lloyd Cassels, Florence Tustison, Dr. Rushing, Judson Samuels, Robert Ferris, and John Payne.

Educator Florence Tustison provided important perspective for the advisory committee and board of trustees. Named a "Woman of Achievement of 1953," she was a teacher with a degree from the University of Toledo and did graduate study at the University of Guadalajara, Mexico.

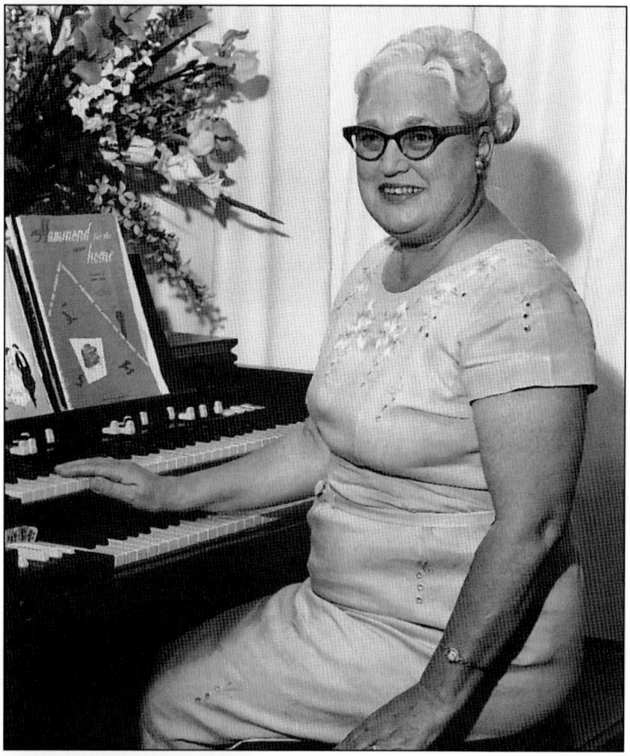

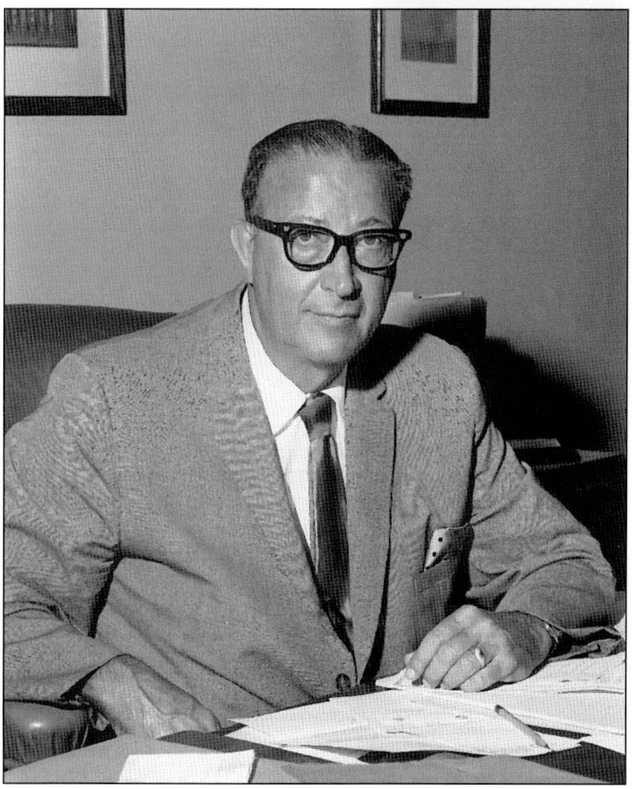

Judson A. Samuels, for whom the South Campus is named, served as a member of the BCC Advisory Committee in 1959 and as a member of the District Board of Trustees from 1971 until his death on April 29, 1974. A graduate of the University of Miami College of Law, he worked many years as an attorney in Hollywood and was a distinguished community activist in southern Broward County.

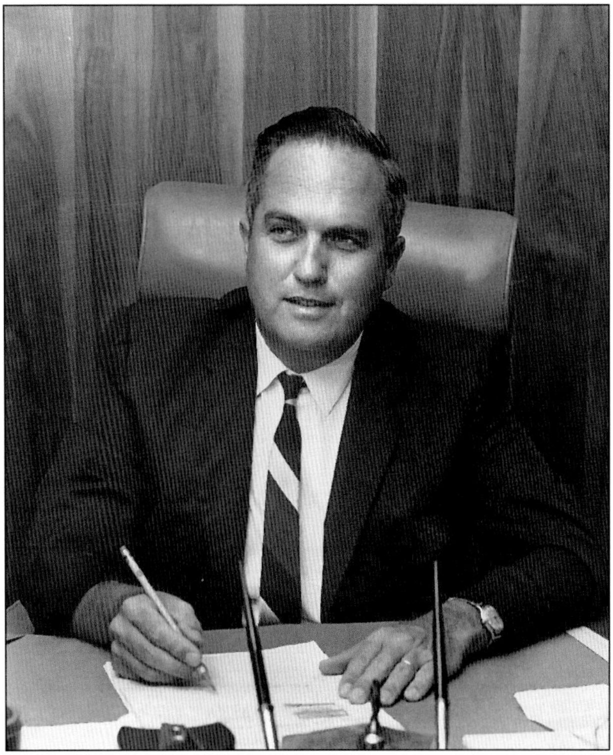

John Payne served as a member of the Advisory Board and also as a member of the BCC District Board of Trustees from 1968 to 1987. An attorney, he is also one of two South Floridians who serves as a trustee to the Emil Buehler Trust, which has provided more than $1 million in support to the college.

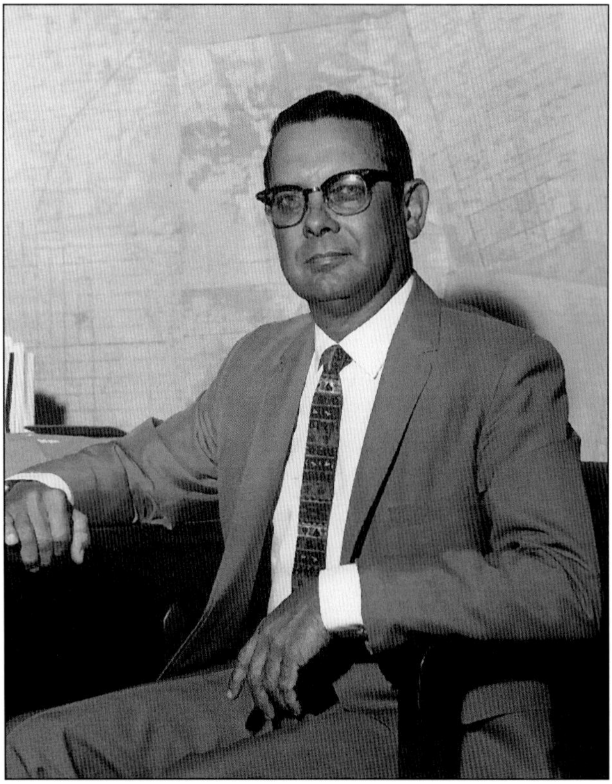

Lloyd Cassels served as a member of the Advisory Committee and as a trustee from 1961 to 1967. Cassels was active in North Broward civic affairs and was president of the Pompano Beach insurance firm of Bateman, Cassels, and Gordon.

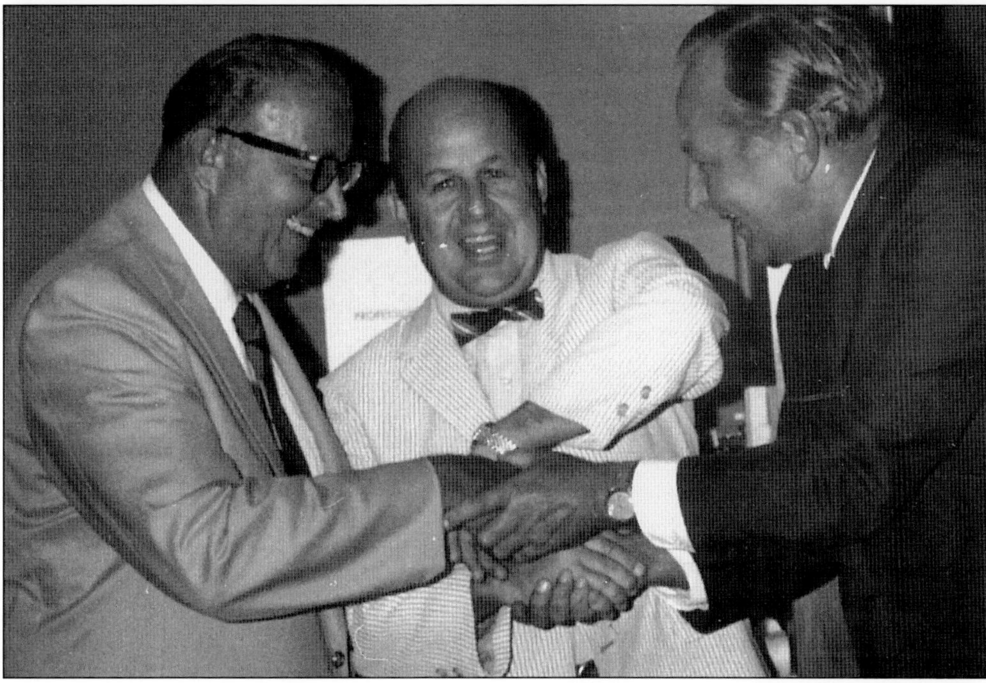

Fort Lauderdale realtor George E. Mayer (center) is welcomed to the board of trustees in 1969 by Chairman Robert E. Ferris (right) and Vice Chairman Judson Samuels. Judge Ferris graduated from the University of Illinois College of Law. Though his background was in law, his interests were in education. In addition to serving on the advisory committee, and later as first chairman of the board of trustees, Judge Ferris served as chairman of the Broward County Board of Public Instruction and as president of the South Florida Educational Center.

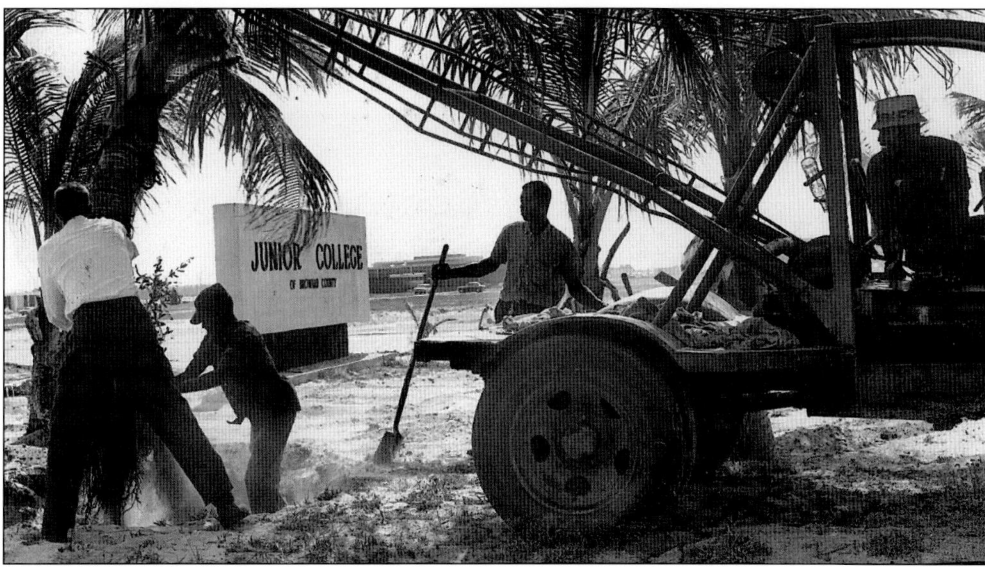


Here, landscape workers plant coconut palms at the east entrance of the campus. When the campus opened in August 1963, it had 7 buildings spread out over 152-acres; it was built on land donated by the United States government. Other fixtures on Central Campus at the time of its opening were temporary trailers for the bookstore and horticulture program.

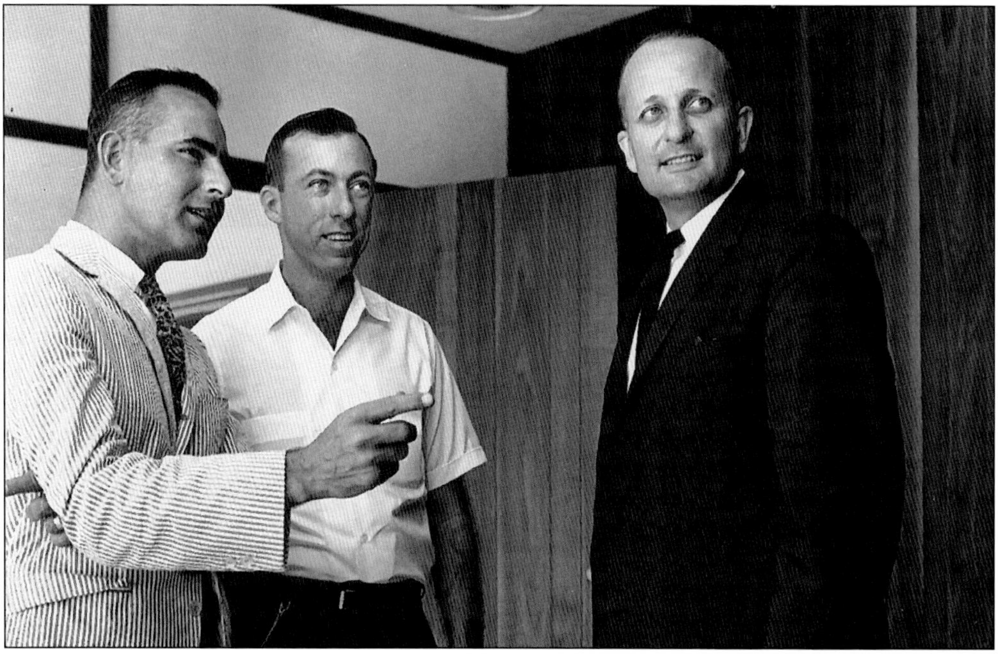

A college architect, Causeway Lumber president Gene Whiddon and Dr. Rushing discuss the president's office at the new Central Campus in Davie in November 1963. Whiddon, a supporter of the college from the start, provided paneling for the president's office. He later became the founding chairman of the Broward Community College Foundation.

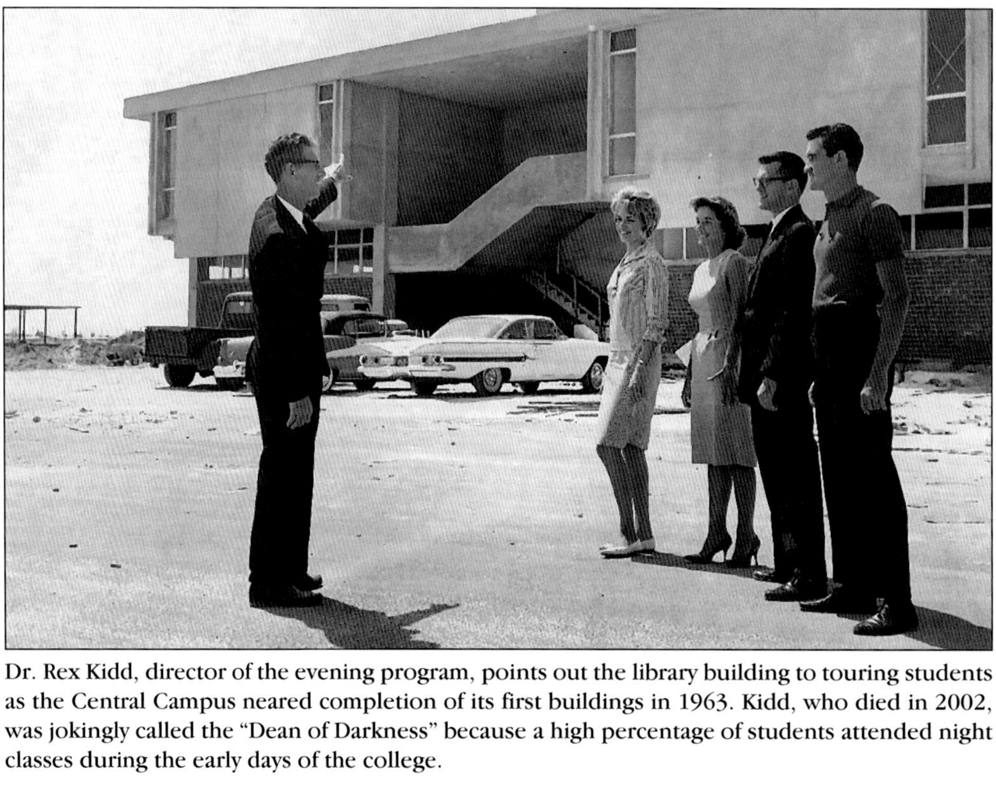

Dr. Rex Kidd, director of the evening program, points out the library building to touring students as the Central Campus neared completion of its first buildings in 1963. Kidd, who died in 2002, was jokingly called the "Dean of Darkness" because a high percentage of students attended night classes during the early days of the college.

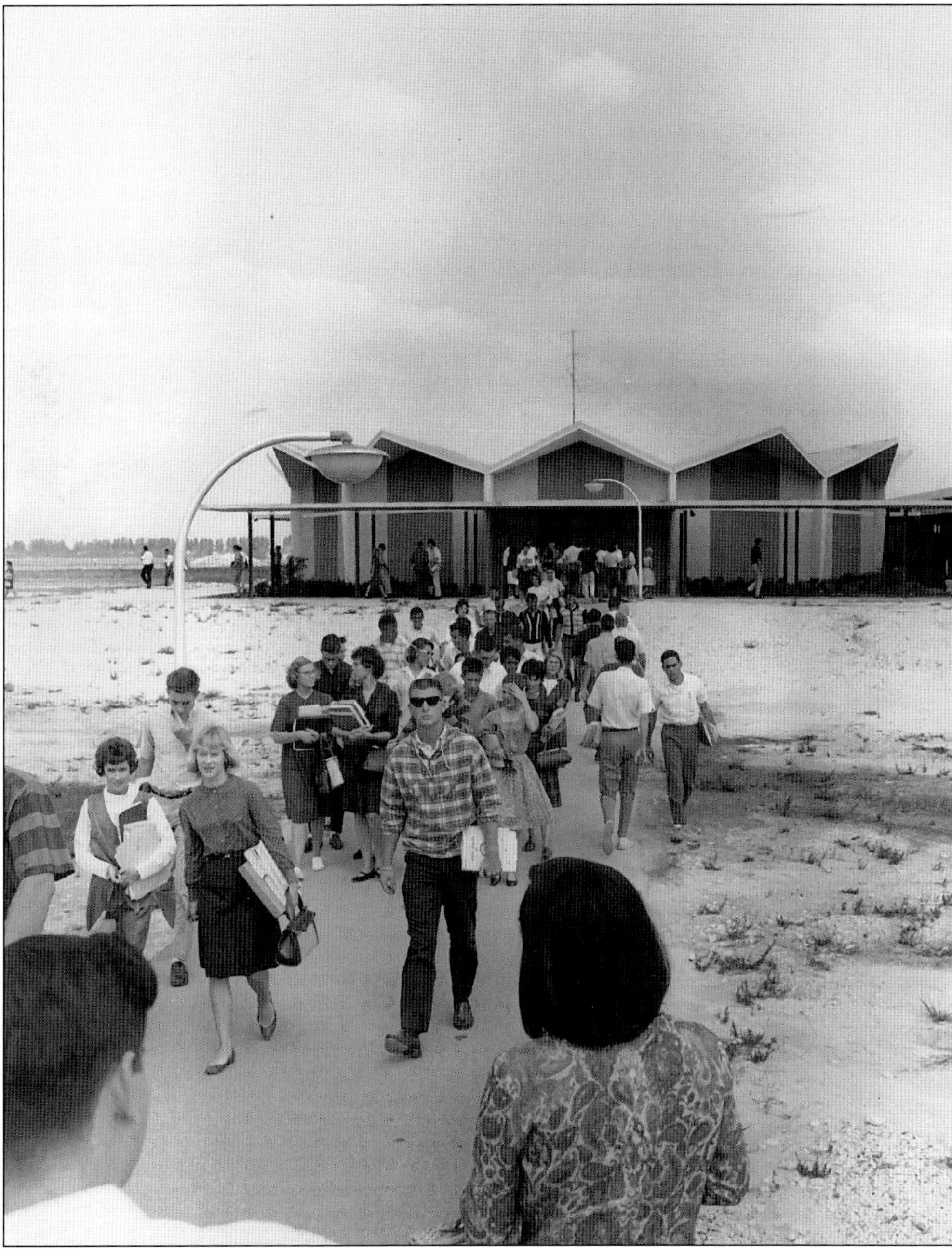

In her autobiography, *Rita Will: Memoir of a Literary Rabble-Rouser*, author, screenwriter, and BCC alumna Rita Mae Brown wrote that the college was "a couple of buildings and a mess of sandspurs." Those sandspurs are evident along the sidewalk from the science lecture theater to the library. The young college, Brown added, "offered little by way of aesthetics, yet a lot by way of education."

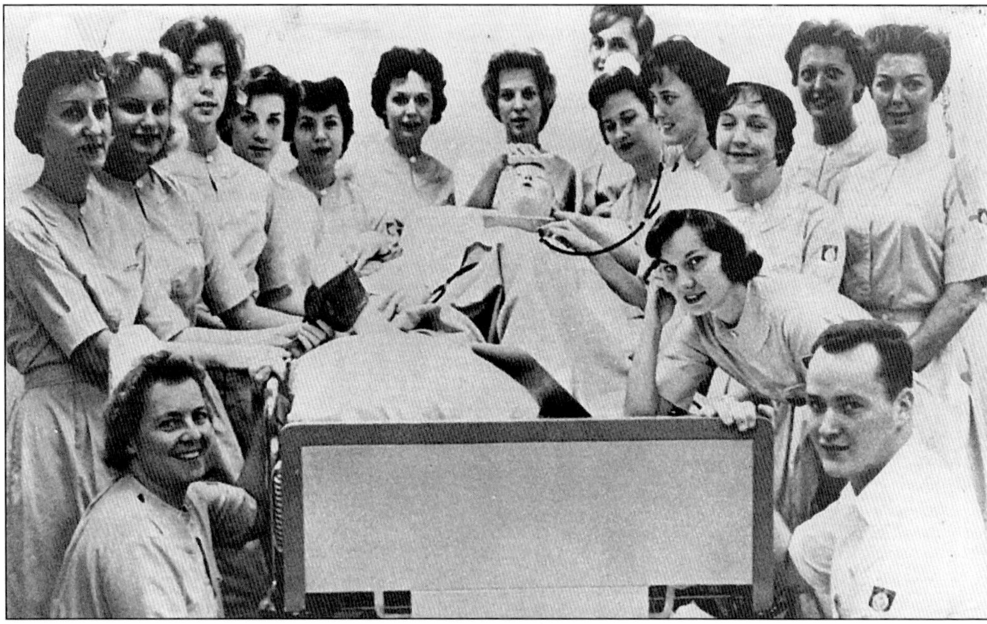

Nursing remains one of the most popular health sciences offered by the college. The first class of nurses began in 1963.

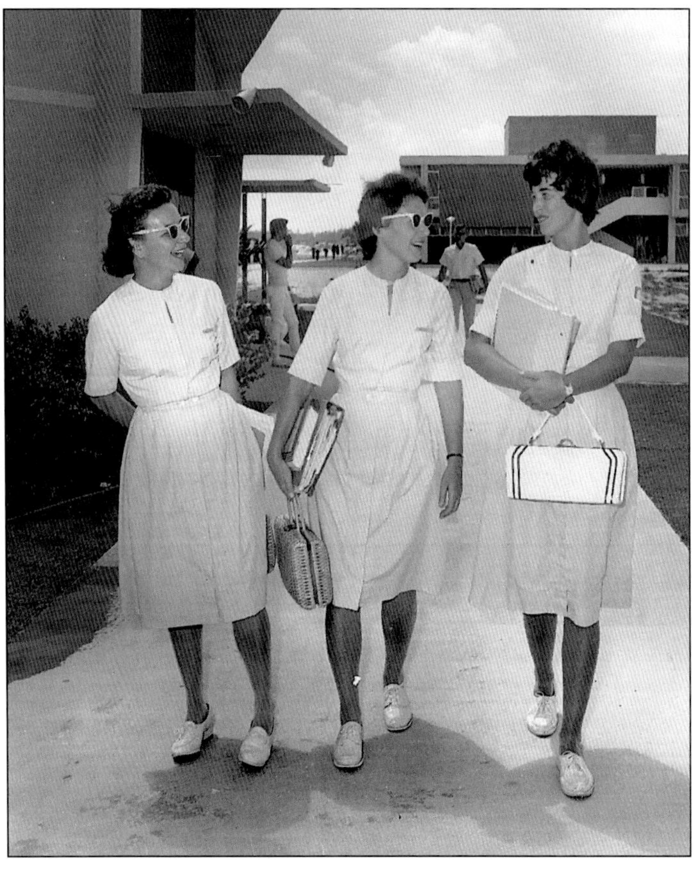

Nursing students chat as they stroll to class on Central Campus. Behind them is the library building and to their left is the distinctive round science lecture theater.

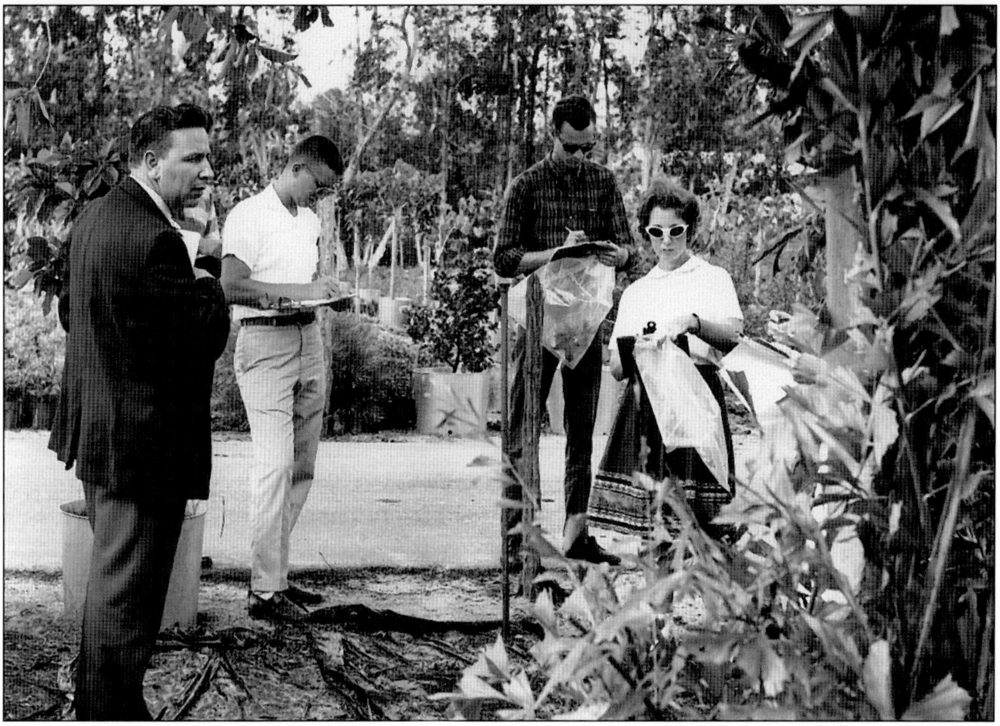

In addition to college-transfer curriculum, the college offered courses of particular value to South Floridians, such as ornamental horticulture. Prof. Albert Will (left) discusses the fishtail palm with his students in 1964. Will served as the ornamental horticulture program's director.

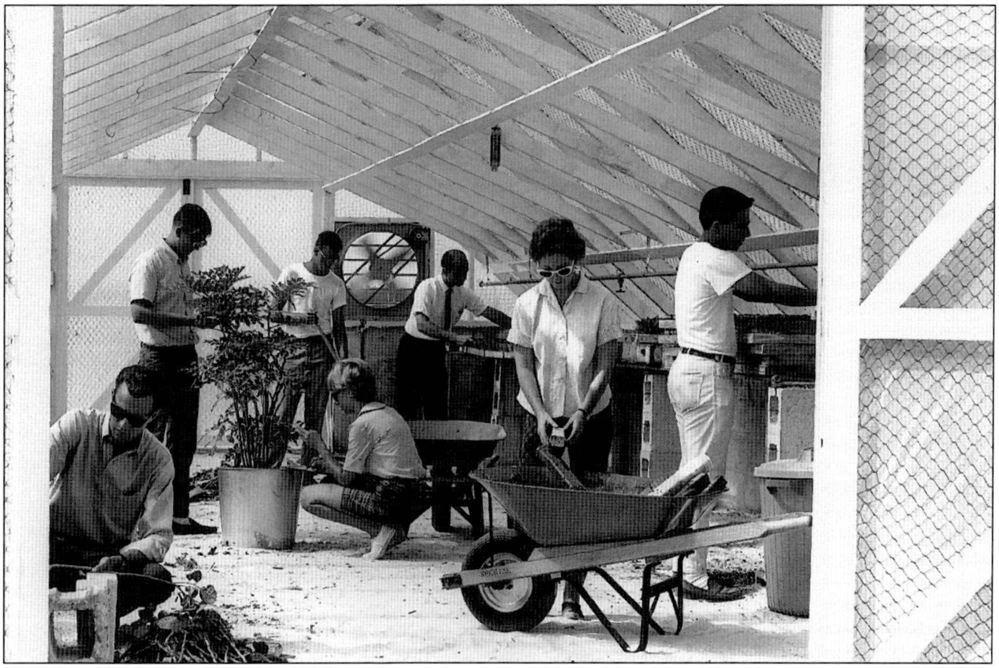

The horticulture students also got practical, hands-on experience working with tropical plants and planning outdoor displays.

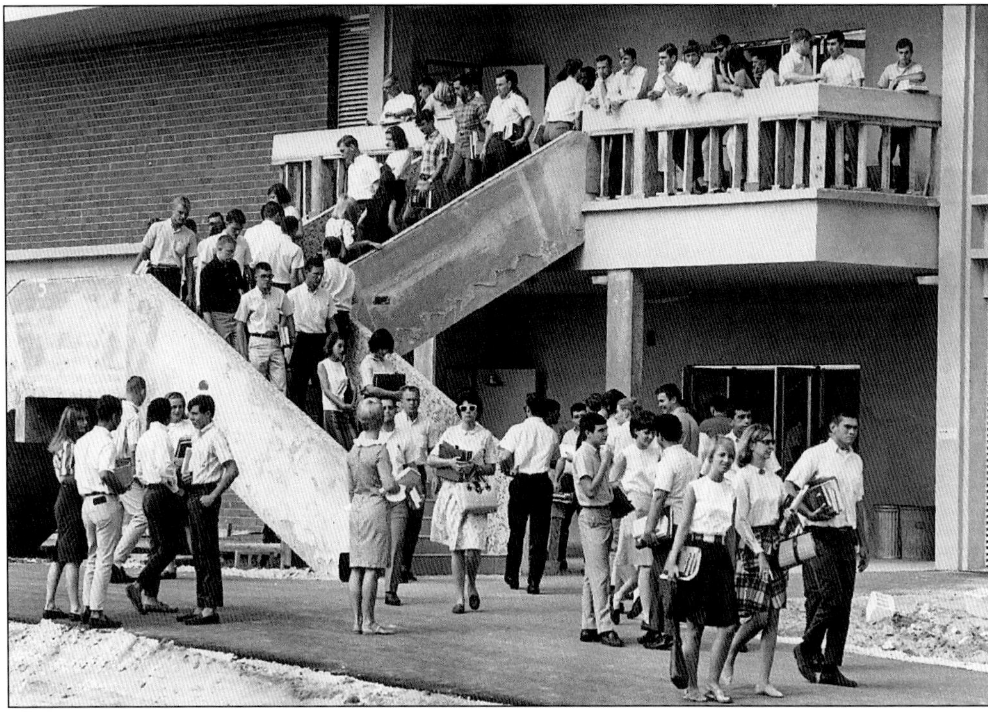

Classes filled quickly at the Davie campus. Even before exterior work was complete and the landscaping was installed, classrooms were filled with students. By the start of the second year, enrollment had doubled to 1,400. More than 2,500 students were enrolled by September 1963.

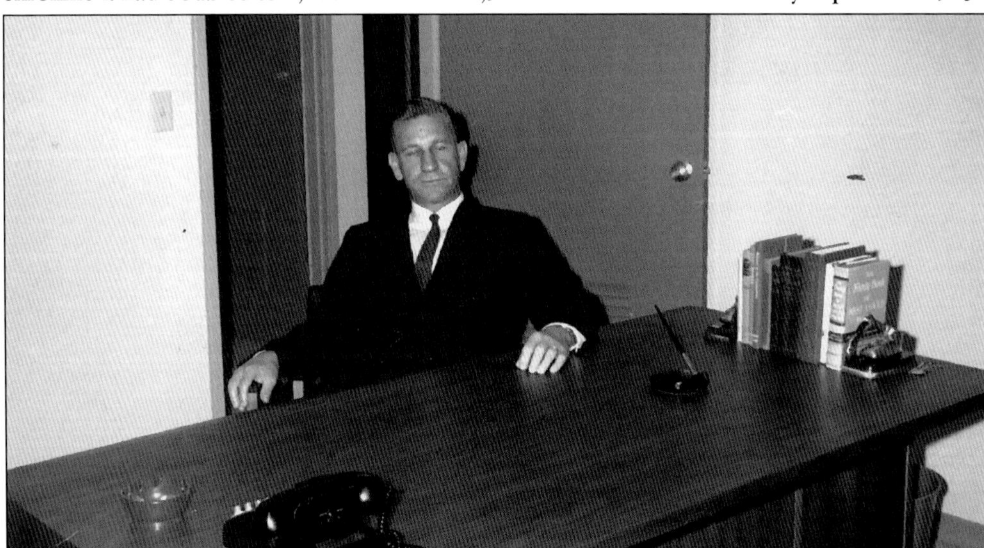

Dr. Elzie Lauderdale, a Mississippian, was BCC's first dean of instruction and helped establish the emphasis on academic excellence. When he called Mildred Bailey Mullikin in May 1960 to recruit her to head the drama department at the college, Mullikin's mother took the call. "Who is Dr. Lauderdale in Fort Lauderdale?" she asked her daughter. Dr. Lauderdale encouraged Mullikin and her mother to visit Fort Lauderdale. "Needless to say," Mullikin wrote years later, "I fell head over heels in love with Fort Lauderdale."

Students participate in a presidential rally at Central Campus, with supporters of candidates Barry Goldwater and Lyndon B. Johnson taking the microphone to extol the virtues of their candidate.

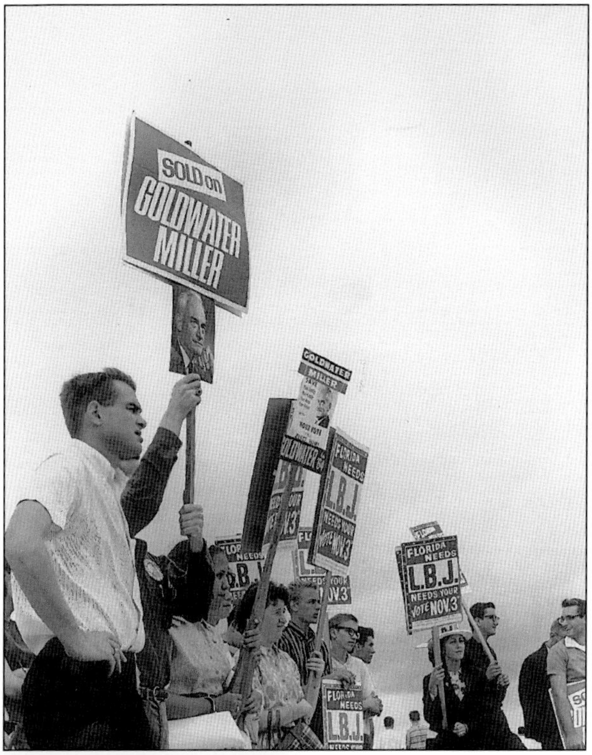


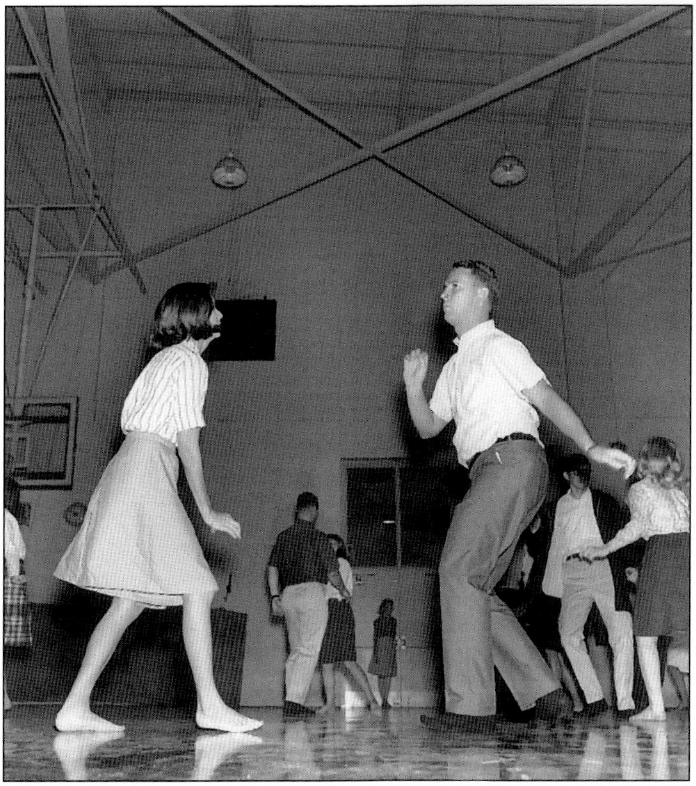

Students kicked off their shoes to do the twist and the other popular dances of the day at a sock hop after a basketball game at Mayer Gymnasium on Central Campus.

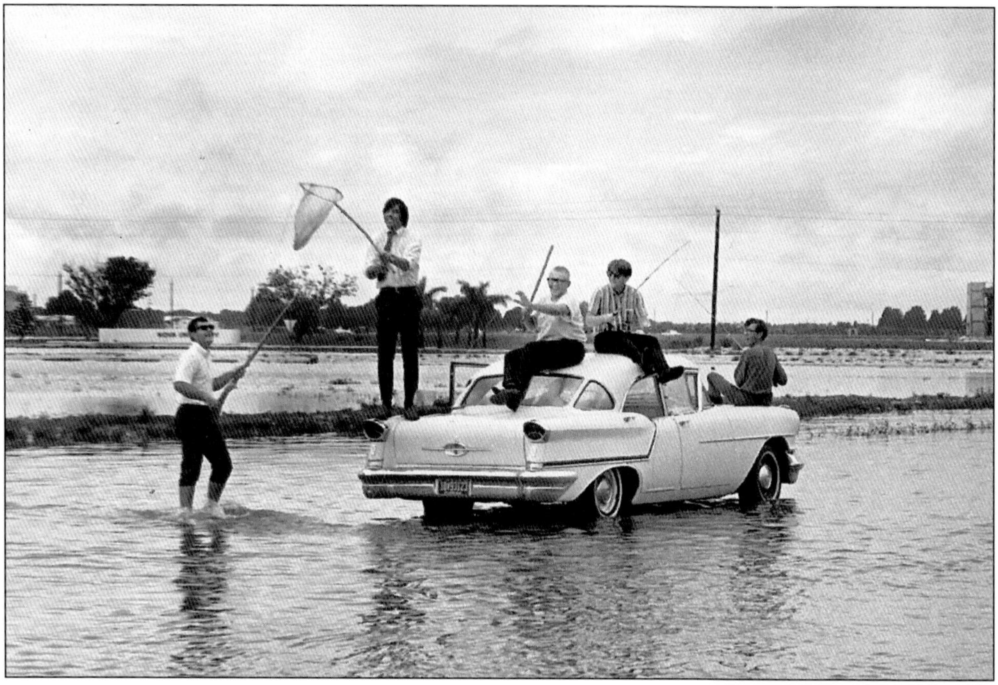

Students brought their fishing poles and nets to take a light-hearted jab at drainage problems at the parking lots on the western side of Central Campus.

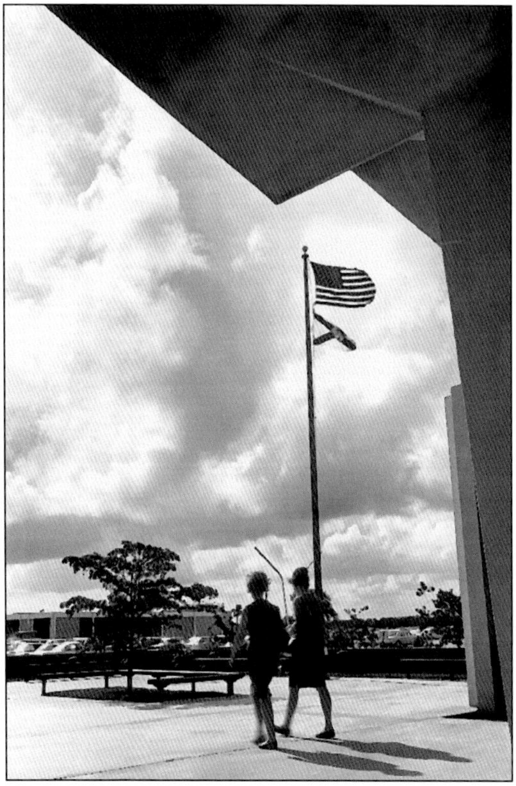

From the front steps of Central Campus one can see the Nova schools to the south.

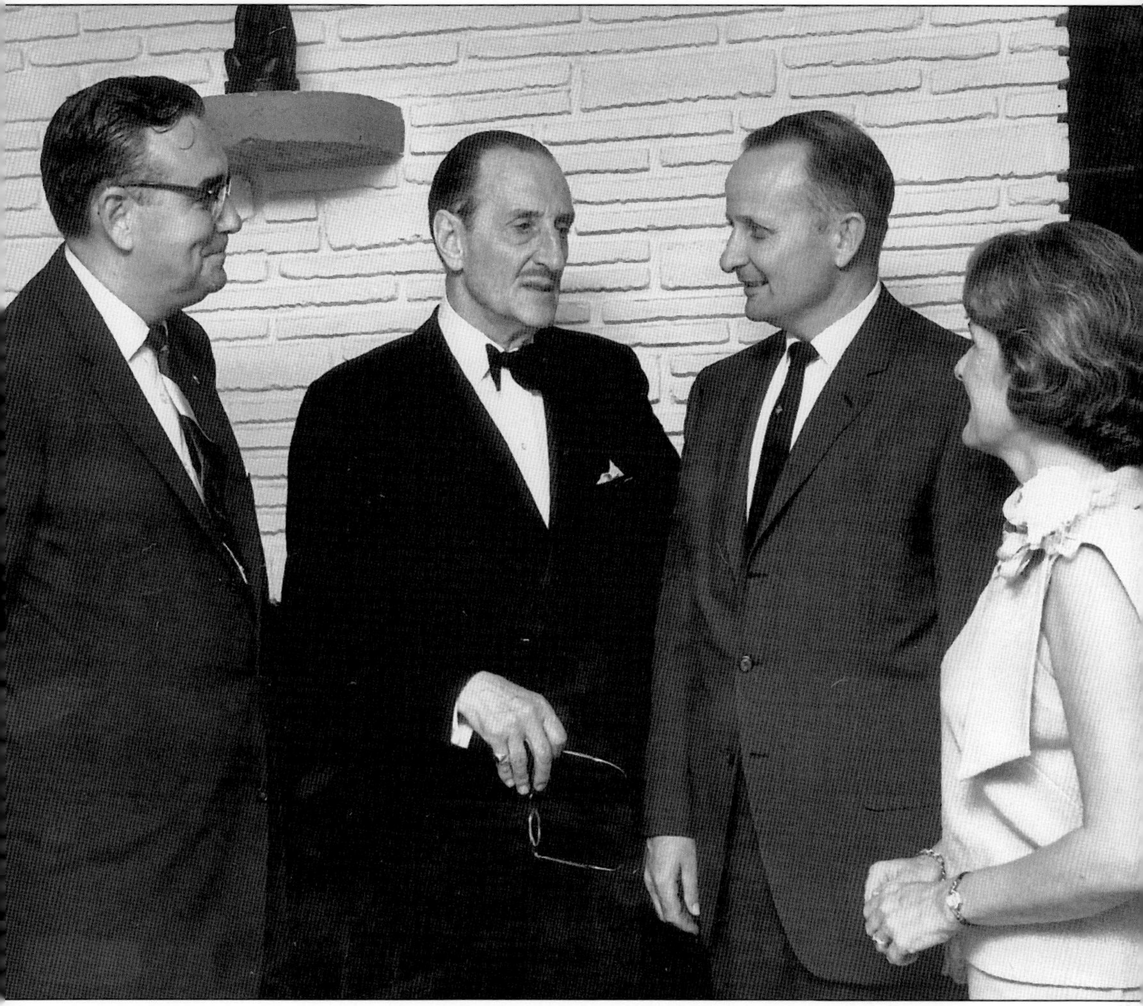

Basil Rathbone, one of the actors who portrayed Sherlock Holmes on film, talks Hollywood with Dr. Rushing and Nan and Hutch Hutchinson in the Hutchinson's Fort Lauderdale home in 1964. Nan Hutchinson was the college's first director of student affairs and helped introduce faculty recruits to the community and the college.

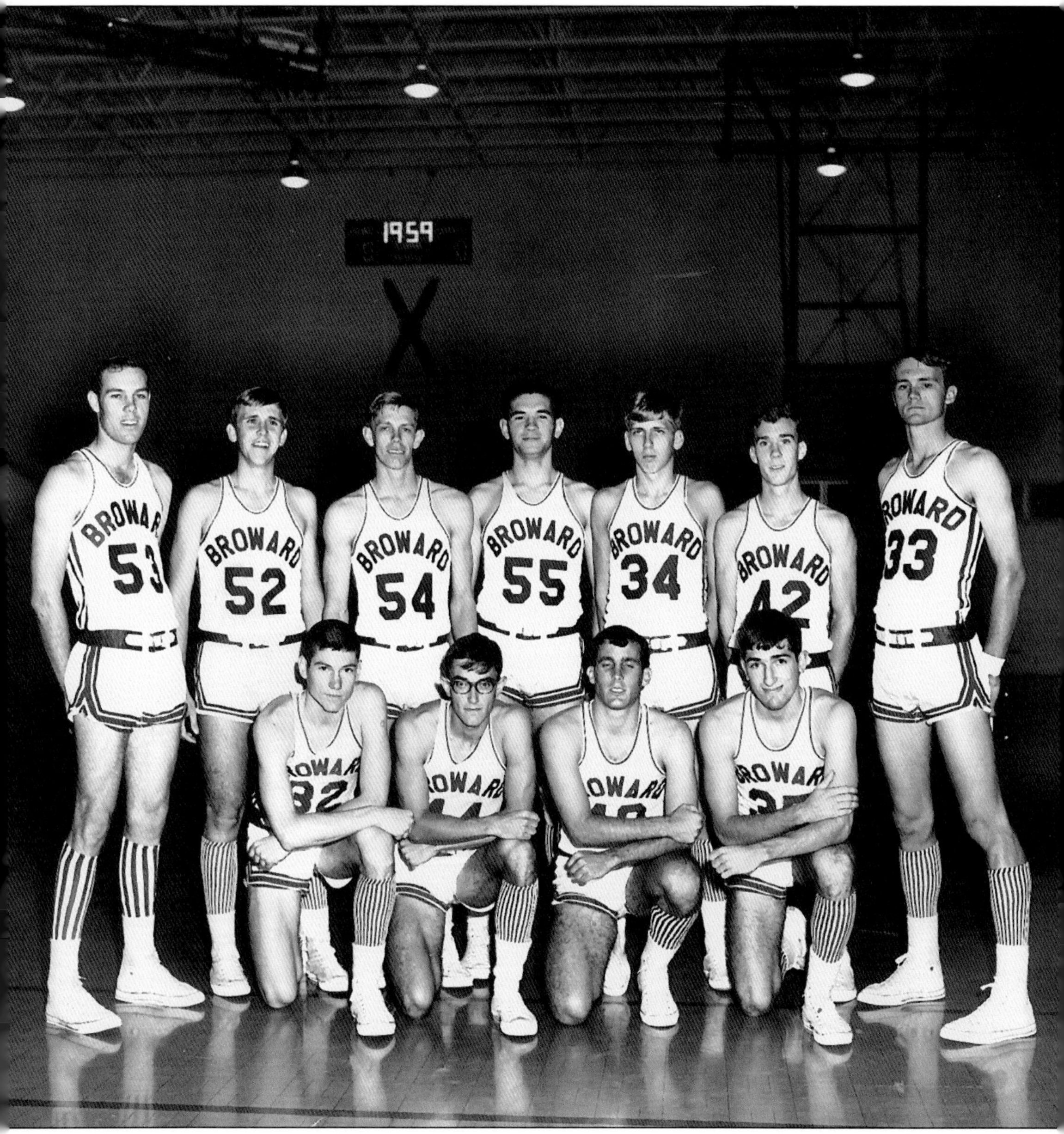


The intercollegiate sports program began in 1962 with men's basketball under the direction of coach Hubert Wright. The first athletic facilities were the tennis courts, which were built over the old Forman Field runways. Early JCBC teams were road warriors, often traveling to practice and play games. For the first few years, the basketball team played its home games at Stranahan High School in southwestern Fort Lauderdale. Hal Blitman, a coach for the men's basketball team, went on to coach the Miami Floridians of the American Basketball Association.

The men's baseball teams flourished under the direction of coach Leroy Wheat. The program sent many players to college teams and also produced several players who reached the major leagues, including Craig Skok and Don Newhowser. Until a diamond was built on Central Campus, the team practiced at New River Middle School and played its games at Holiday Park in Fort Lauderdale.

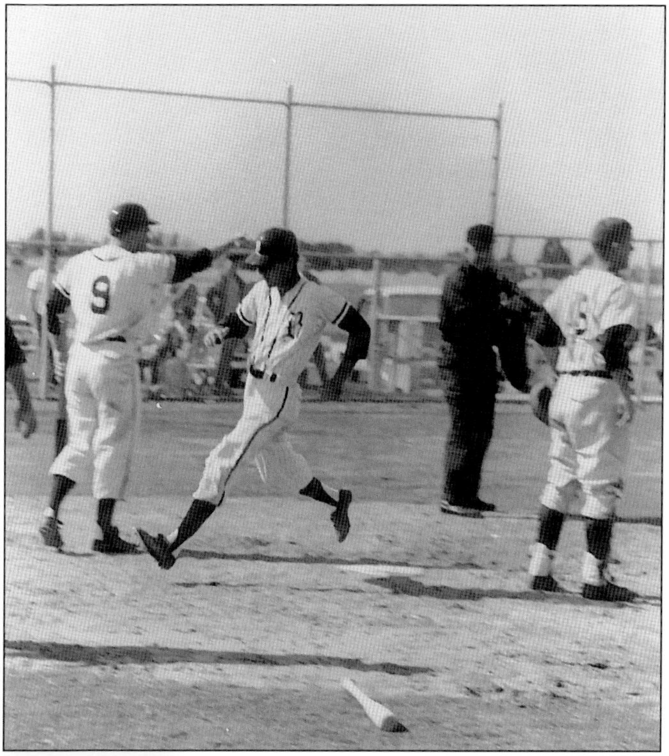

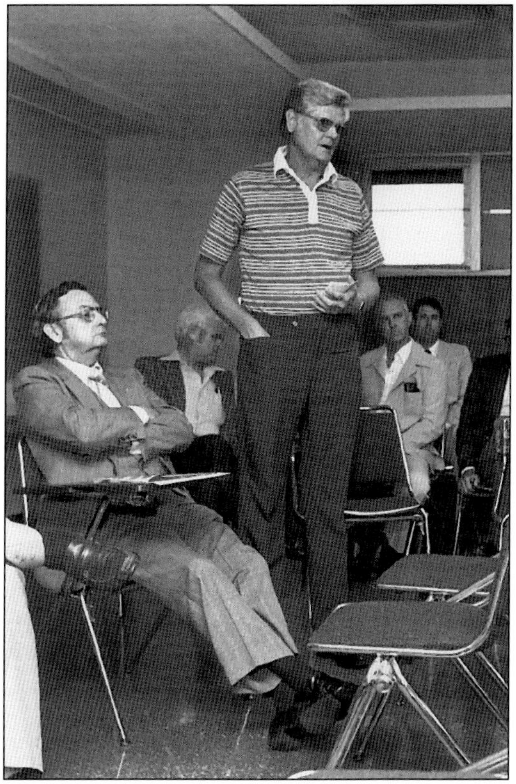

Coach Wheat (standing) pitched for the Philadelphia Athletics during his major-league career and was known to grant extra credit to students who could produce his major-league baseball card.

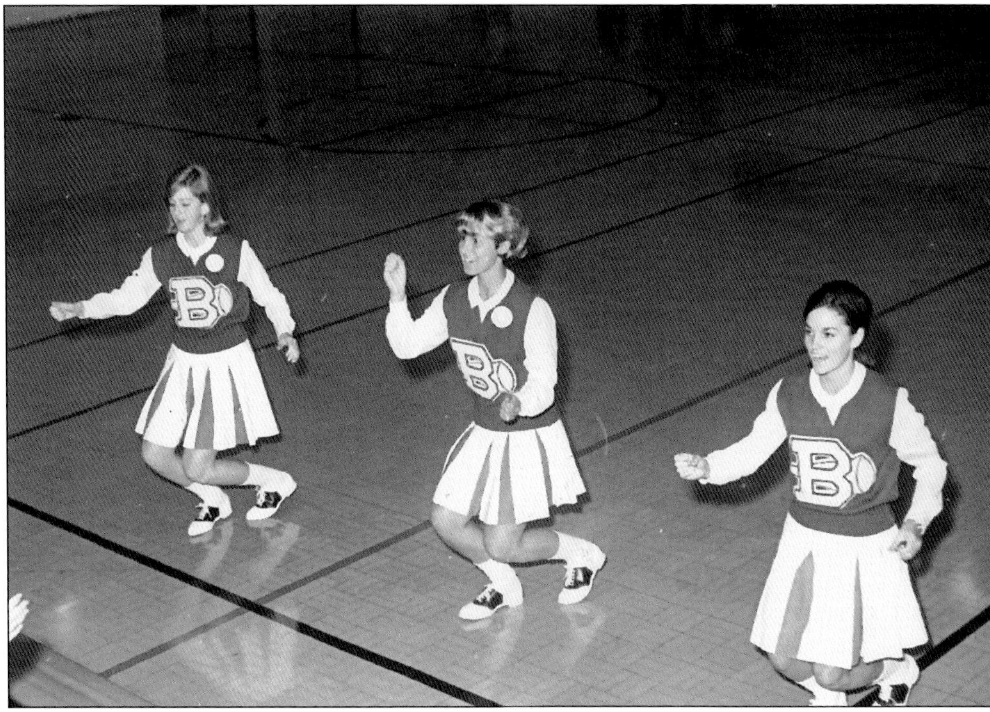

More programs were added over the years, including wrestling, women's badminton, soccer, tennis, golf, and swimming and diving for men and women. The college selected the seahorse as its mascot.

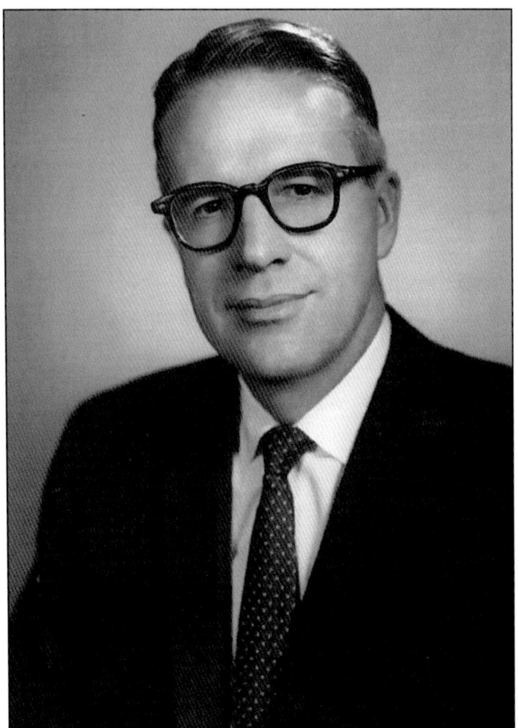

Dr. Edmund J. Gleazer (left), president of the American Association of Junior Colleges, was the speaker at JCBC's 1961 commencement ceremonies. The first class to begin JCBC as freshmen graduated June 10, 1962. Dr. John Allen, president of the University of South Florida, addressed 73 graduates at commencement ceremonies at War Memorial Auditorium in Fort Lauderdale. The first student to receive a diploma was Judith Abel of Fort Lauderdale. Also in the first graduating class was Central Catholic High graduate Parris Nelson Glendening, who went on in 1967 to become the youngest recipient of a doctorate in political science at Florida State University. In 1994, Glendening was elected Maryland's 59th governor.

# *Two*

# The Blee Era

## From Harmony to Discord

*In September 1965, Dr. Joe Rushing announced his intention to return to Texas. Dean of Students Dr. Jack Taylor was named acting president until a successor was chosen.*

*In May 1996, the college advisory board eschewed the top in-house candidates, Dr. Taylor and Dean of Instruction Dr. E.P. Lauderdale, to nominate Dr. Myron Blee for the presidency. An expert in educational policy, former president of the Florida Institute for Continuing University Studies, and former director of Learning Resources at Florida Atlantic University, Dr. Blee was serving as director of the Office of Emergency Planning in Washington at the time of his appointment to the presidency. He requested leave until he could complete his assignment in Washington.*

*Controversy had begun long before Dr. Blee arrived on campus and had ample time to build and fester during his leave. Rumors swept the campus. Upon arrival at the college, he began making massive changes, causing further discord.*

*The roiling clouds that hung over the college affected it in other less-apparent ways. One of the college's benefactors, Emil Buehler, notified the school board that he no longer wished to provide the college with airplanes or classroom space at Fort Lauderdale Executive Airport.*

*Angered faculty became active, venting their indignation to the media as well as professional and educational regulatory organizations and politicians. On April 27, 1967, the Broward County Board of Public Instruction, by a 3-2 vote, refused to renew Dr. Blee's contract.*

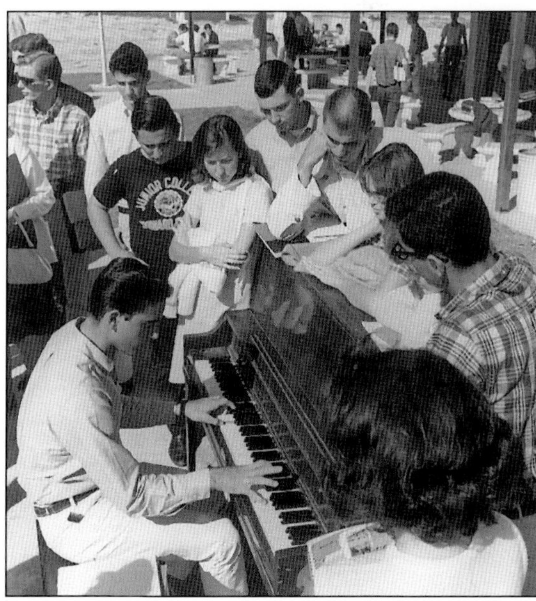

Dr. Rushing left behind a college with a new campus and a dynamic faculty and staff, but the mood on campus wasn't as rosy and upbeat as it seemed. During the period between Dr. Rushing's departure and Dr. Blee's arrival, the seeds of discord sprouted and began growing. Ultimately, from October 31, 1965 to June 15, 1968, the college was without consistent leadership.

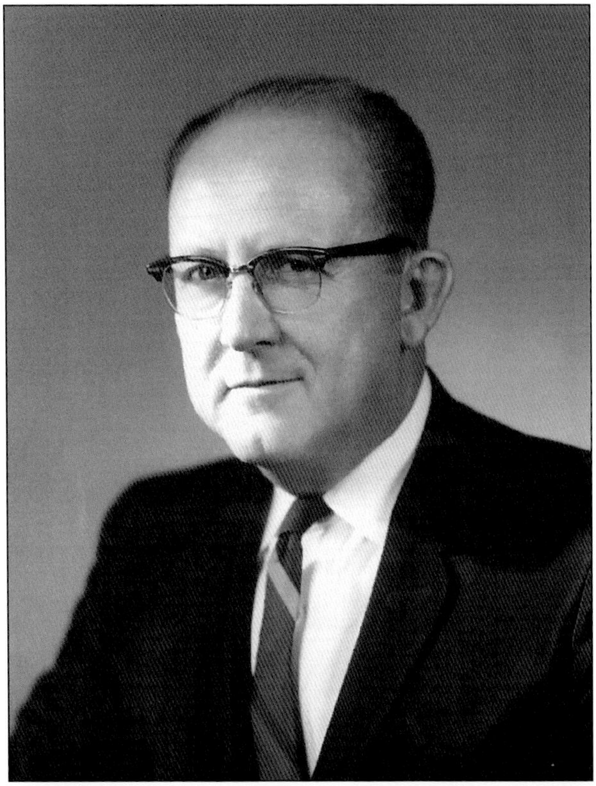

Dr. Myron Blee was selected to succeed Dr. Rushing as the JCBC's second president. Although he had varied high-level experience in educational policy and administration, the Illinois native had never served as a college president before taking the reins at JCBC.

Dr. Blee and graduation speaker Dr. James Wattenbarger, father of the Florida community college system, chat with a student at 1966 commencement ceremonies.

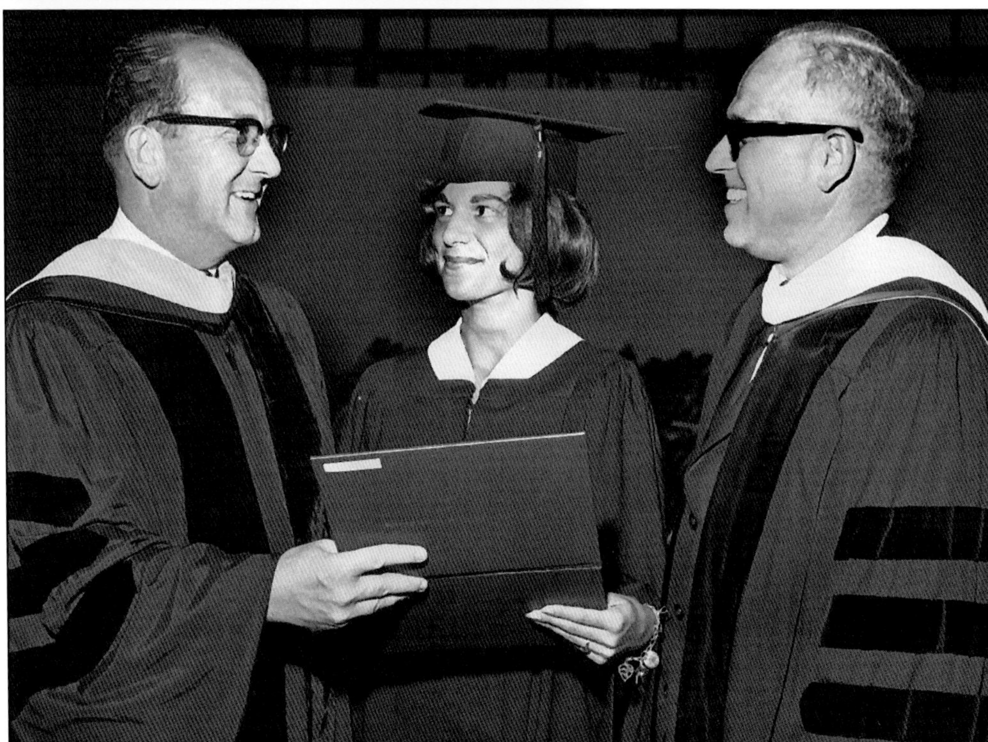

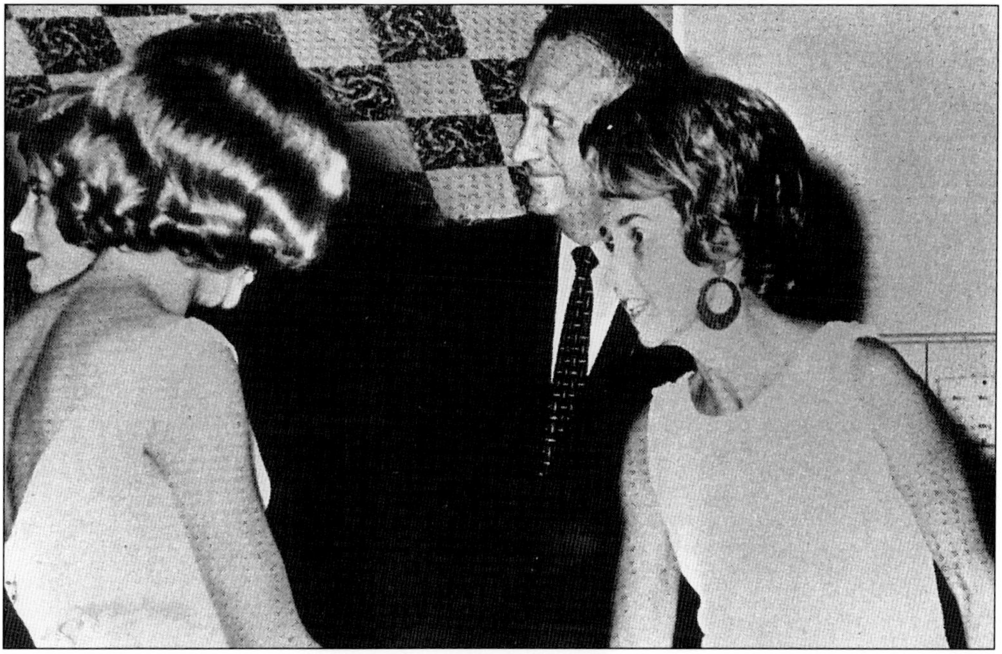

Dr. and Mrs. Jack Taylor greet students at a college event. Dr. Taylor, the dean of students, served as acting president until Dr. Blee arrived at JCBC. He and Dr. E.P. Lauderdale were the choices of many of the faculty and staff to succeed Dr. Rushing. After Dr. Blee arrived on campus, Dr. Taylor returned to his post, but Dr. Lauderdale resigned.

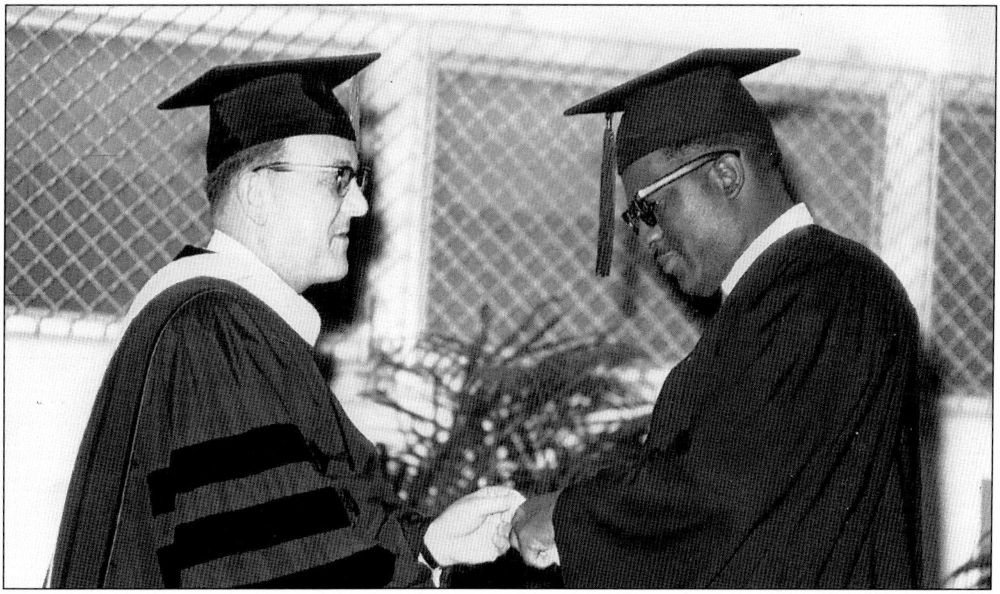

A system of junior colleges serving African-American students was established by the state in 1949. In Broward County, JCBC offered courses for its African-American students at a branch campus of Dillard High School, which opened in August of 1961. The Civil Rights Act of 1964 mandated desegregation of all publicly supported educational institutions. By the 1966–1967 school year, the "Magnificent 12" black junior colleges in Florida had ceased operations or had folded into formerly all-white junior colleges.

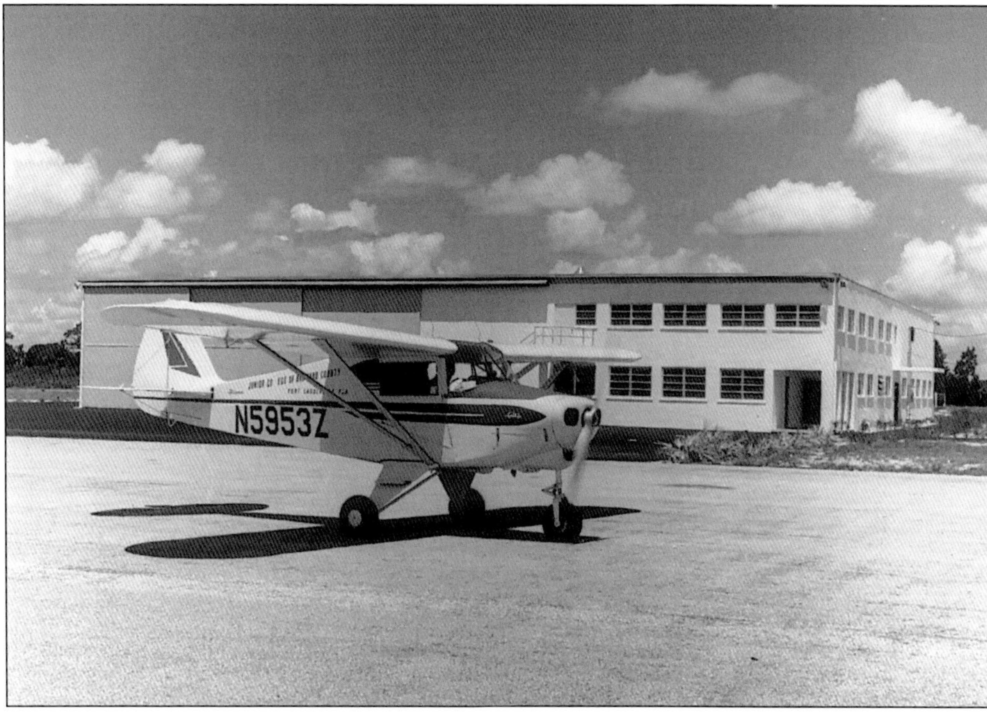


The contentious, unsettled conditions at the college prompted Emil Buehler, a German-born aviator, architect, inventor, and philanthropist, to threaten to withdraw his support from the aviation program for which he had provided the planes and classroom space for at Fort Lauderdale Executive Airport. "He never did, though," said trustee John H. Payne. "He never would have done anything to hurt the college."

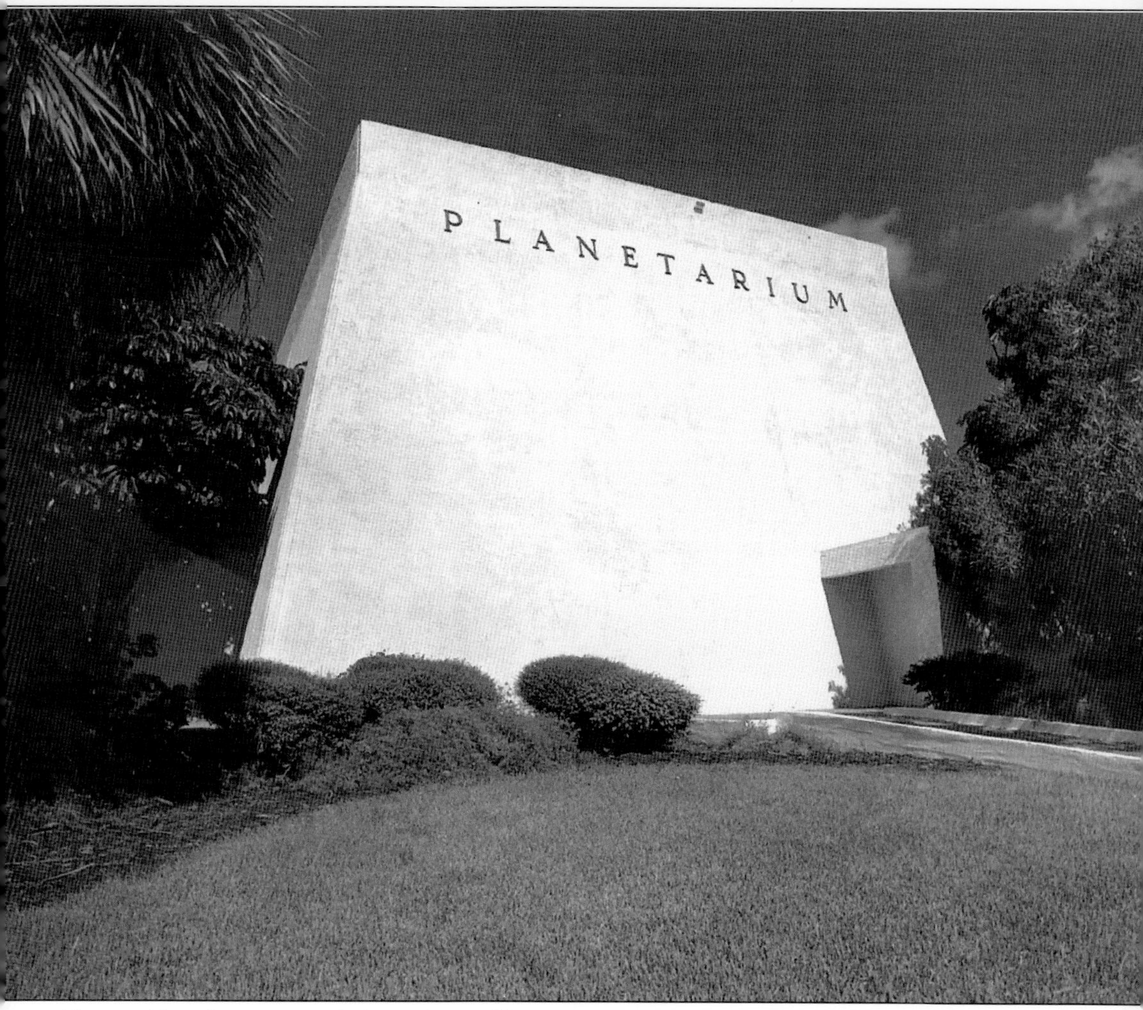


The Buehler Planetarium, dedicated in 1966, remains a favorite for South Florida school children, who learn about the heavens from the planetarium's extensive educational programs.

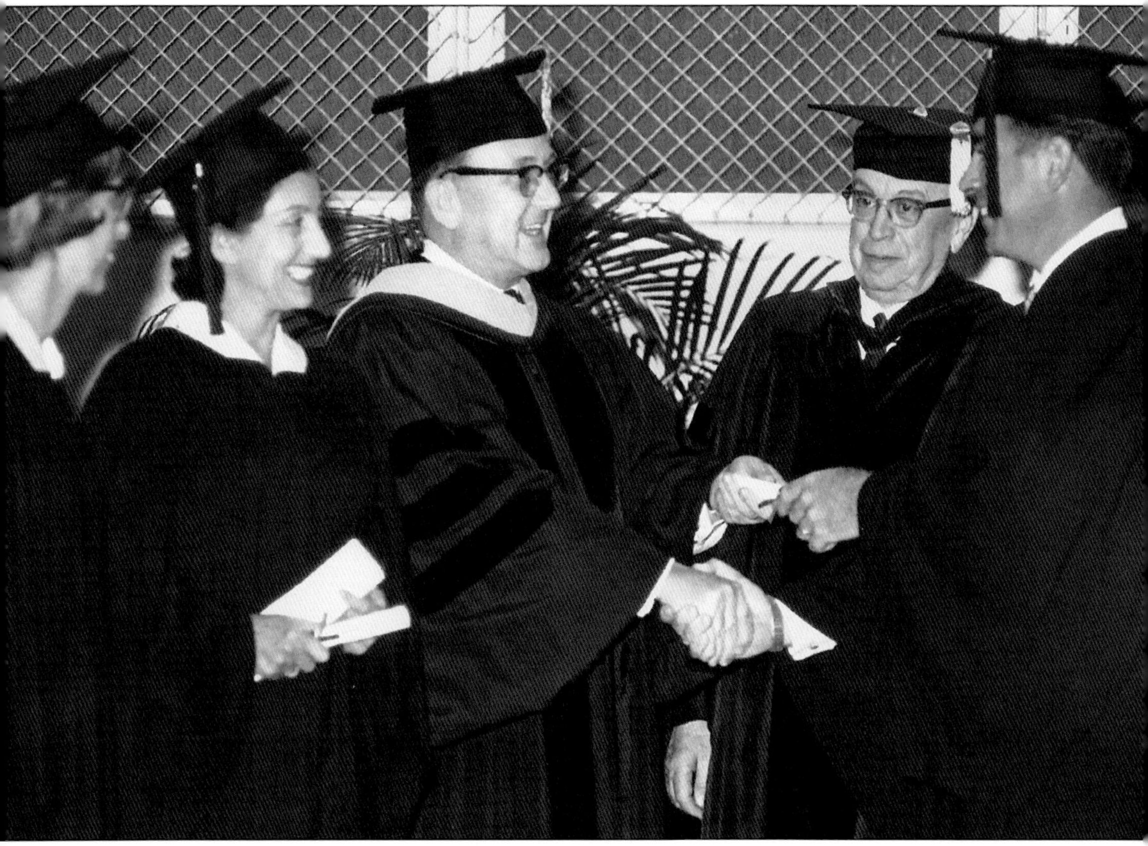

Dr. Blee was all smiles at commencement ceremonies, but his brief presidency resulted in hard feelings and strained relations for many. Blee sued the college after the school board refused to offer him a new contract. The parties eventually settled out of court. Dr. Myron Ashmore served as acting president while a search to replace Dr. Blee was underway.

# *Three*

# The Adams Era

## Bigger and Better

*The Junior College of Broward County needed someone with broad shoulders to take on the responsibility of putting the college back on track after a period of anger and confusion.*

*The college found him in A. Hugh Adams. After earning his Associate in Arts degree at the University of Florida, Adams went north to Tallahassee, where he completed work on his bachelor's and master's degrees as well as his doctorate at Florida State University. Adams was more than just a good student, he was captain and most valuable player on the Seminoles football team and named to the Little All-America team. After graduation, he served as a varsity assistant football coach from 1955 to 1958. He then moved on to the FSU faculty, where he served until 1964.*

*In 1965, Adams became the first appointed superintendent of public instruction in Charlotte County. He left there in April 1968 to tackle the challenges that lay ahead at JCBC. A month after his arrival, the college underwent another noticeable change—it became Broward Junior College. Two months later, the legislature removed the junior colleges from governance by local school boards. The advisory boards then became the governing board of trustees.*

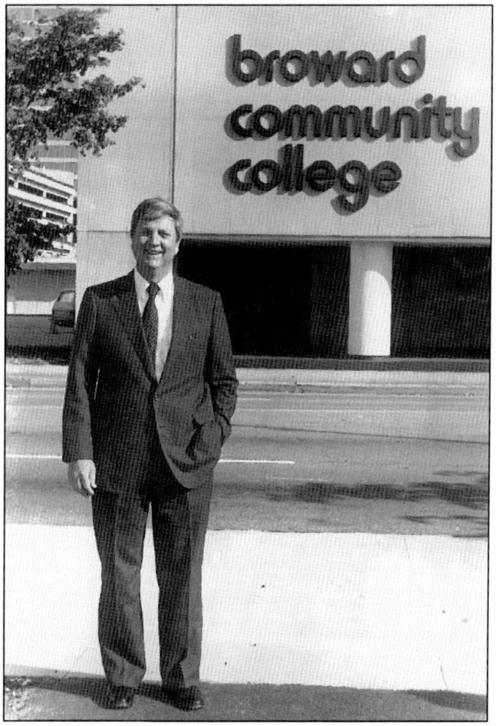


One of the greatest accomplishments of Dr. Adams was making the college a multicampus institution. He stands across East Las Olas Boulevard from the Downtown Center, dedicated in 1973 as the college administrative headquarters and an instructional site.

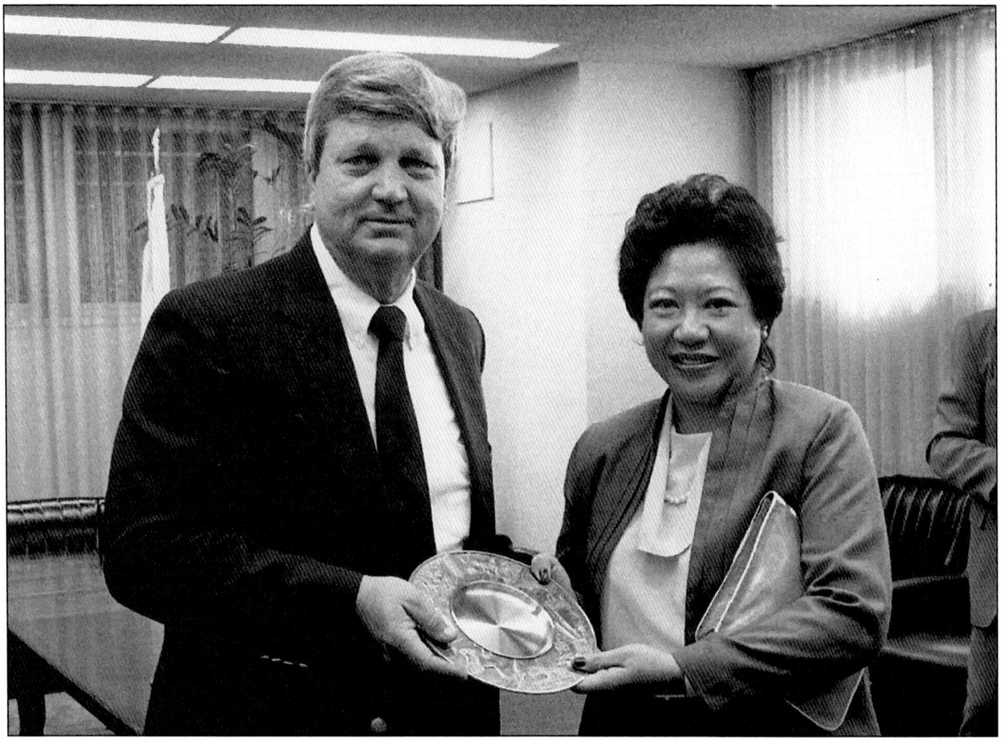

International education has long been a focus of the college. Terri K.T. Ng Hew, president of Kalej Damansara Utama in Selangar, Malaysia, presents Dr. Adams with a memento of her visit.

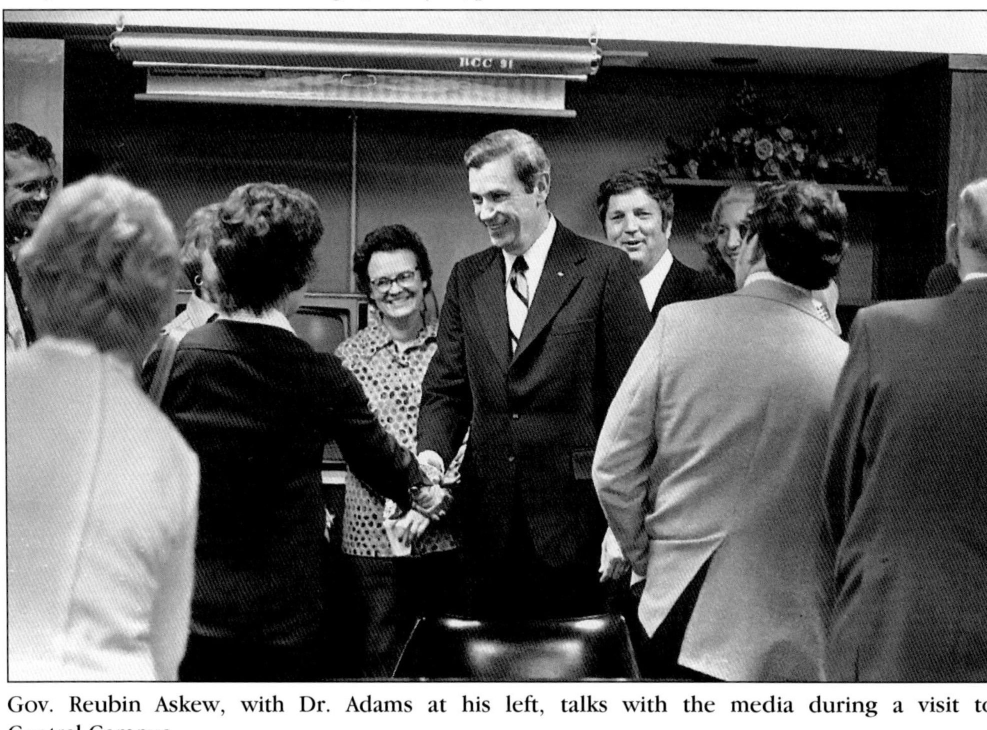

Gov. Reubin Askew, with Dr. Adams at his left, talks with the media during a visit to Central Campus.

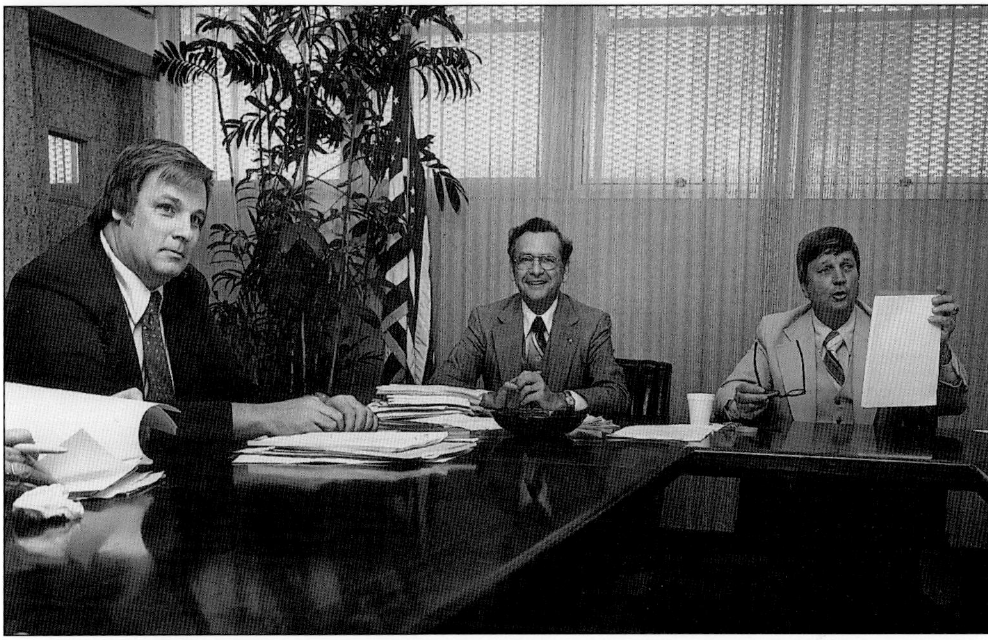

Two of Dr. Adams's top administrators were Dr. Clinton Hamilton (next to Dr. Adams) and Dr. George Young. Dr. Hamilton, a native of Mississippi, came to the college as academic dean, but spent most of his quarter-century career there as executive vice president. Dr. Young, the vice president for student affairs, was the son of Virginia Young, chair of the Broward County Board of Public Instruction who also served as mayor of Fort Lauderdale.

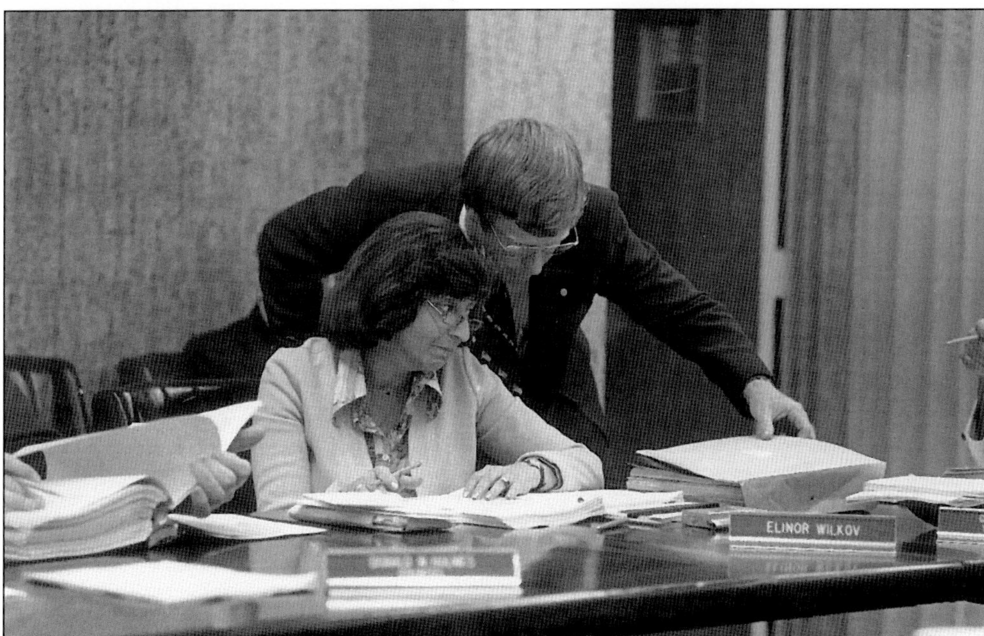


Another top administrator was Dr. Willis Holcombe, who served as an assistant to Dr. Adams before moving to Florida's other BCC—Brevard Community College—as vice president. In this 1975 photo, he counsels Elinor Wilkov at a BCC District Board of Trustees meeting.

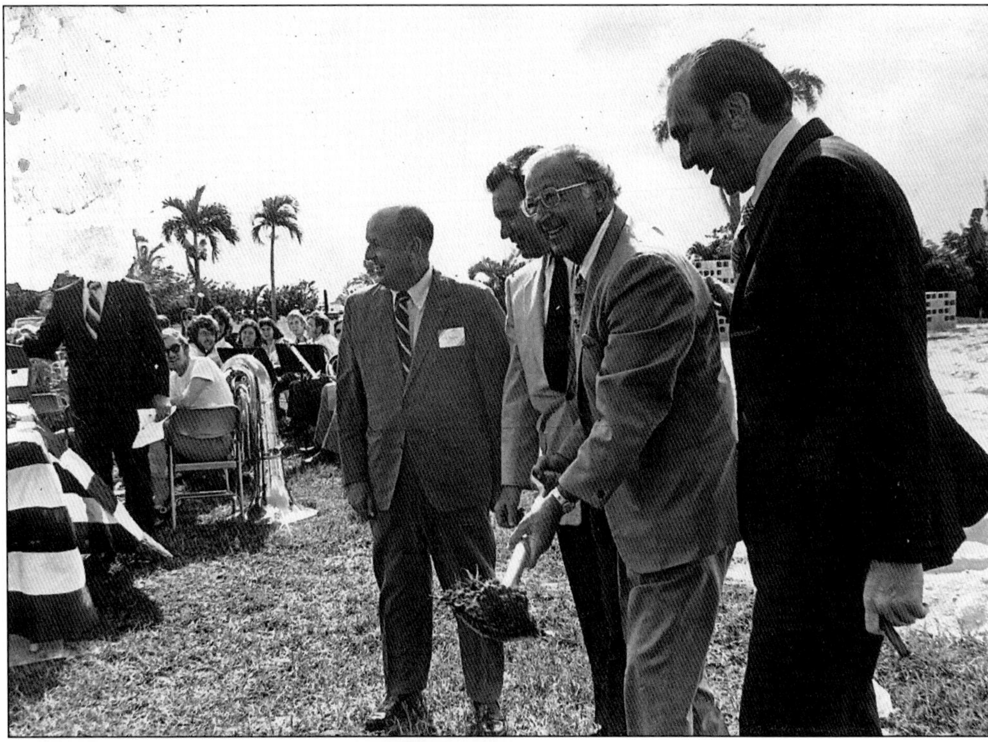

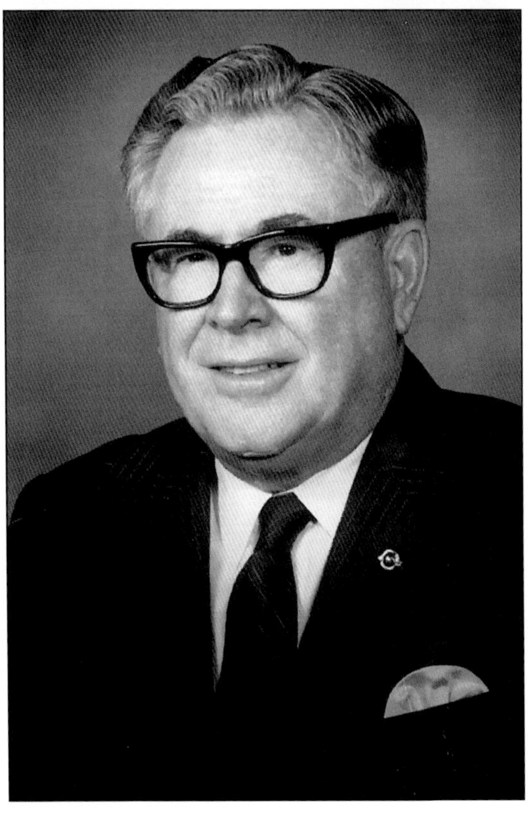

Because of the rapid growth of the college during the 1960s and 1970s, groundbreaking was a common occurrence. In this picture, from left to right, trustees George Mayer, Jules J. Polachek, Judson A. Samuels, and Sheldon Schlesinger do the spadework.

Charles W. Lantz served as a member of the BCC District Board of Trustees from June 1981 to May 1989.

The first president of the Urban League of Broward County, civic activist Margaret Blake Roach was also the first African American named to the BCC District Board of Trustees. After her appointment to the board of trustees by Gov. Reubin Askew, the State Board of Education appointed her to the Community College Council.

English professor Judith VanAlstyne confers with Judson A. Samuels before a district board of trustees meeting. After leaving the classroom, VanAlstyne remains active in college affairs as a member of the Broward Community College Foundation board.

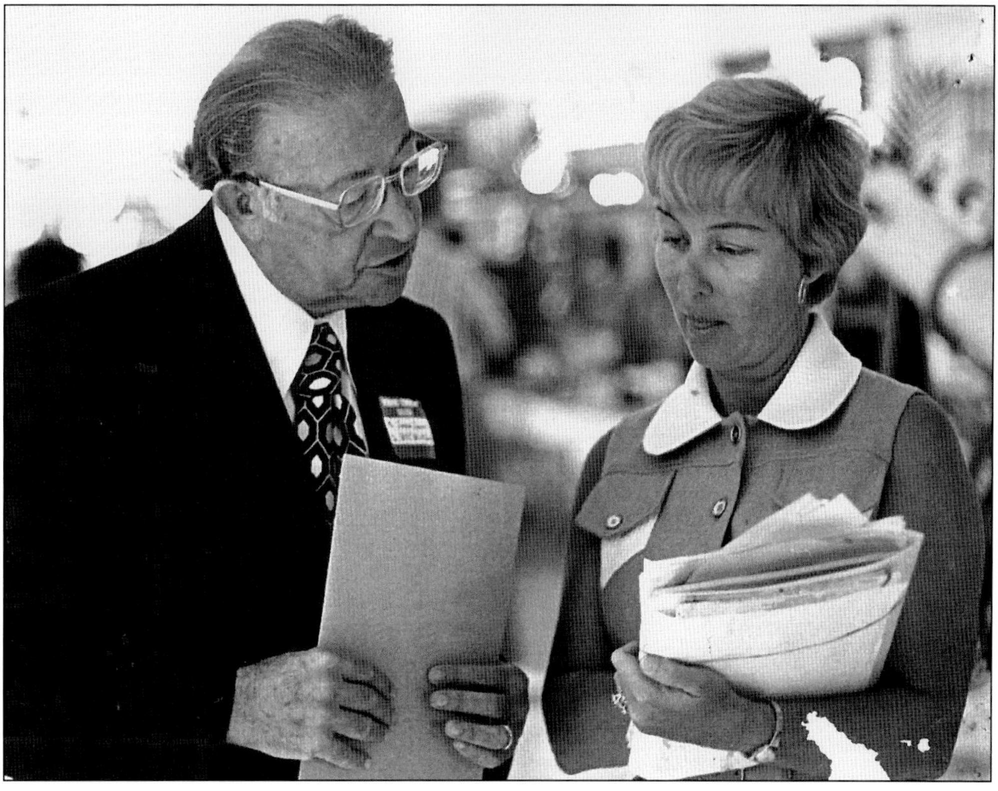

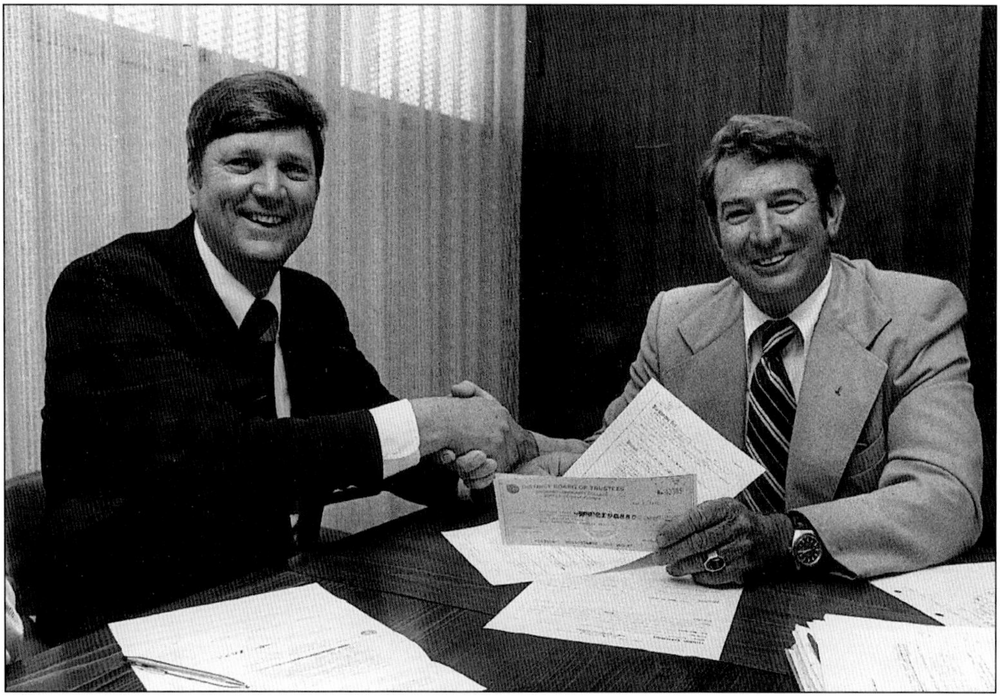

Dr. Adams hands over a check to Lucius Weeks to purchase the Downtown Center from Landmark Bank in 1977. The Downtown Center was to become the college's administrative headquarters as well as an instructional site.

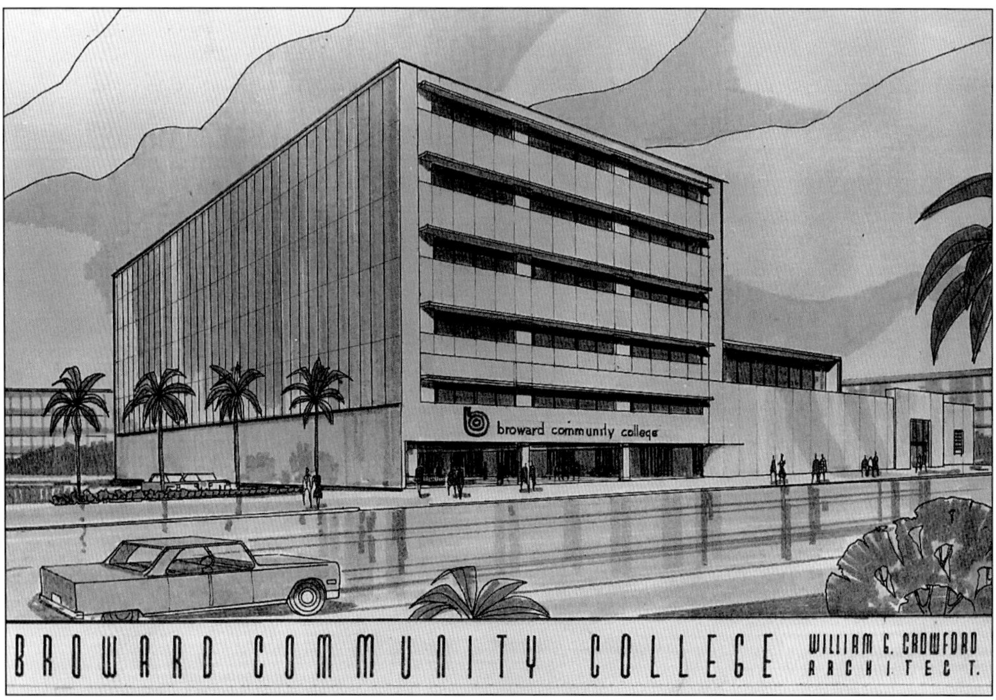


Architect William G. Crawford, who designed many of the buildings on Central Campus, modernized the building's facade and transformed the drive-through to a registration area.

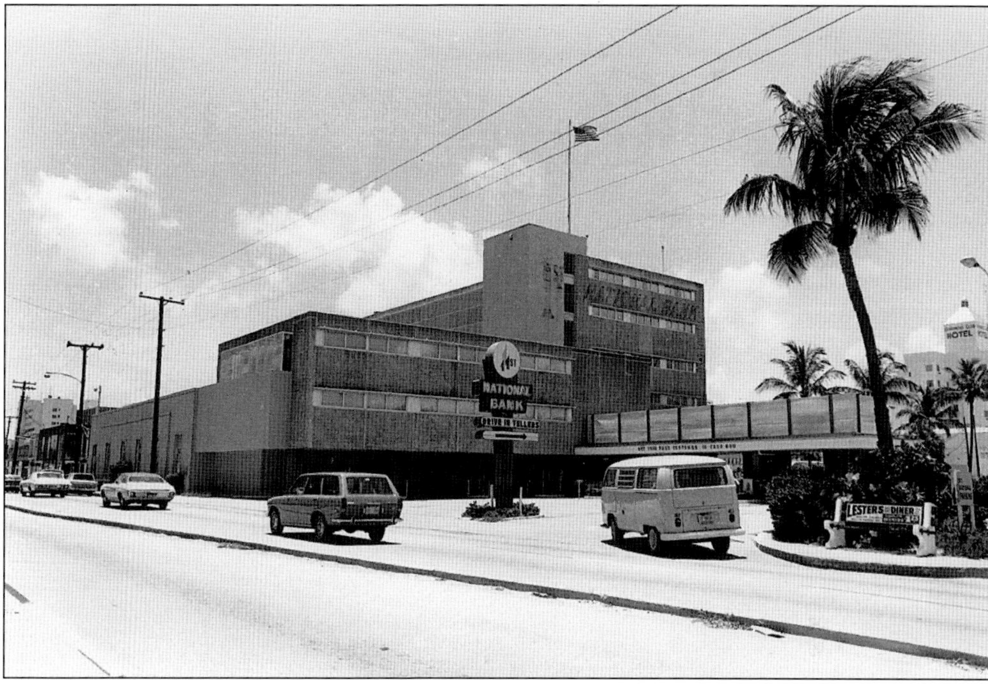


Originally home to First Federal Bank of Broward, the Downtown Center was easily adapted to its new use.

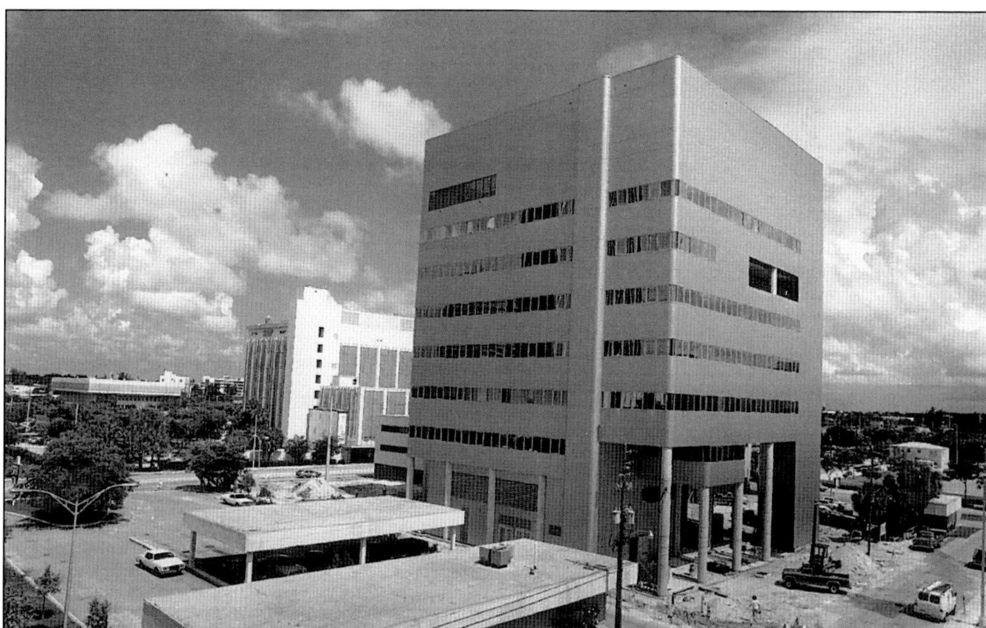

When Florida Atlantic University looked to expand its offerings in downtown Fort Lauderdale, BCC was pleased to share its site.

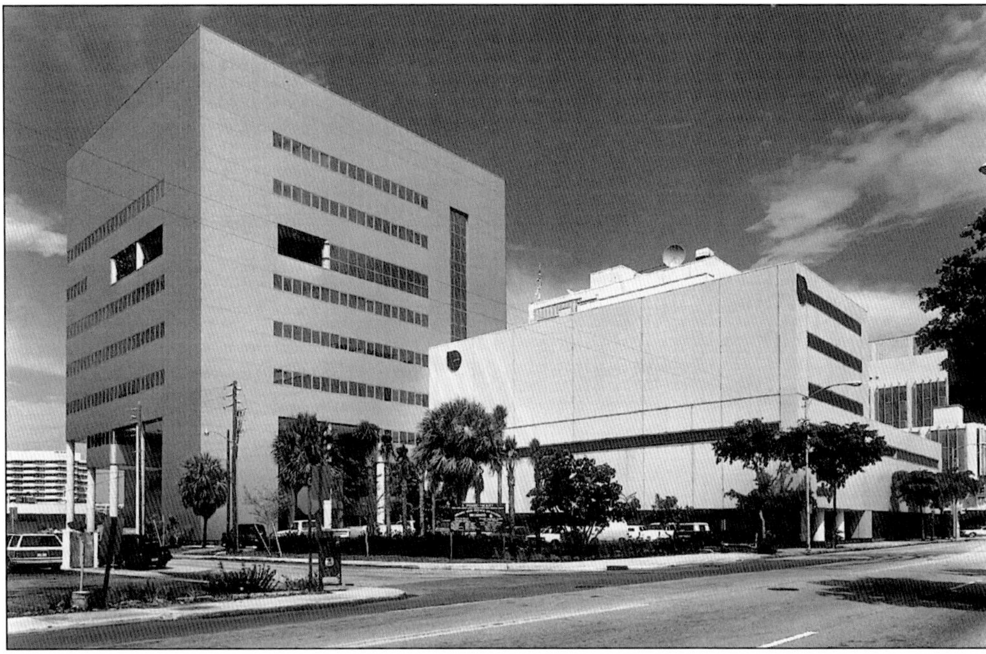

Once complete, the BCC and FAU buildings joined seamlessly. The two institutions have gone on to successfully partner on other projects.

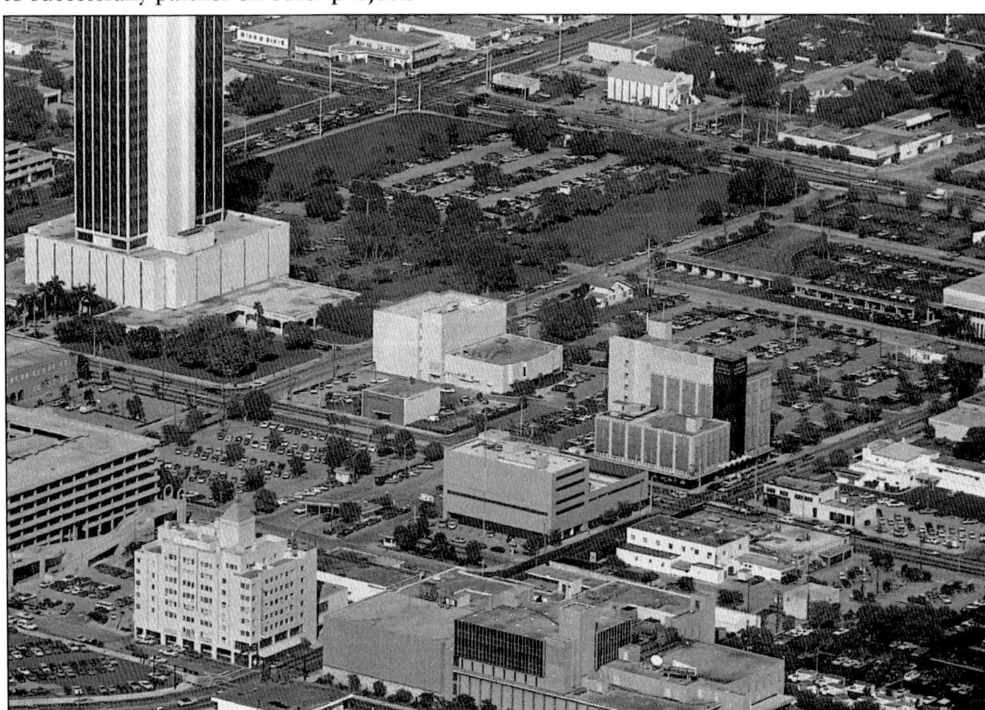

The Downtown Center sits in the heart of Fort Lauderdale. The larger building in the foreground is the *Fort Lauderdale News* building. Next to it is the Governor's Club Hotel, razed to provide the site for the joint FAU/BCC Higher Education Center, which was dedicated in 2001.

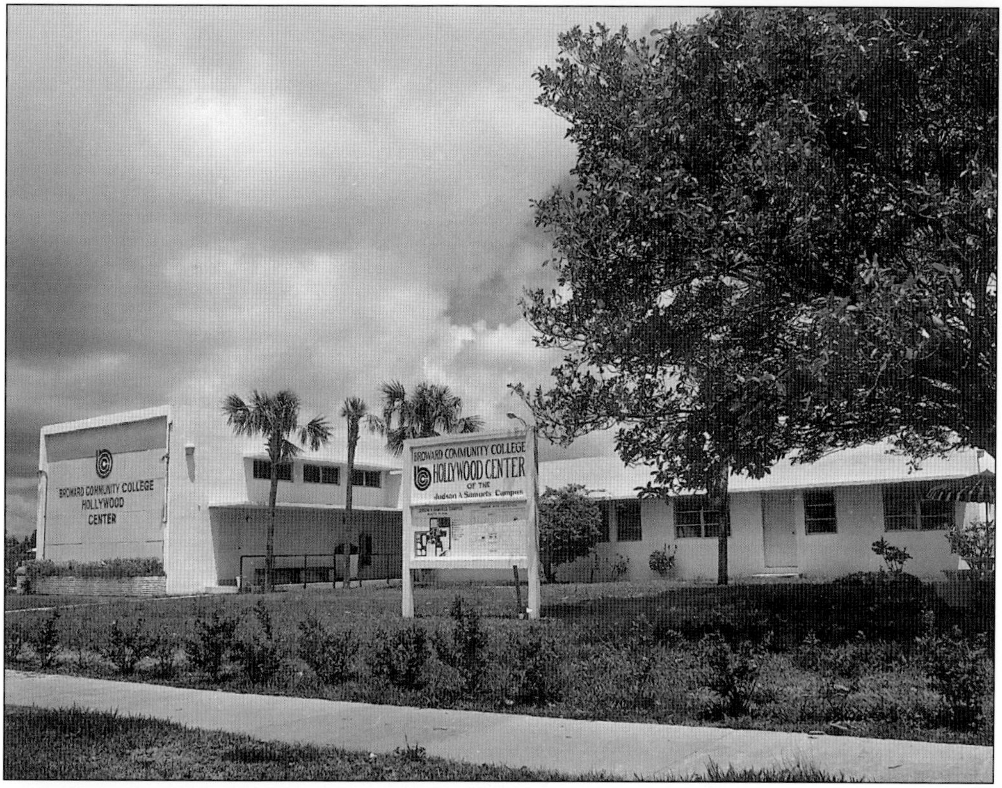


BCC's presence in Hollywood was established in 1970 at the Hollywood Center, at 3601 Johnson Street, in a building leased from next-door neighbor Memorial Hospital.

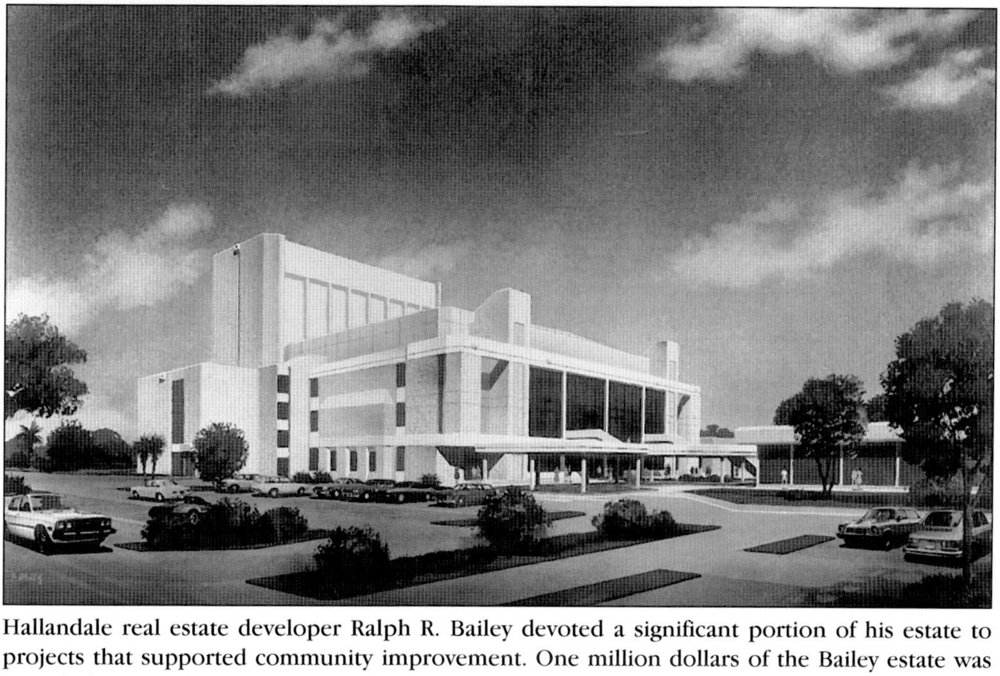

Hallandale real estate developer Ralph R. Bailey devoted a significant portion of his estate to projects that supported community improvement. One million dollars of the Bailey estate was provided to BCC for construction of a concert hall and theatre.

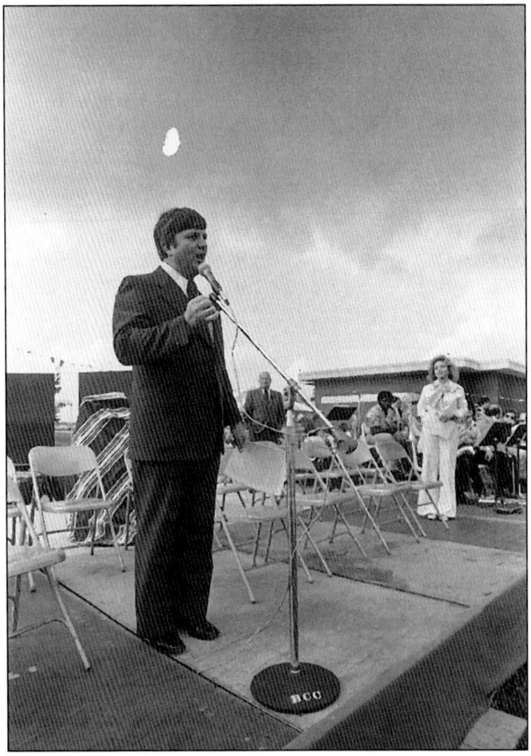

The Bailey Estate's donation was matched with $2 million from the Community Educational Facilities Act of 1975, sponsored by then state senator Bob Graham. Ground was broken in November 1979. In this photo, Dr. Adams addresses the crowd at the groundbreaking ceremonies.

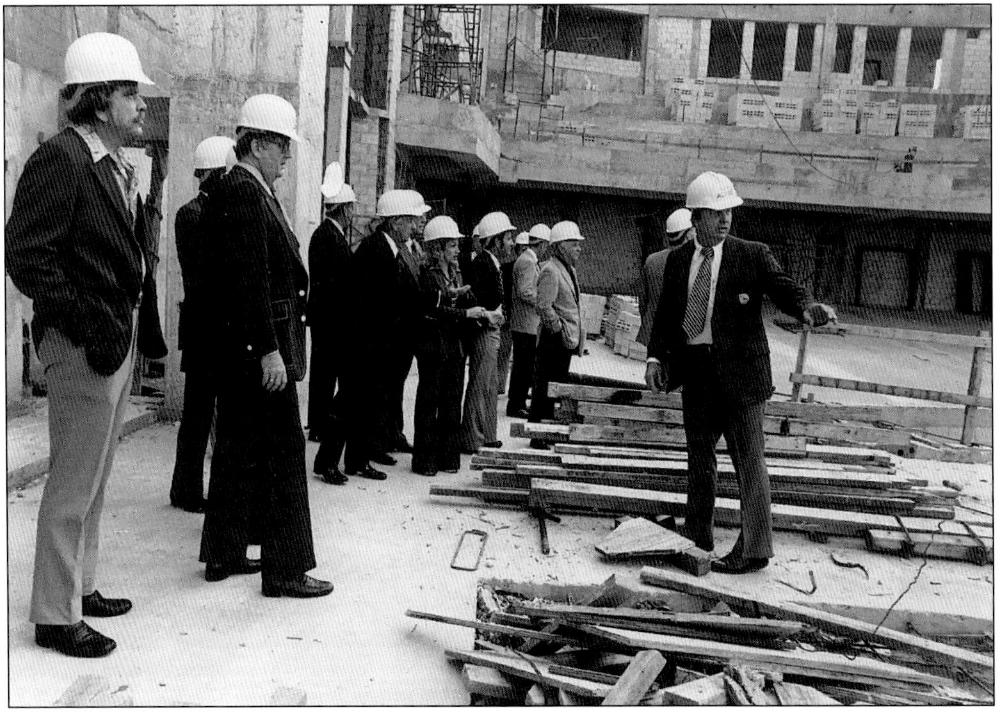

Dr. Adams leads a tour for visiting dignitaries of the $6-million facility during construction.

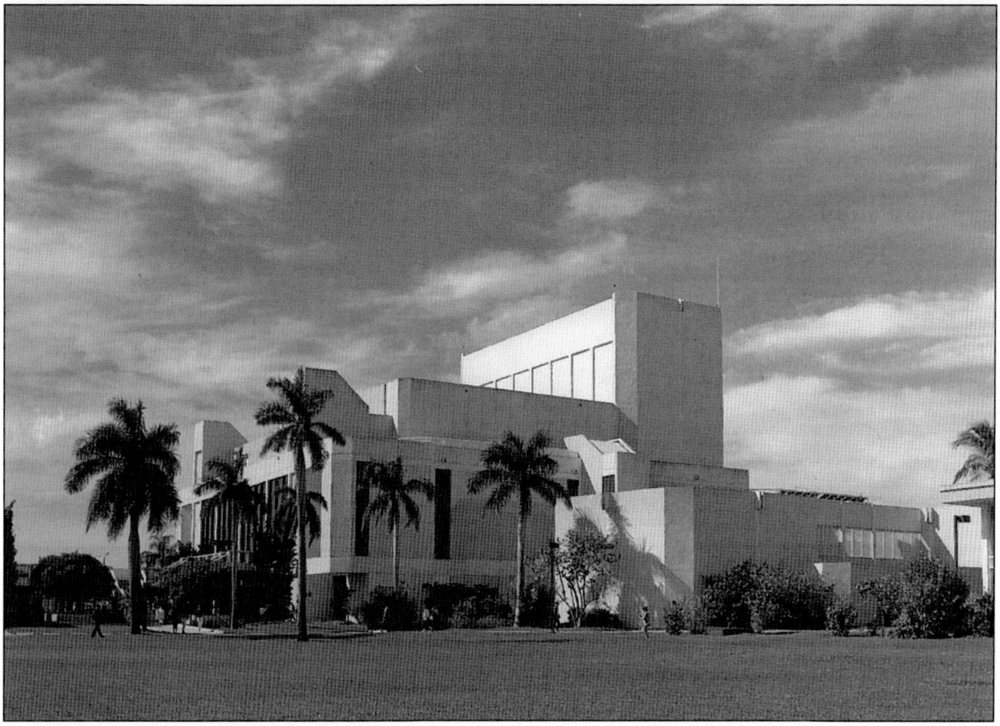

The Ralph R. Bailey Concert Hall has grown to become the focal point for the performing arts in southwestern Broward County.

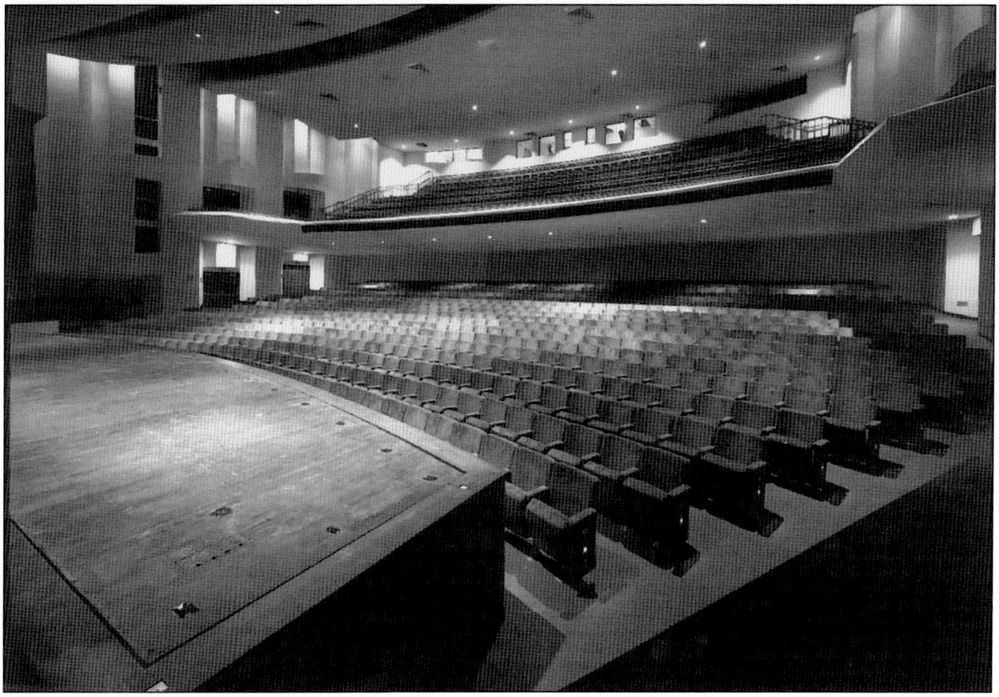

In October 1979, the 1,200-set performing arts center was dedicated. Each seat has clean sight lines and excellent sound.

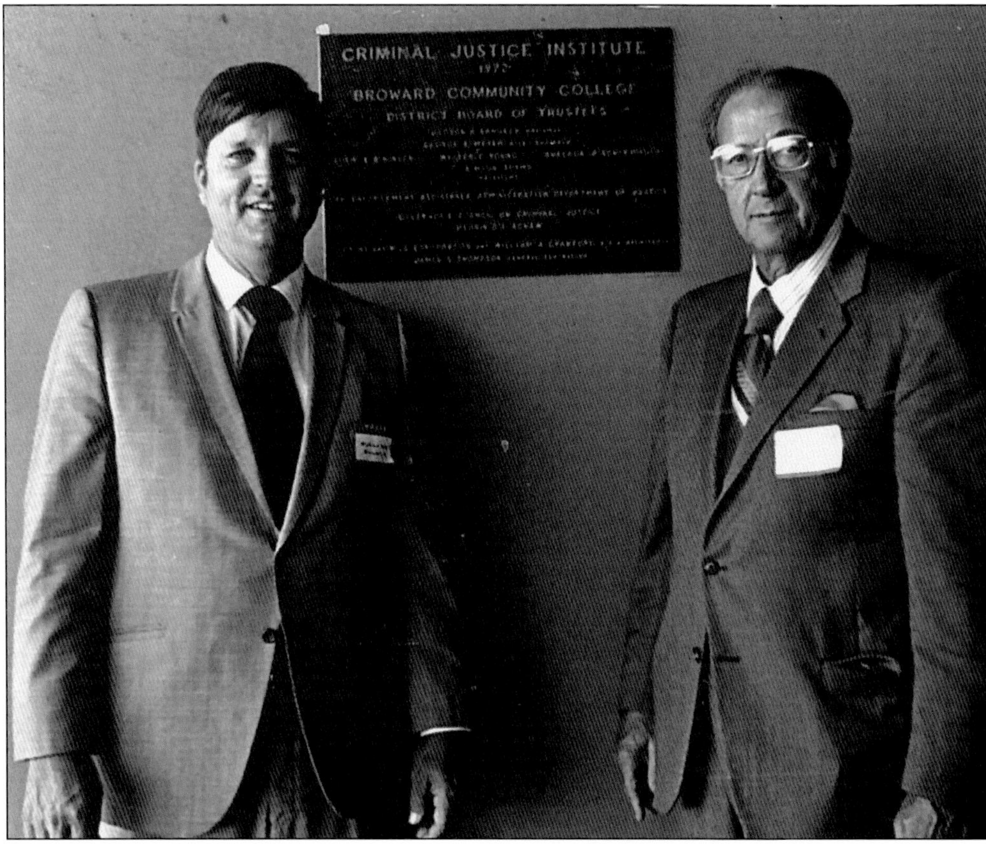


Dr. Adams and District Board of Trustees Chairman Judson A. Samuels are pictured here at the dedication of the Criminal Justice Institute on Central Campus in 1972. Now called the Public Safety Institute, the center trains all of Broward County's law-enforcement officers.

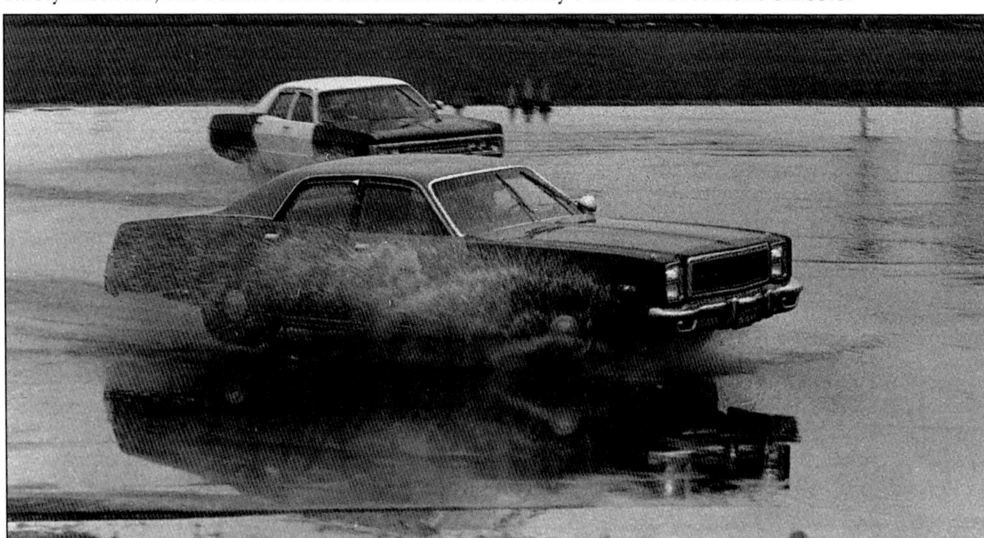

The Criminal Justice Institute has grown to become a complete facility for training all of Broward's law enforcement personnel.

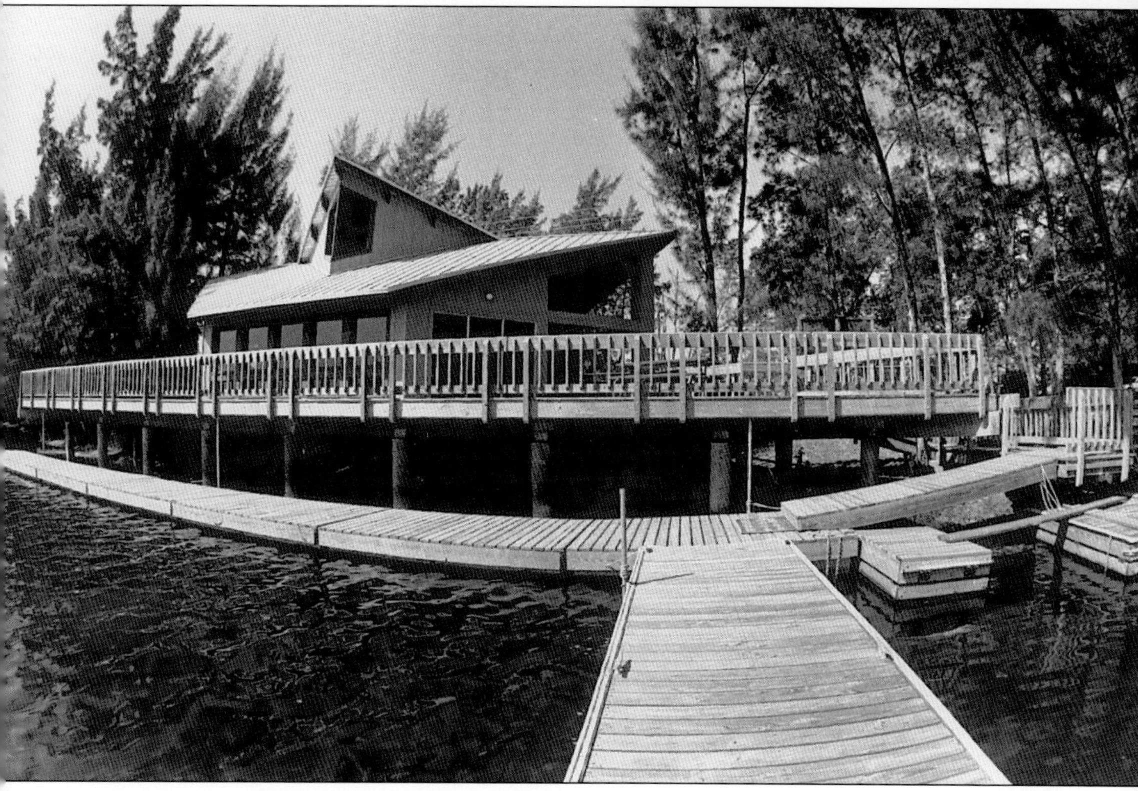

Broward County leased a portion of Tigertail Lake in Dania Beach to BCC in 1975 so the college could begin a sailing program. A portable trailer and small boathouse were added later. The Otto M. Burkhardt Conference Center, dedicated in November 1986, was constructed for classes, workshops, seminars, meetings, and conferences with about 40 conferees.

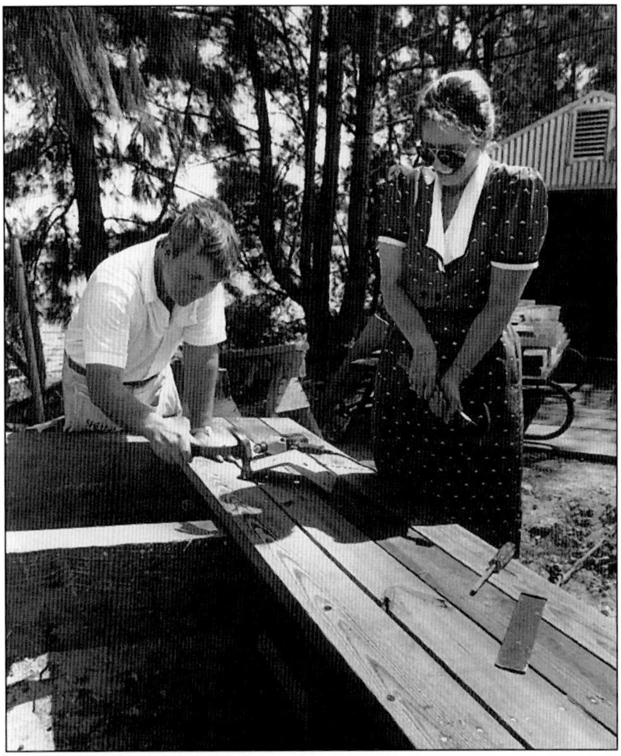

The conference center building effort got a hand in construction from the administration and trustees. Dr. Katherine Hunter, the vice president for academic affairs, takes the lead from Dr. Adams in the art of driving nails.

Dr. Adams congratulates art professor Lamonte Anderson and his "Fatcats" intramural team, winners of the President's Intramural Cup.

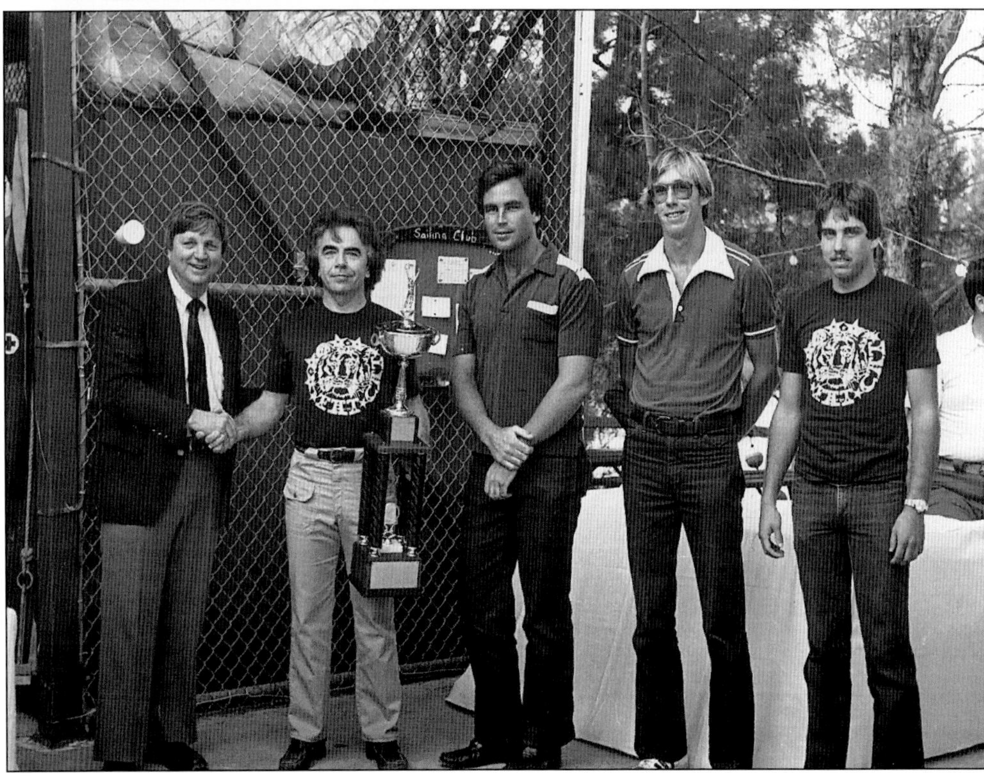

The Floyd County Sound Bluegrass Band put the Tigertail boathouse to good use at the center's rededication ceremonies in November 1986.

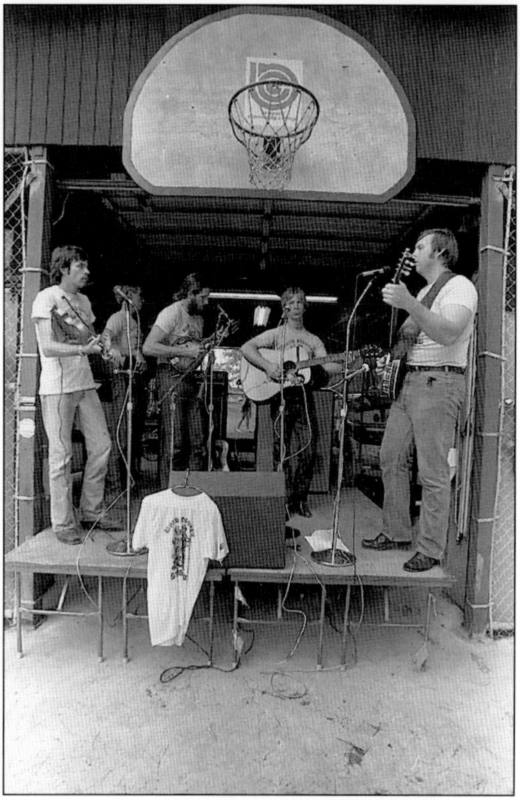

With both the Fine Arts Theater and Bailey Hall, the college gained greater drawing power and attracted impressive names. Here, Trustee Sheldon Schlesinger chats with Vincent Price.

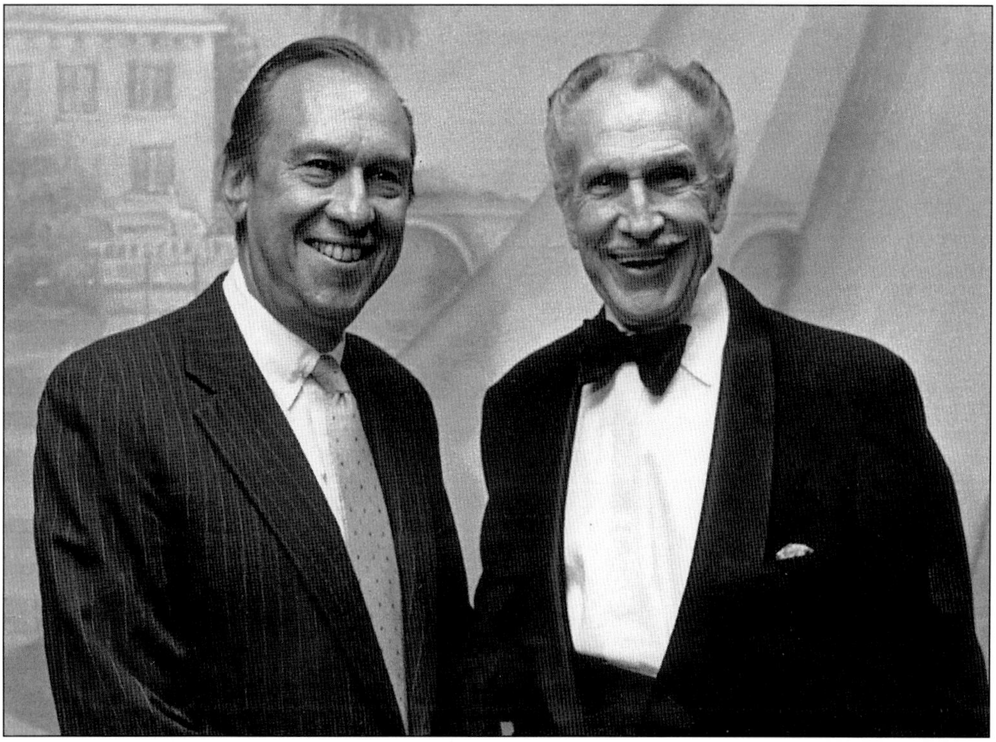

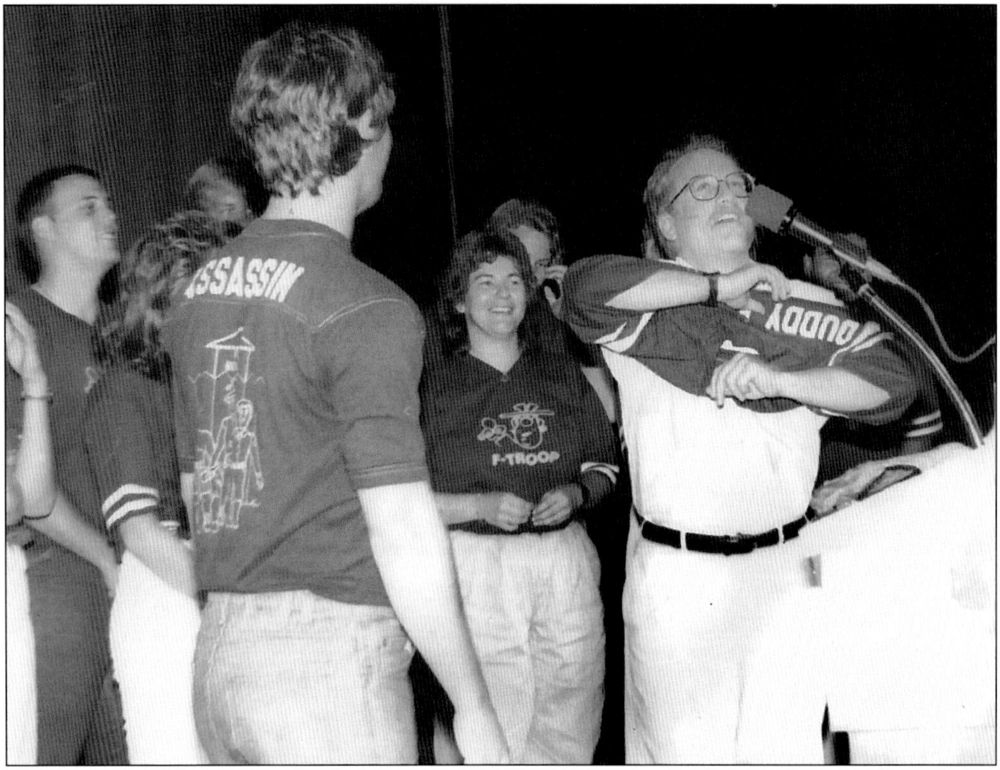


Richard Dreyfuss dons a jersey presented to him by F-Troop members during a visit to the college. The name on the back of the jersey refers to Dreyfuss's title role in the 1974 film *The Apprenticeship of Duddy Kravitz*, based on the 1959 book by Mordecai Richler.

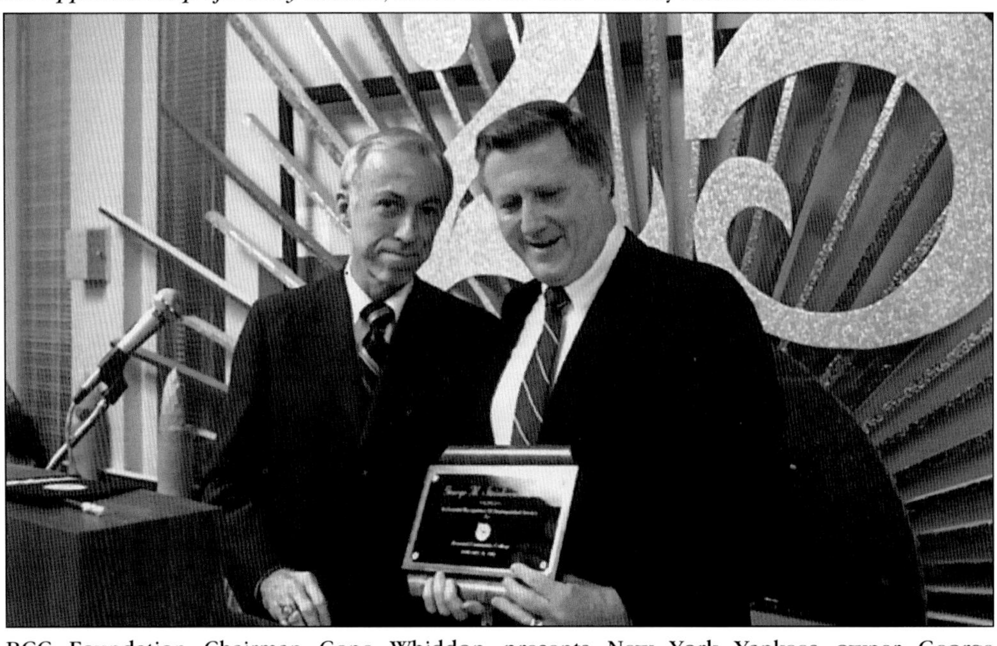

BCC Foundation Chairman Gene Whiddon presents New York Yankees owner George Steinbrenner with a memento from the college.

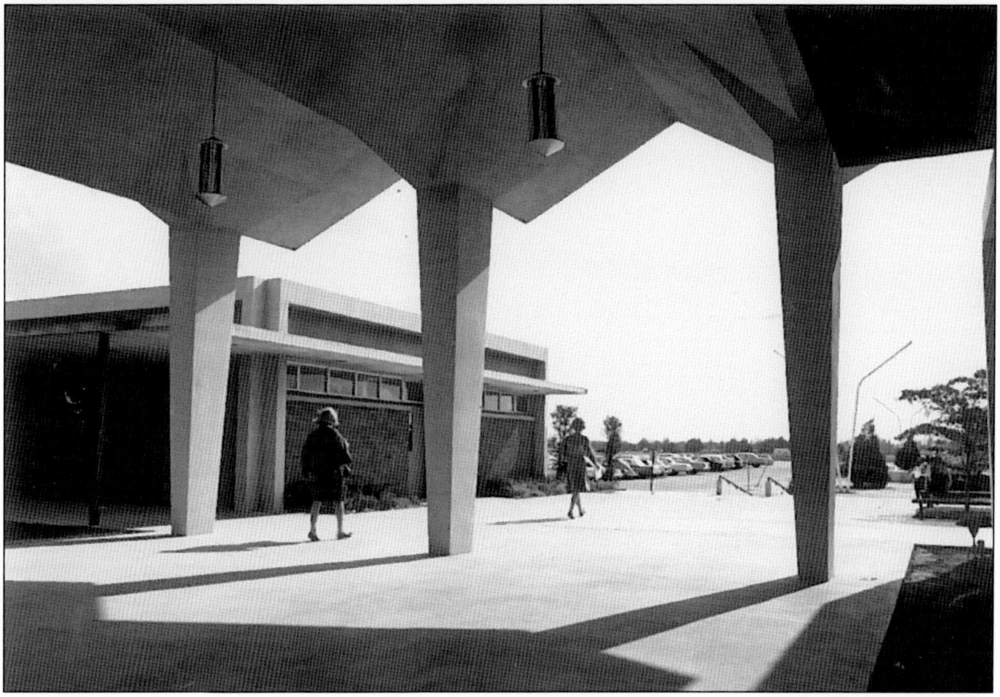

In 1980, as part of the college's 20th birthday celebration, buildings on Central Campus were dedicated to honor individuals of importance to the college. The Central Campus administration building was named Joe B. Rushing Hall in honor of the founding president of the college.

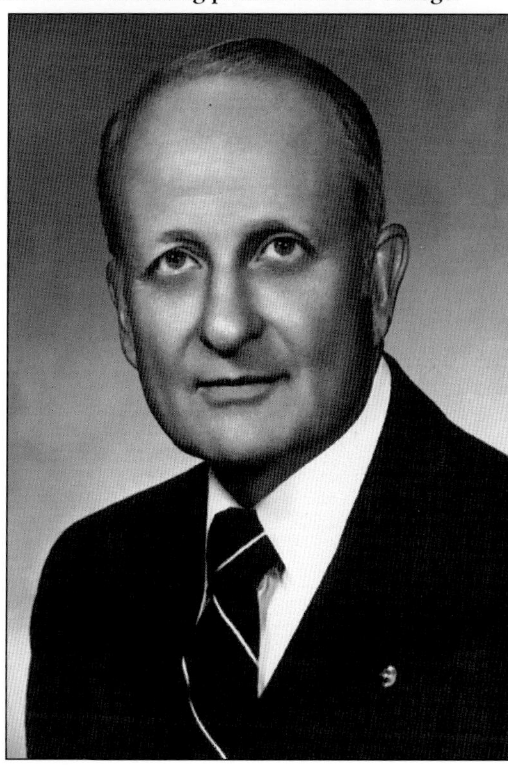

Now retired and raising bulls in Texas, Joe Rushing still maintains ties to BCC.

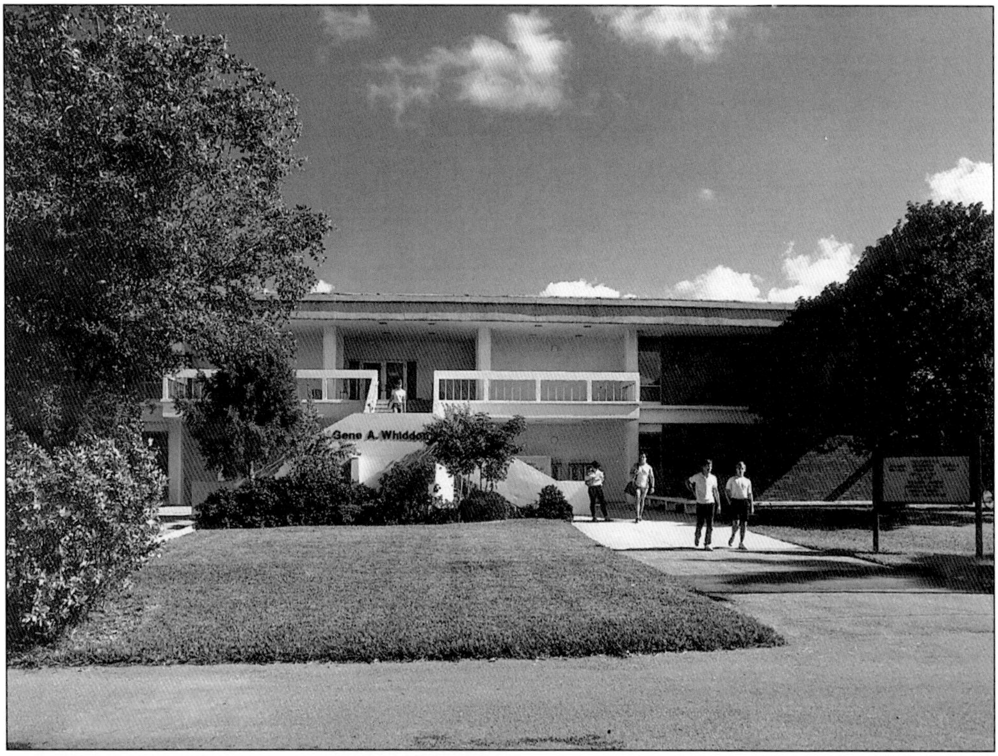

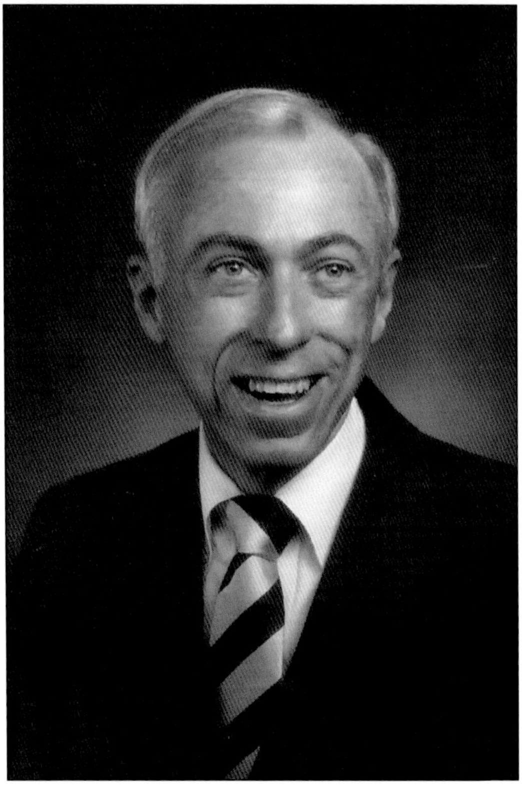

Gene A. Whiddon Hall was named to honor the founding chairman of the BCC Foundation. Whiddon brought together a group of 15 prominent Broward citizens and college officials in 1971 for the purpose of creating an organization to assist the college in its mission of serving the community.

Gene Whiddon, who was also president of Causeway Lumber Co., served as chairman of the BCC Foundation through his death in 1989. He was named the first recipient of the college's Distinguished Service Award in 1973 and the Seahawk Award in 1978. Whiddon Hall is home to Central Campus business programs.

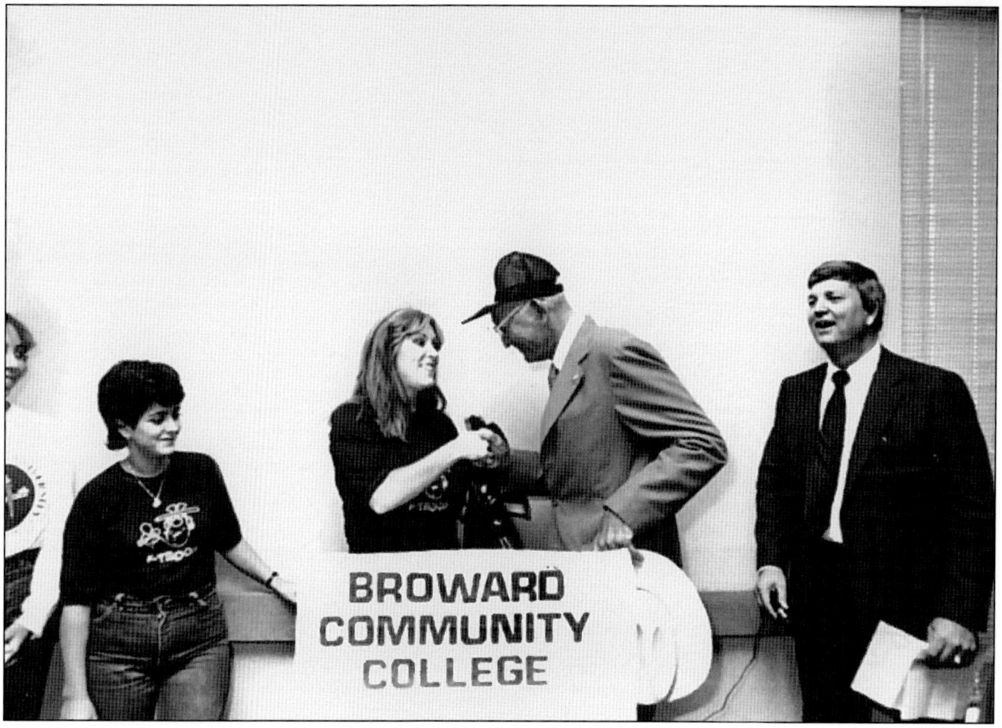


Dr. Adams joins with members of F-Troop in welcoming Dr. Charles Forman to the dedication ceremonies for the Charles R. Forman Center.

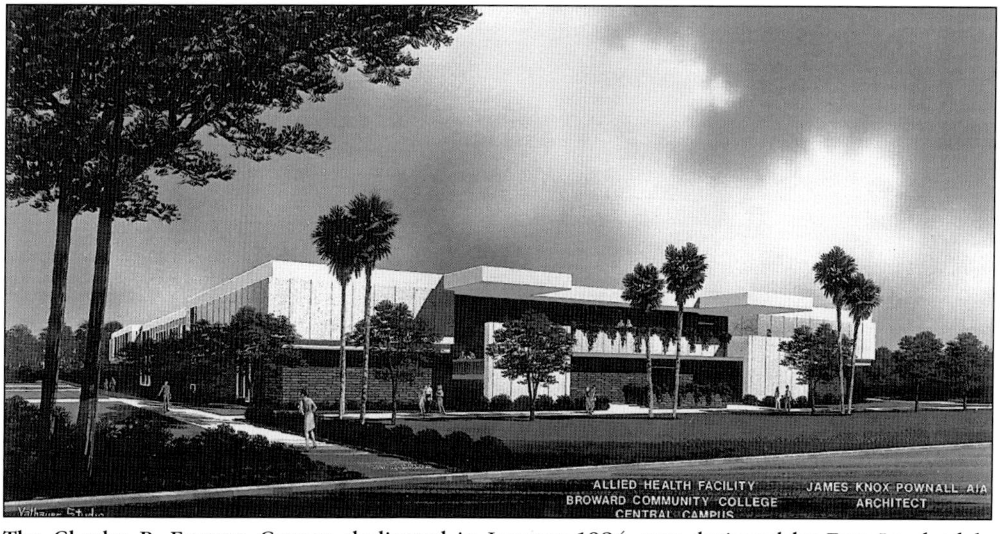


The Charles R. Forman Center, dedicated in January 1984, was designed by Fort Lauderdale architect James Knox Pownall. The center was planned as the home for the variety of health science programs offered by the college, offering classroom and laboratory space.

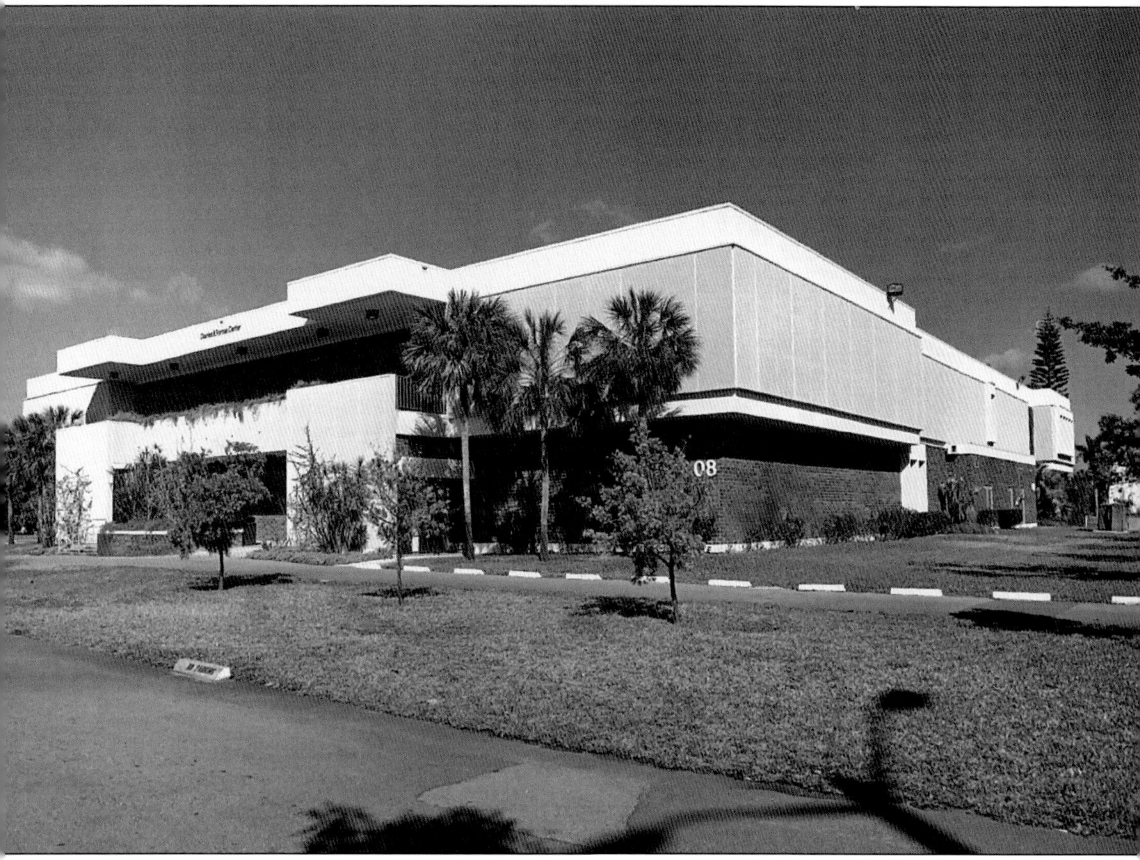

The Forman Center was re-dedicated in 1999 as the Lucy W. and Charles R. Forman Center, reflecting the contributions of Dr. Forman and his wife, Lucille Watson Forman. Dr. Forman, a veterinarian, school board member, and a member of one of Broward's pioneer families, was a staunch supporter of educational issues in Broward and was influential in the growth and development of Broward Community College.

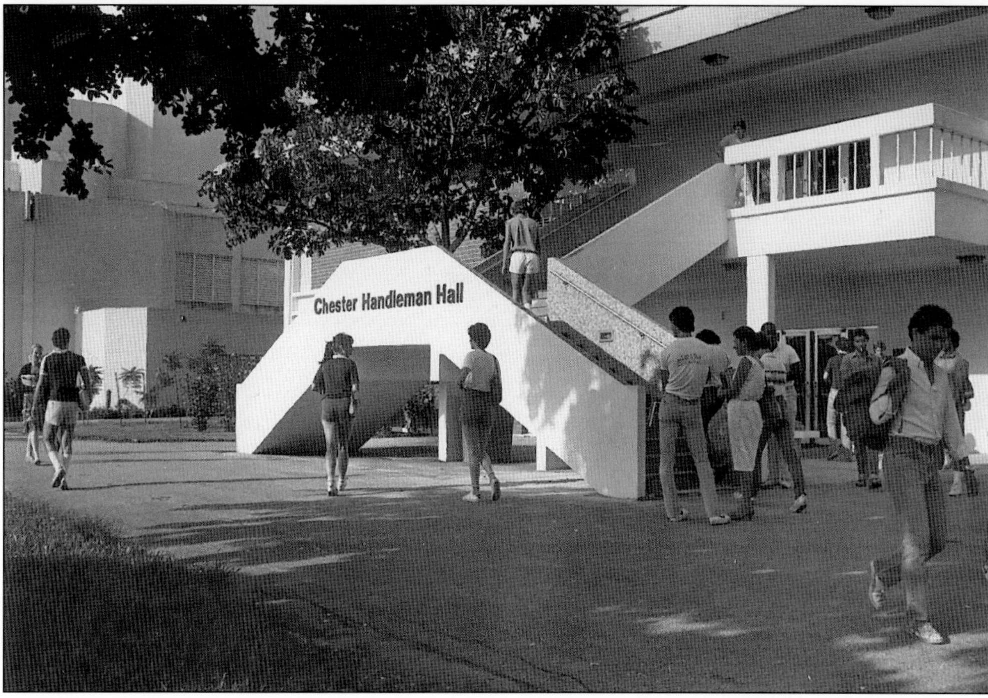


Handleman Hall is home to a variety of classes, including English, mathematics, and history.

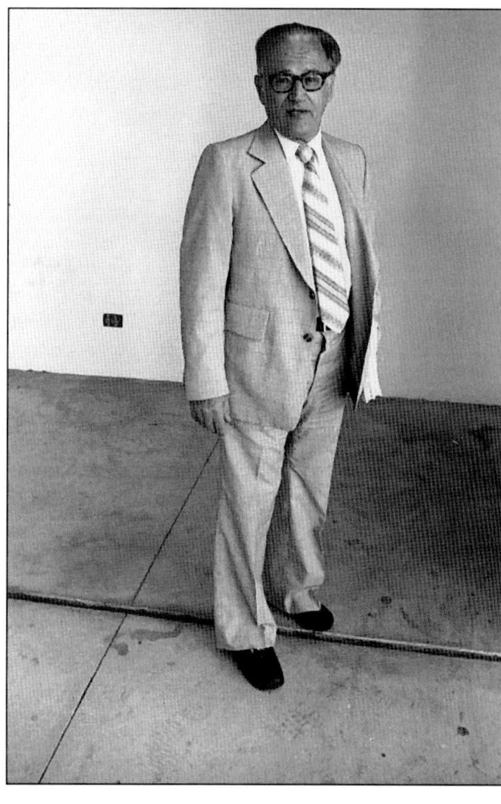

Chester Handleman was a congenial yet cerebral history and political science professor who was loved by his students, respected by his colleagues, and active in many facets of college life. Educated at Clark College, Massachusetts State, and Nova University, Dr. Handleman was a widely published expert in the areas of international relations and national politics. He was a member of the faculty from 1961 until his sudden death while on sabbatical at Durham, North Carolina.

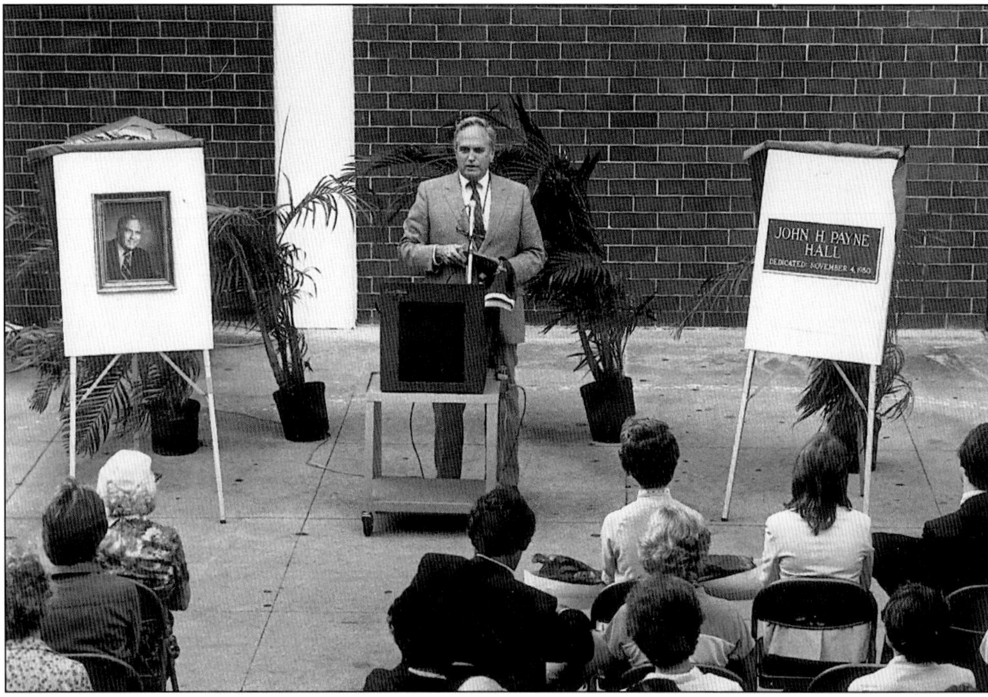


John H. Payne addresses the audience at dedication ceremonies for the building that bears his name. A member of the college's advisory committee, Payne also served as one of the college trustees through September 1987 and remains a staunch supporter of the college.

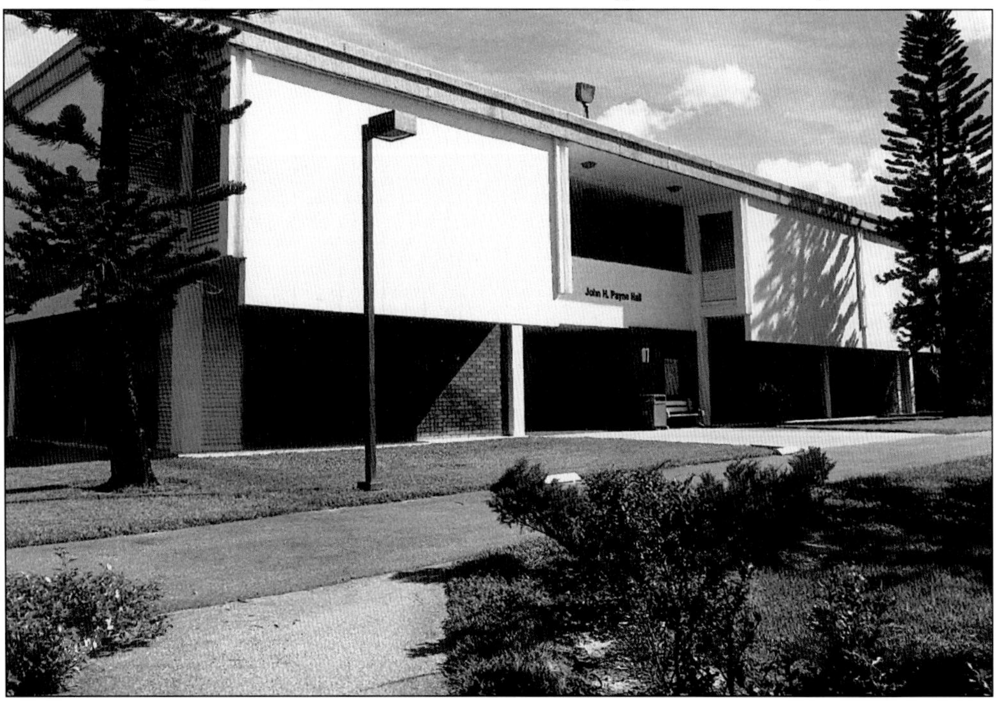


Located within Payne Hall is the Leon Watts Career Center, named in honor of a longtime college employee who also served as one of the college's trustees.

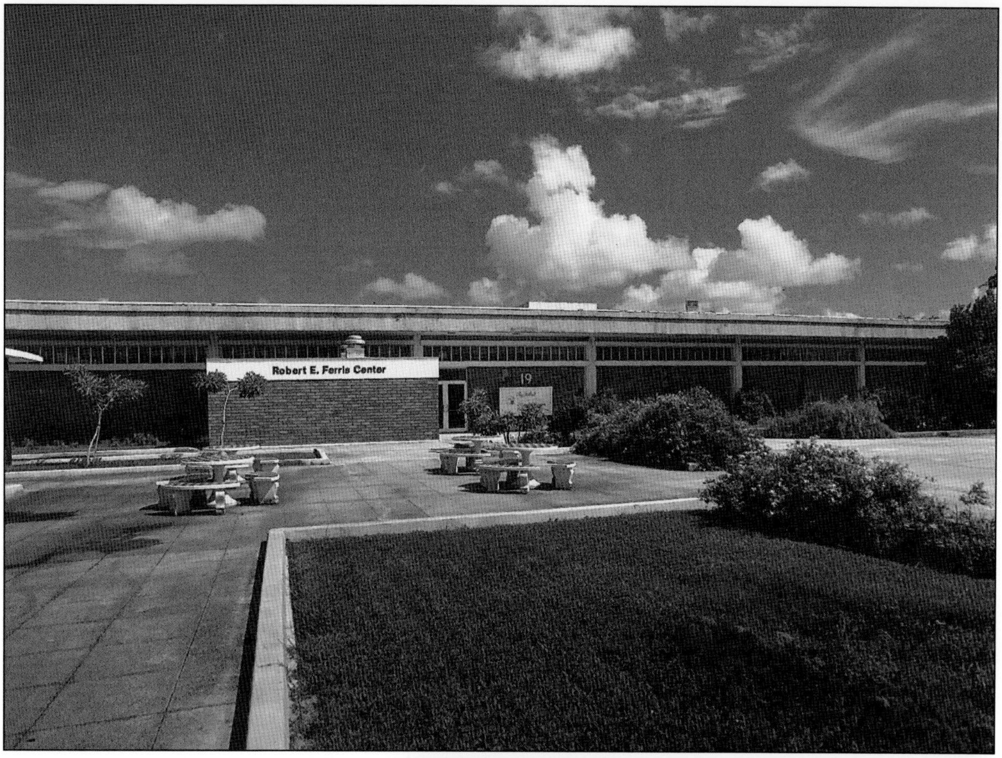


The Robert E. Ferris Center, more widely known as the Hospitality Center, was the center of student activities on campus.

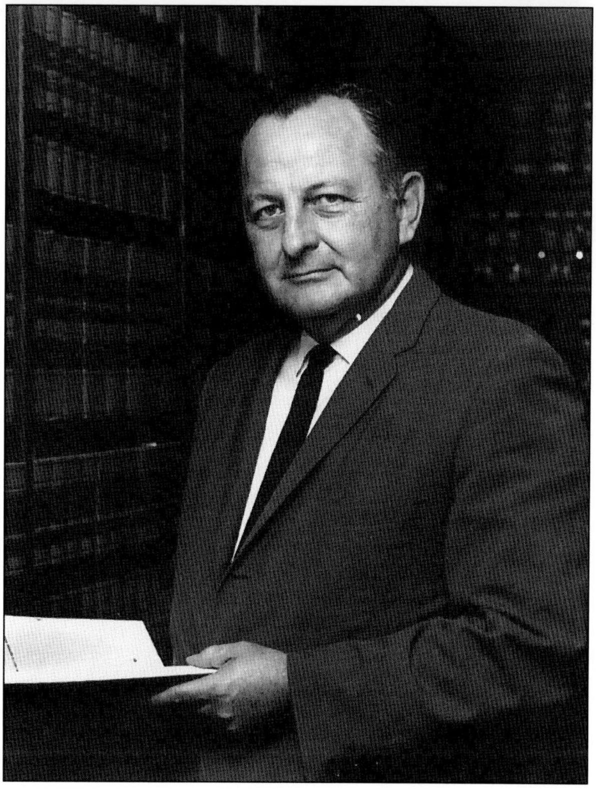

Robert E. Ferris, a Broward County attorney and judge, served on the Board of Public Instruction and was named to the JCBC Advisory Committee in 1959. He also served as a member of the BCC District Board of Trustees from 1968 to 1971.

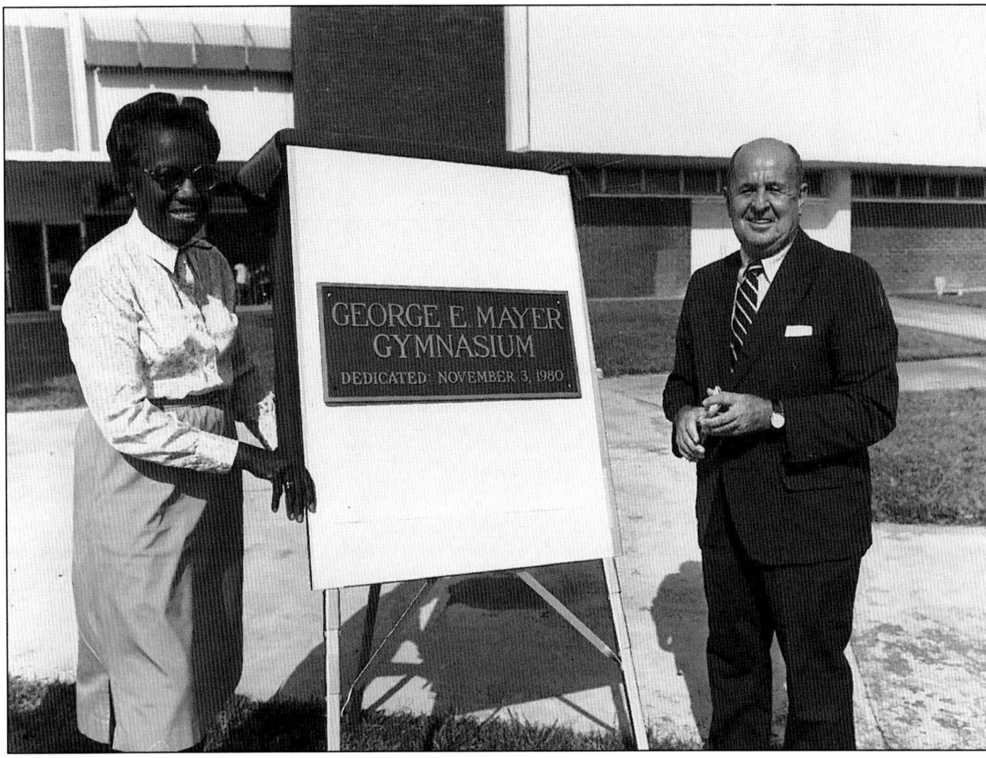


Trustee Margaret Roach joins George Mayer to unveil the plaque for the George E. Mayer Gymnasium.

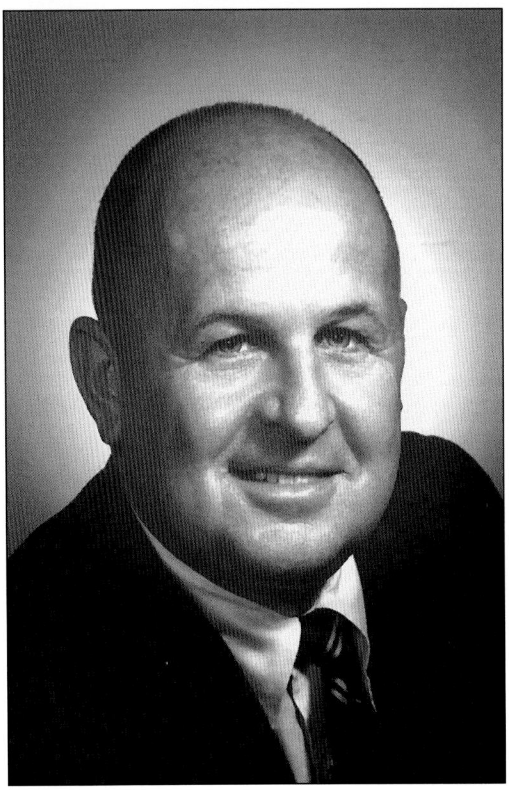

George E. Mayer, owner of a Broward real estate company, served as a trustee from 1969 to 1981.

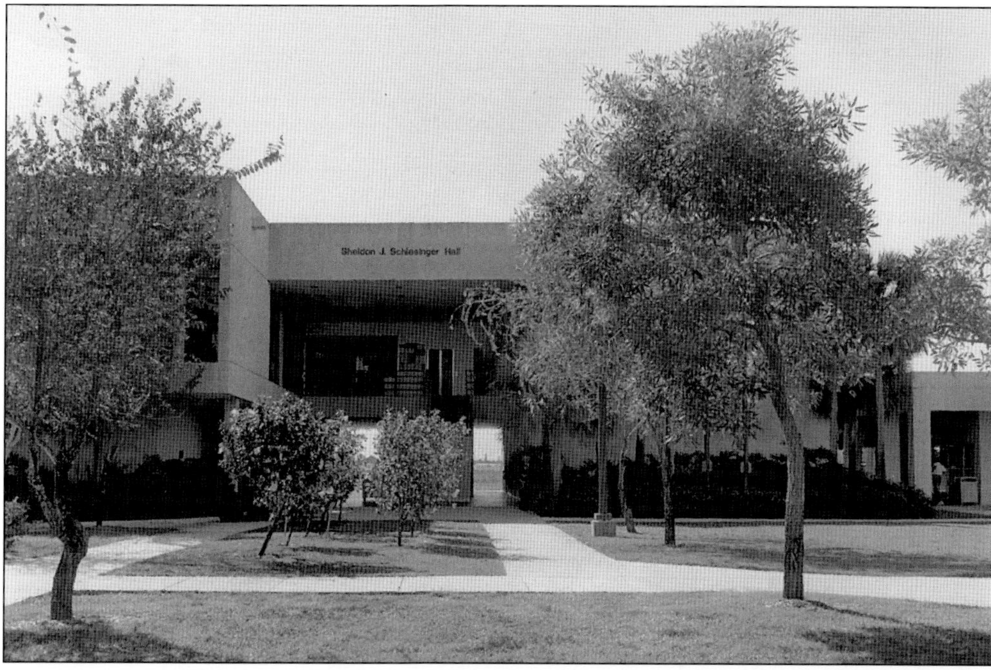


On August 24, 1977, South Campus opened its doors to about 700 students. Classes were held at the First United Methodist Church in Hollywood. On June 3, 1979, ground was broken for the first permanent facility on the North Perry Airport property. The building, later named Sheldon J. Schlesinger Hall, contained classrooms, student services facilities, and faculty and administration offices, and was ready for the start of fall classes in 1980.

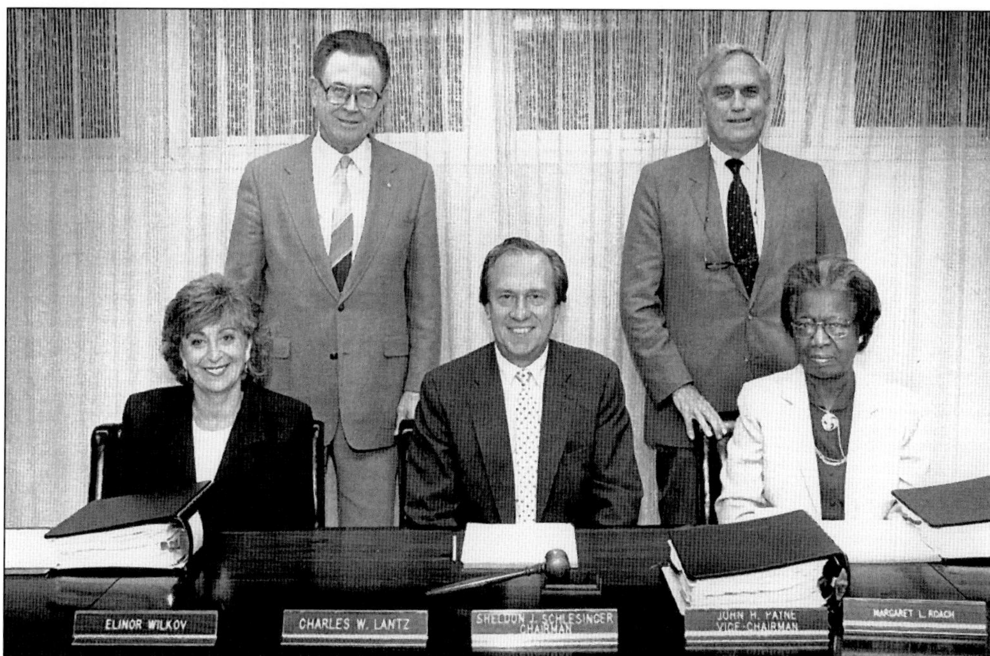


Broward County civil attorney Sheldon J. Schlesinger served on the board of trustees from 1971 to 1987.

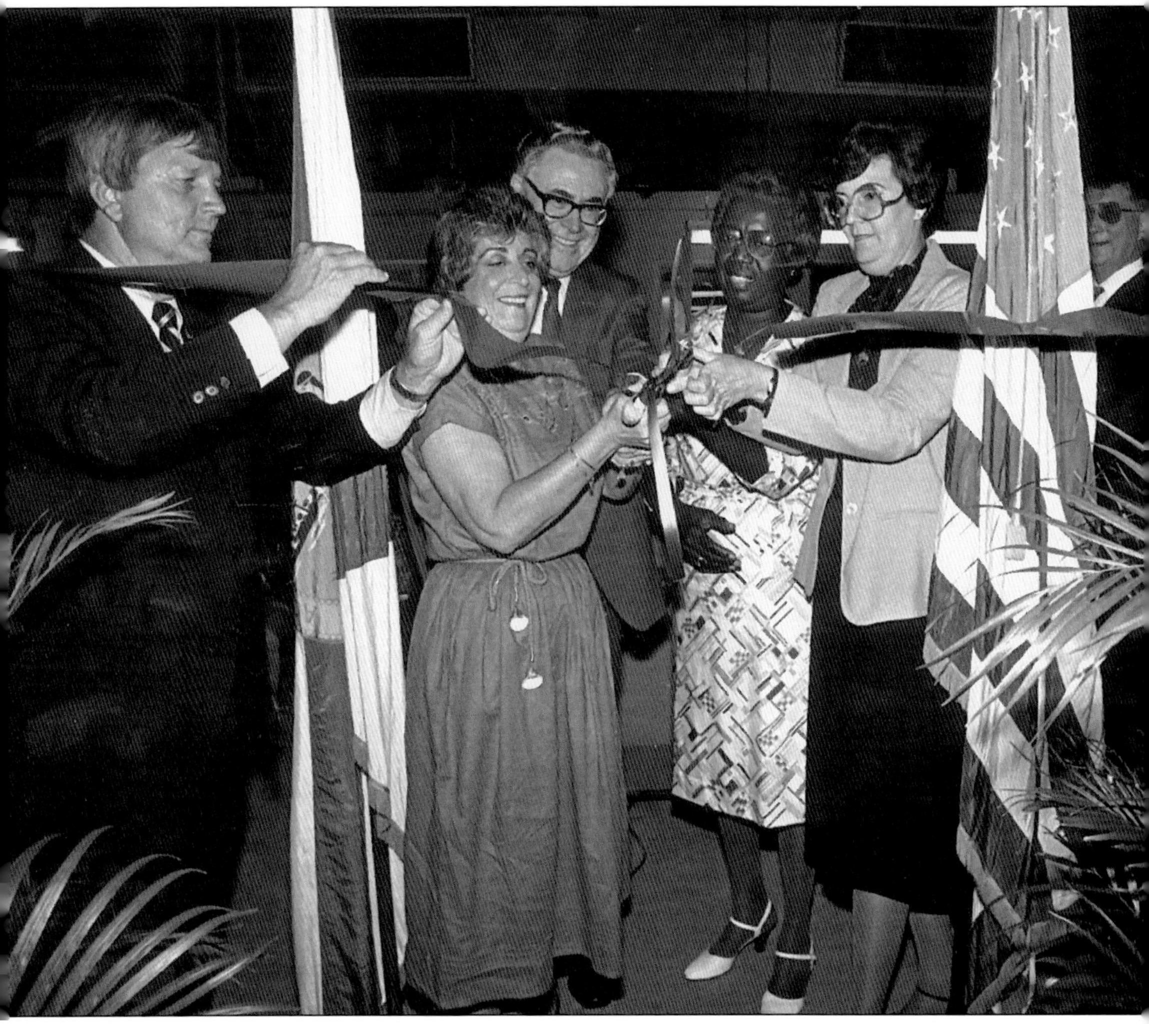

The Broward County Commission in March 1982 leased to the college the vacant auto inspection station on Pembroke Road at University Drive for the aviation institute. BCC's Aviation Maintenance Technology program was the first public post-secondary program in the state. The program opened its doors in the fall term of 1982 to a class of 65. At the ribbon-cutting ceremonies, from left to right, Dr. Adams, trustees Elinor Wilkov, Charles Lantz, and Margaret Roach joined with Broward County Commissioner Marcia Beach to carry out their ceremonial duties.

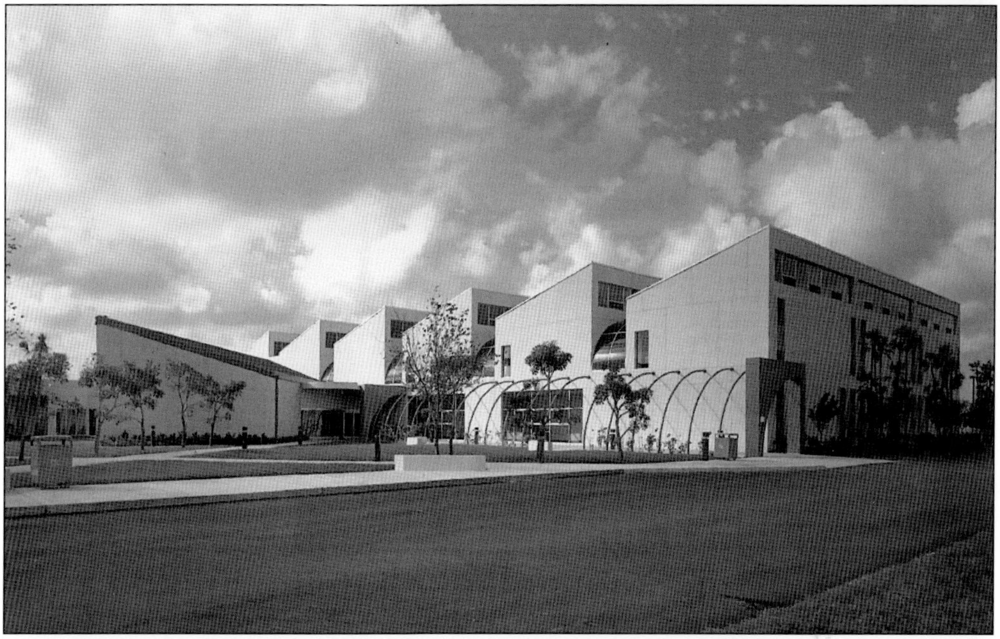

Groundbreaking ceremonies were held in April 1982 for the BCC/South Regional Library, a partnership between the college and the Broward County Library. The facility was completed in July 1983 and serves the college and the community. The partnership turned out to be so mutually beneficial, the entities partnered again on North Campus.

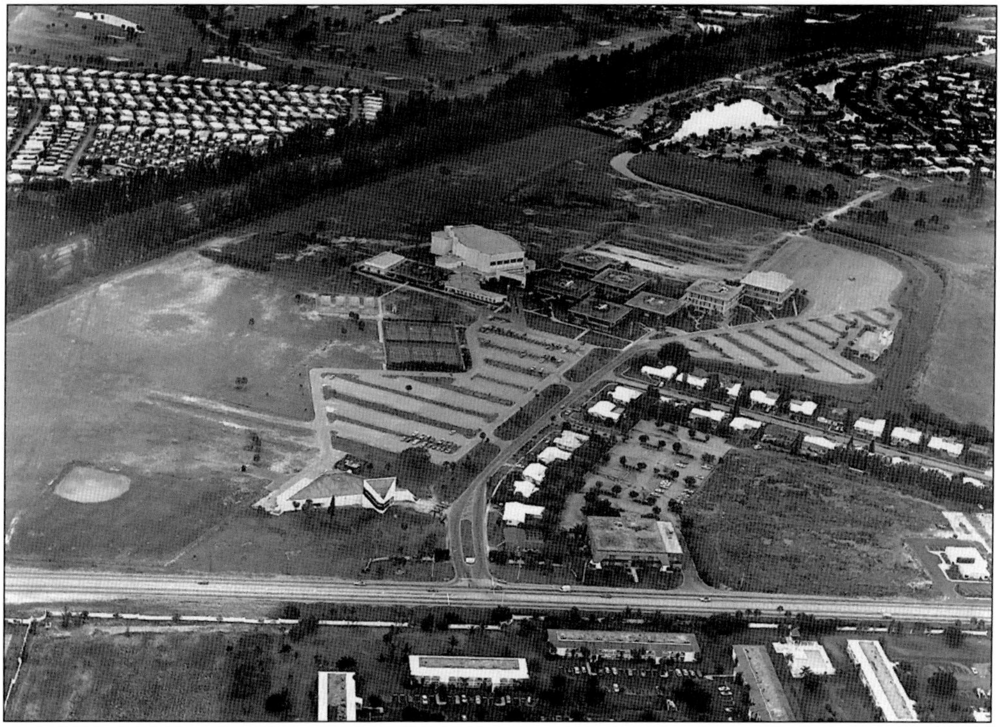

North Campus, dedicated in February 1972, is pictured early in its development. Building 41, the first building constructed on campus, is the tiny triangle at the lower left center of the picture.

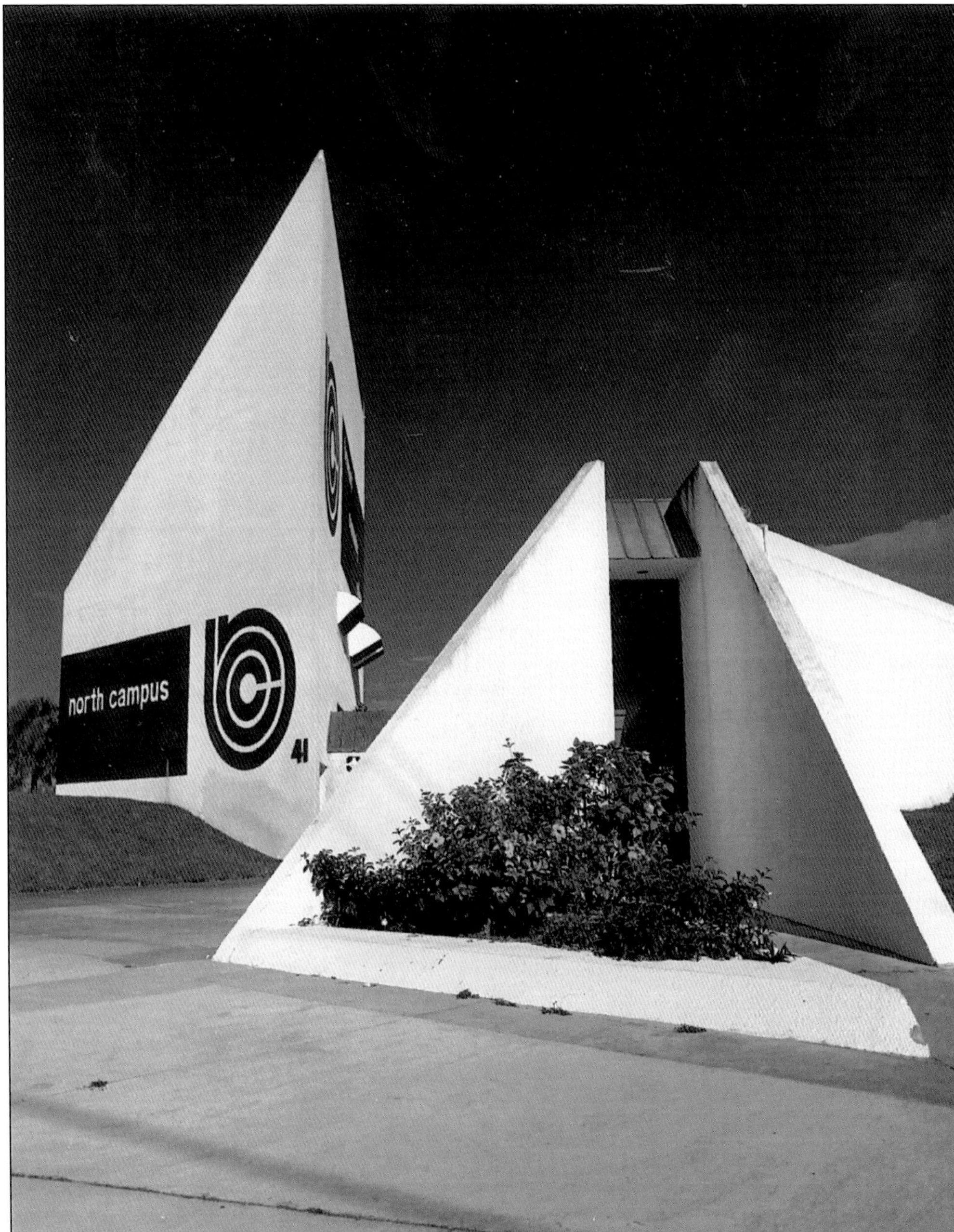


Building 41, used originally as an administration and student services building,was constructed of a series of triangles and was an attention-getter on Coconut Creek Parkway. The building was razed to make way for the Health Science Center II.

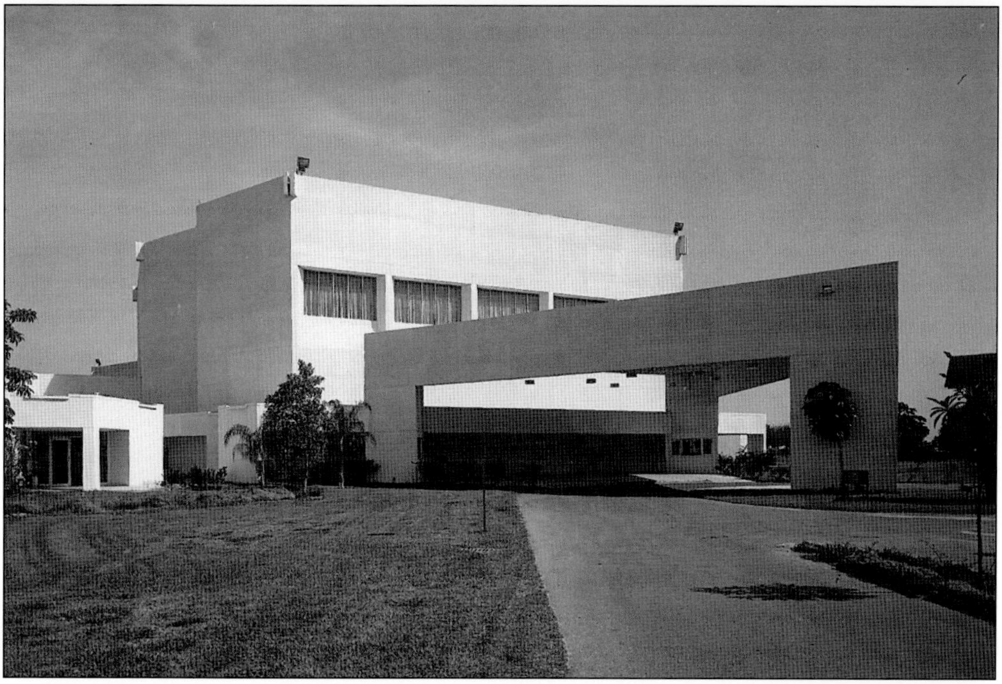

The Omni Auditorium, opened in 1980, serves as home to BCC's men's basketball and women's volleyball teams. The multipurpose facility seats 2,000 and also is used for graduation ceremonies and a variety of civic and cultural events.

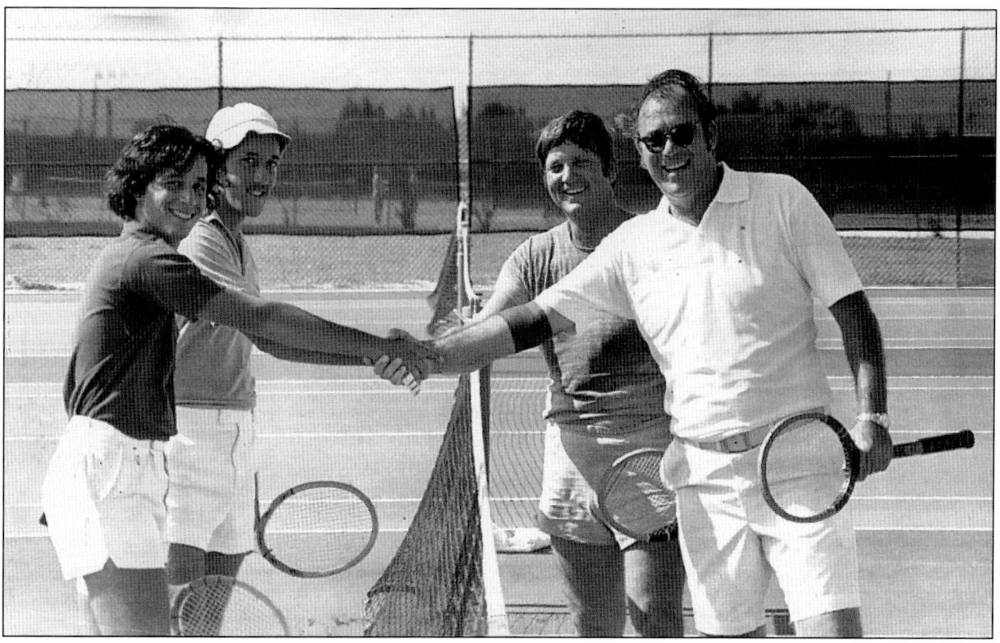

Dr. Adams and Dean Harry Smith, at far right, congratulate Dale Thisler and Steve Medoff after their match at the rededication of the Central Campus tennis courts.

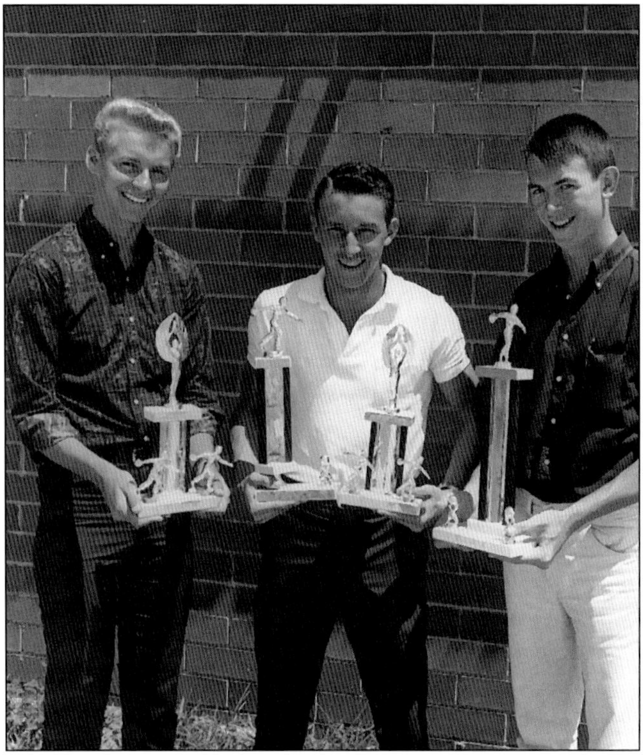

The quality of BJC's popular intramural sports program was demonstrated by these students, who brought home the state intramural bowling title

Dr. Tom Ryan, a history professor who also served as director of College Life and athletic director, takes time out to join in an intramural volleyball game. Behind Ryan, wearing a tie, is Dr. George Young, vice president for student affairs. The building in the background is Chester Handleman Hall.

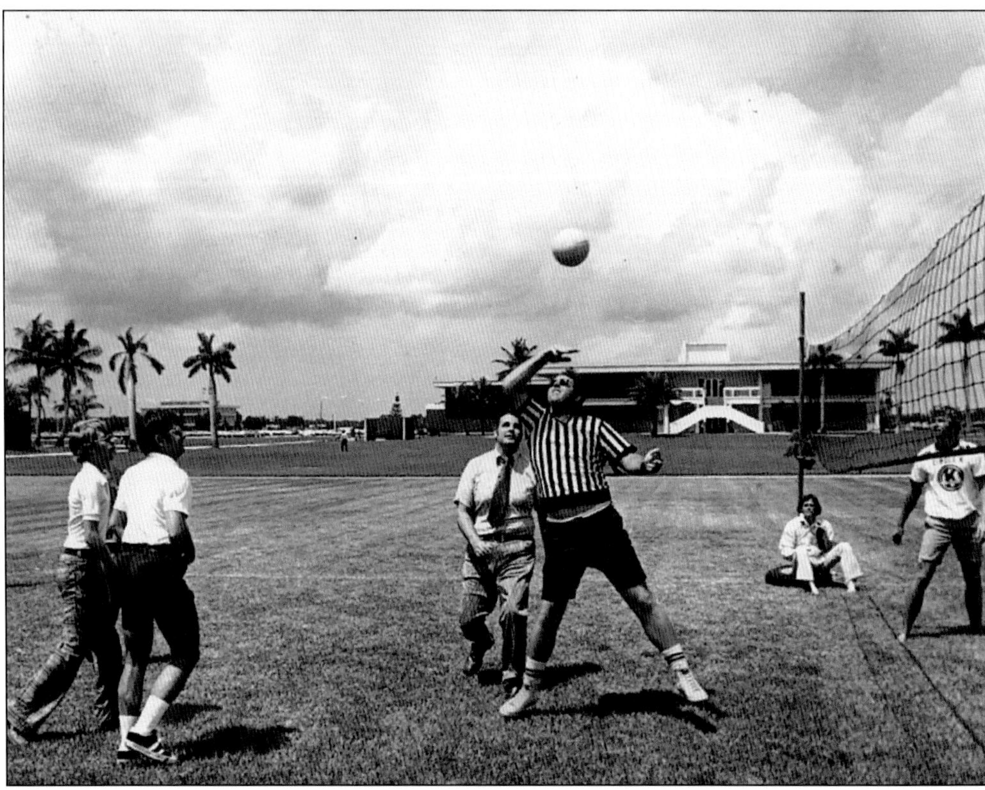

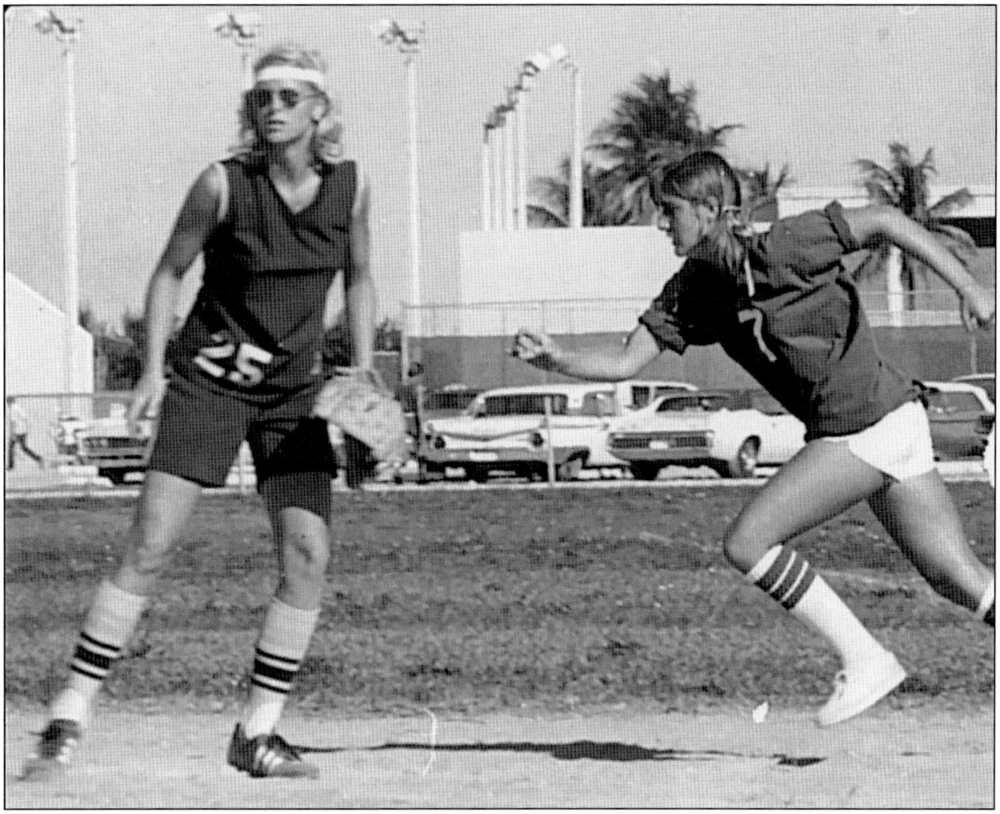


The Seahorses' third baseman waits for the throw in a softball game on Central Campus in the early 1970s. The site where the softball diamond was located is now a parking lot.

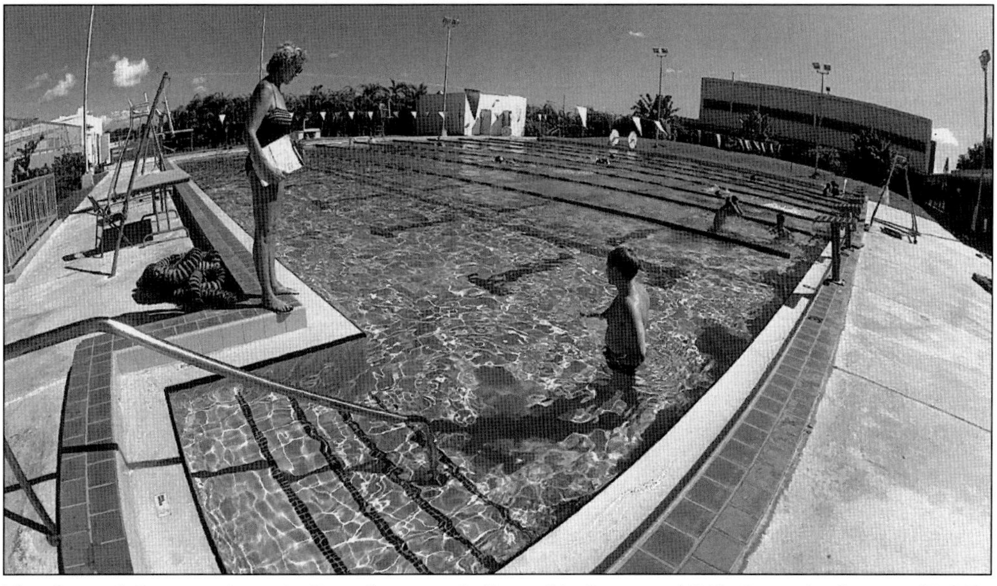

The Central Campus Aquatic Complex was dedicated in January 1976. Once the home of BCC's powerhouse swimming and diving teams, it now serves the college and community as a hub of aquatic activity.

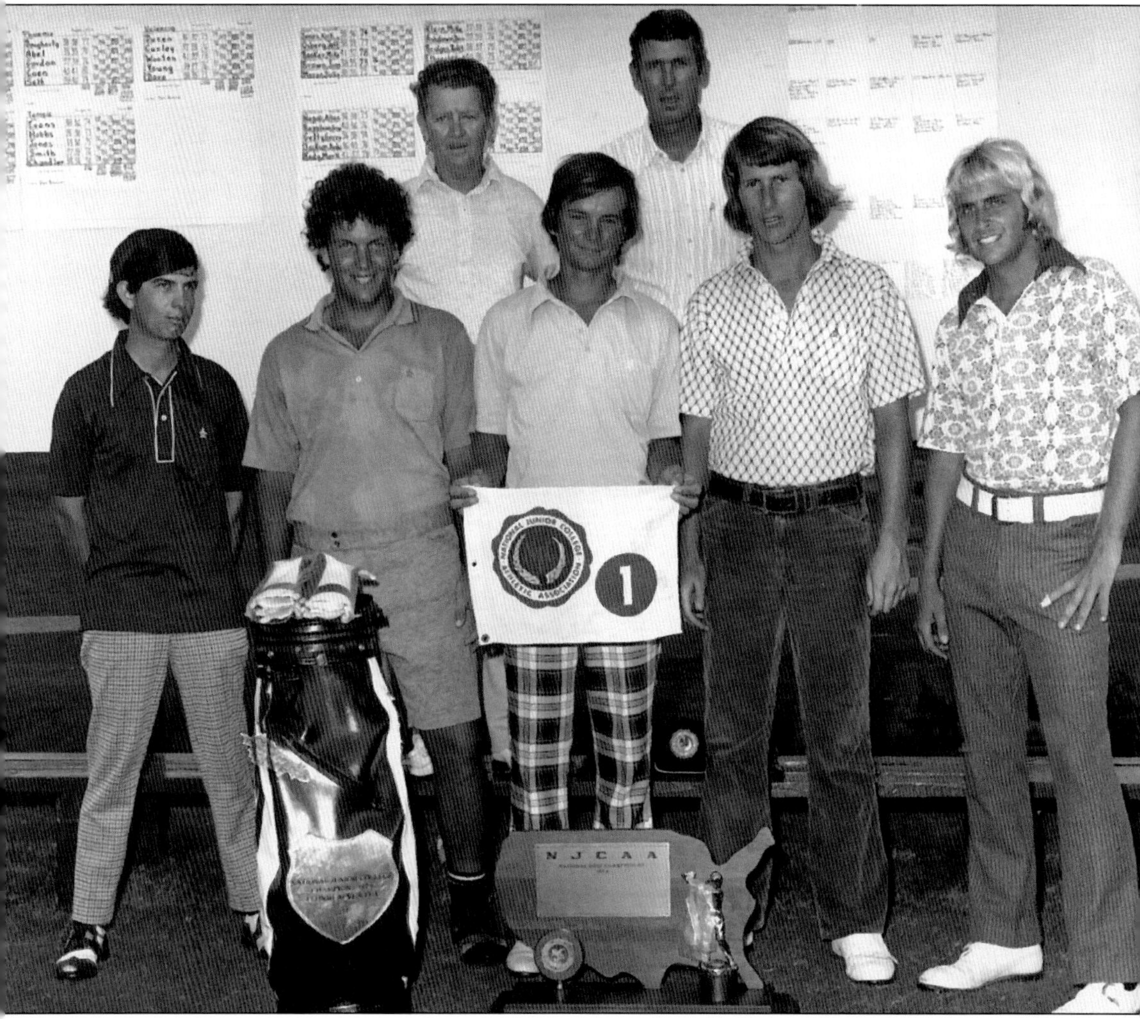


The men's golf team won the first of two National Junior College Athletic Association championships in 1974, at Lehigh Acres, Florida. Holding the flag is medalist Mike Donald, of Hollywood. Donald, a two-time all-American at BCC, won a Chris Schenkel scholarship to Georgia Southern College and later played on the PGA Tour. He turned pro in 1978 and joined the PGA Tour in 1980. He won the 1989 Anheuser-Busch Classic and tied The Masters record for low first-round score (64) for a rookie. Other members of the BCC championship squad are, from left to right, Don Beattie, Russ Hulser, John Duggan, and Bob Perlsanter. Coach Bud Marsee, at top right, went on to become the first coach of Auburn University's women's golf team.

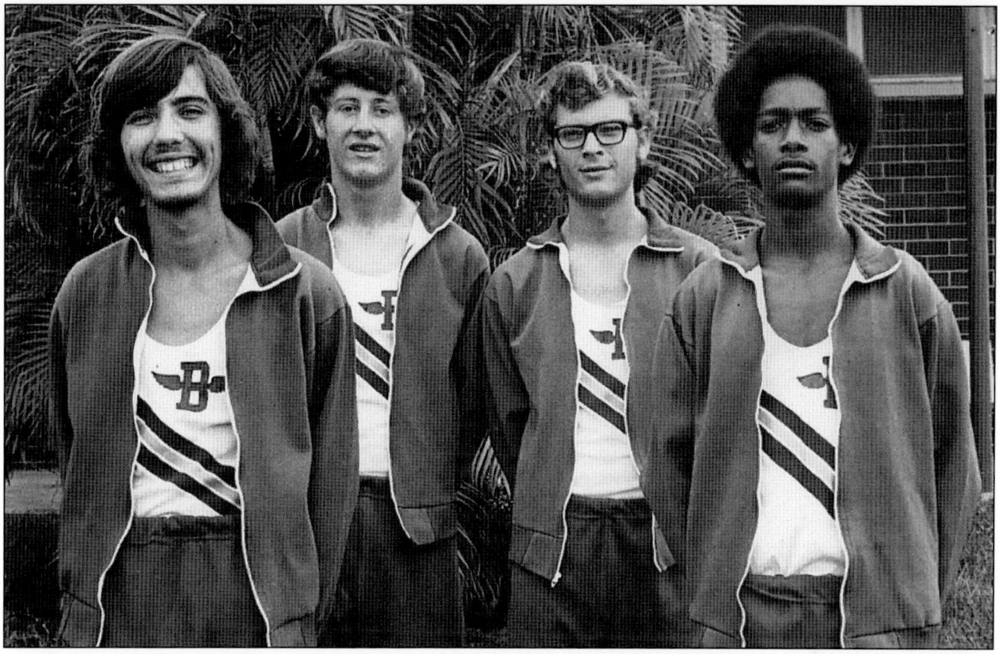

Over the years, the college has offered a variety of sports, including soccer, swimming, and diving for men and women; women's badminton; and men's cross-country and wrestling. From left to right are Rex Duff, Steve Christian, Don Edgar, and Ed Everett.

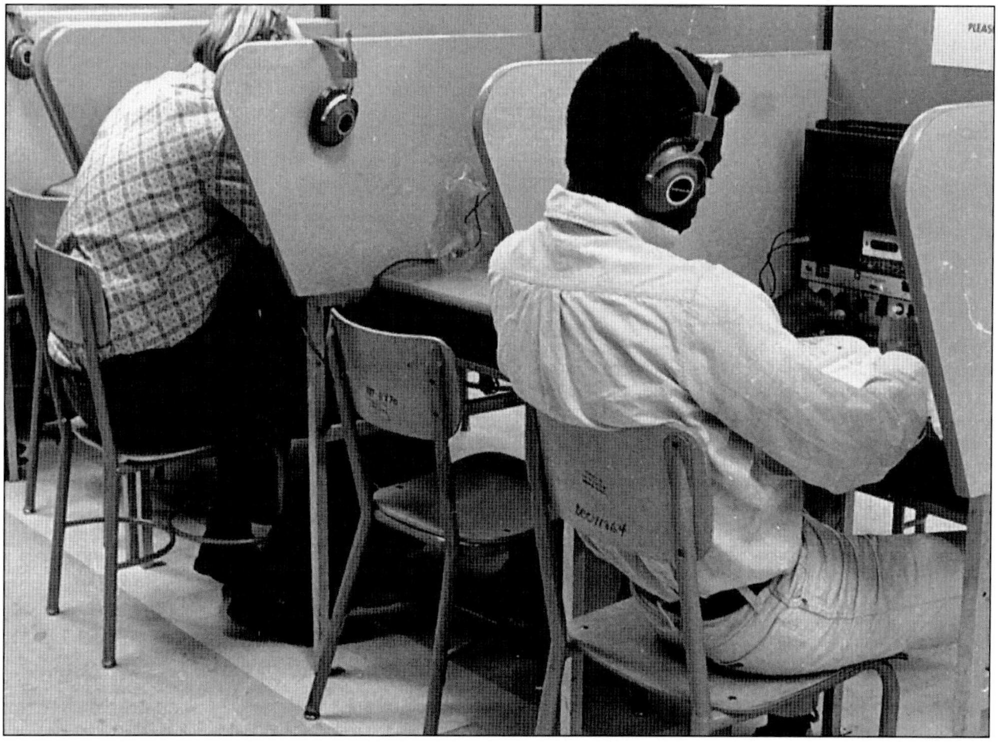

Students gained practical experience learning modern foreign languages in self-paced laboratory programs.

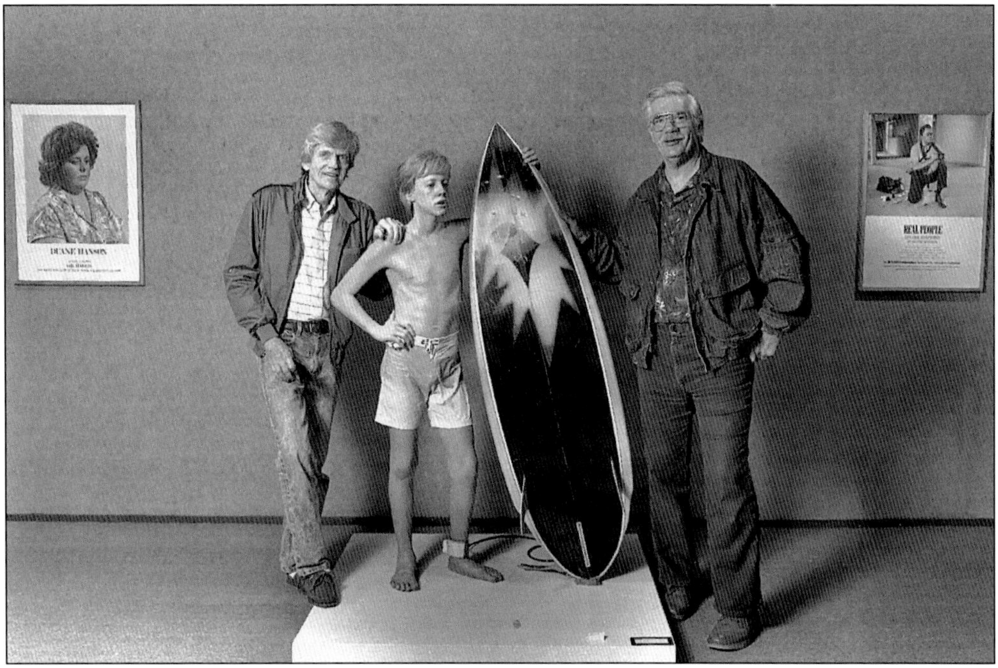

Sculptor Duane Hanson (left) was a regular guest at the Central Campus art gallery. A Davie resident and neighbor of BCC art professor Larry Tobe (right), Hanson often spoke to BCC art students. The sculpture *The Surfer* used Hanson's son as model. Tobe and his wife also served as Hanson models.

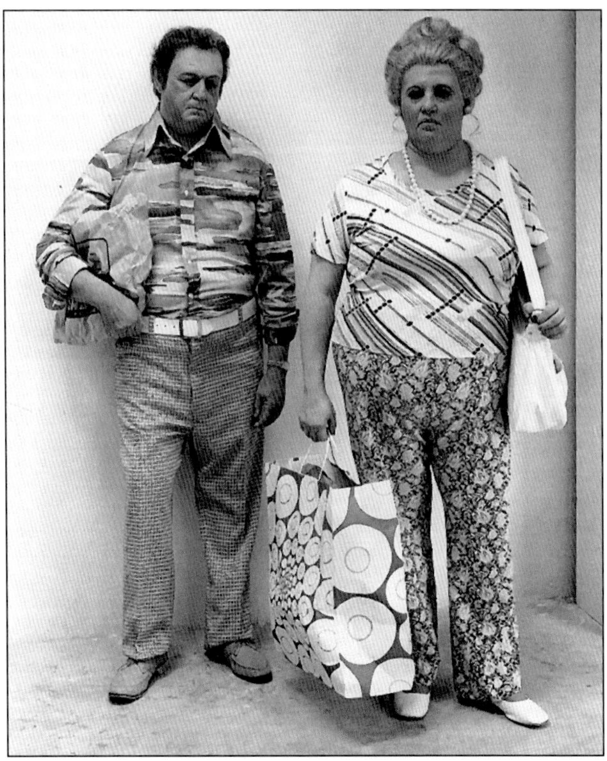

Hanson modeled his sculptures with gray polyvinyl body filler, airbrushed and painted skin, and then added hair and other details. Finally, he dressed them and added accessories. Hanson died in 1996, 11 days before his 71st birthday.

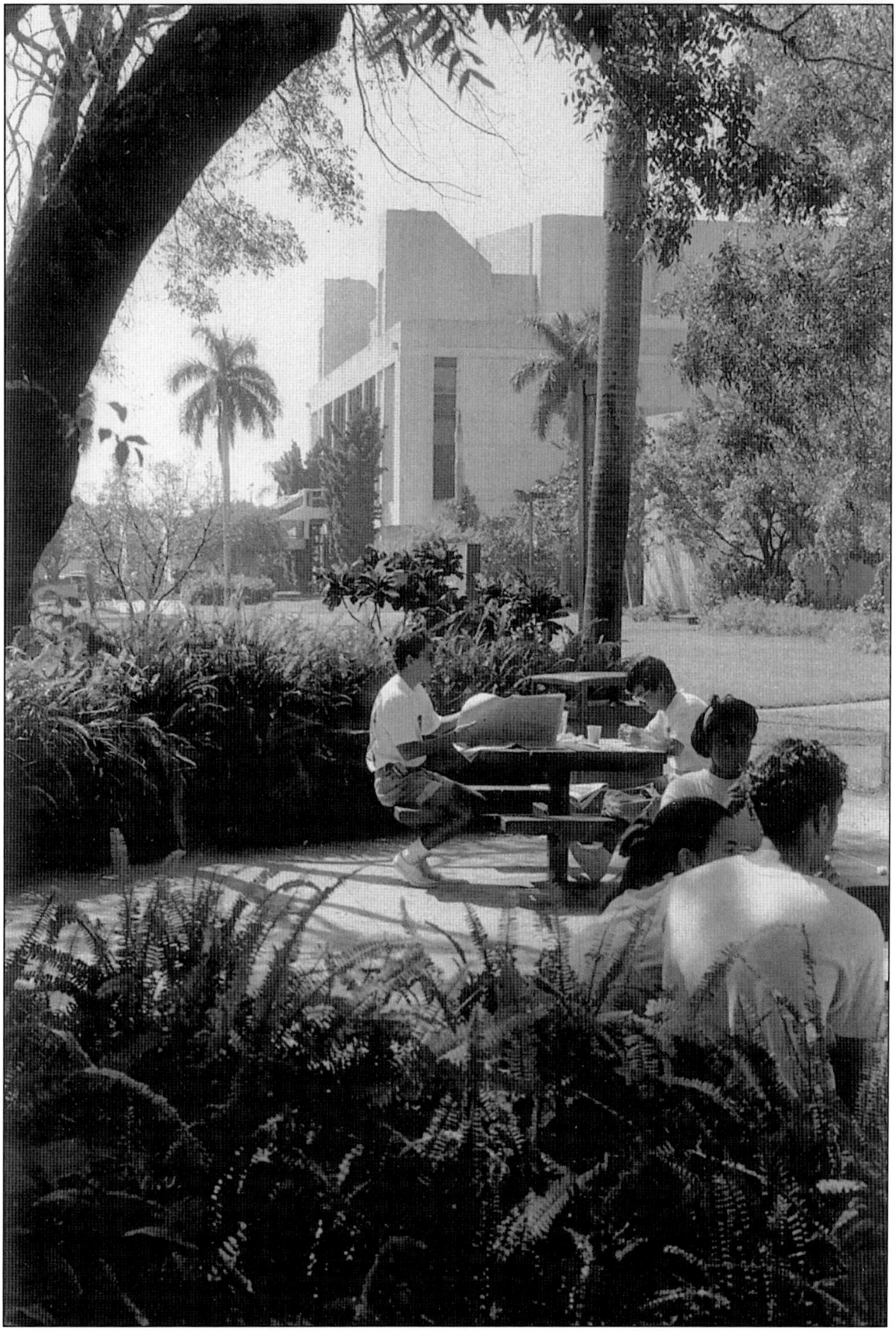

From the planting of the first tree on Central Campus—a black olive—BCC has grown to become among the state's best-landscaped community colleges.

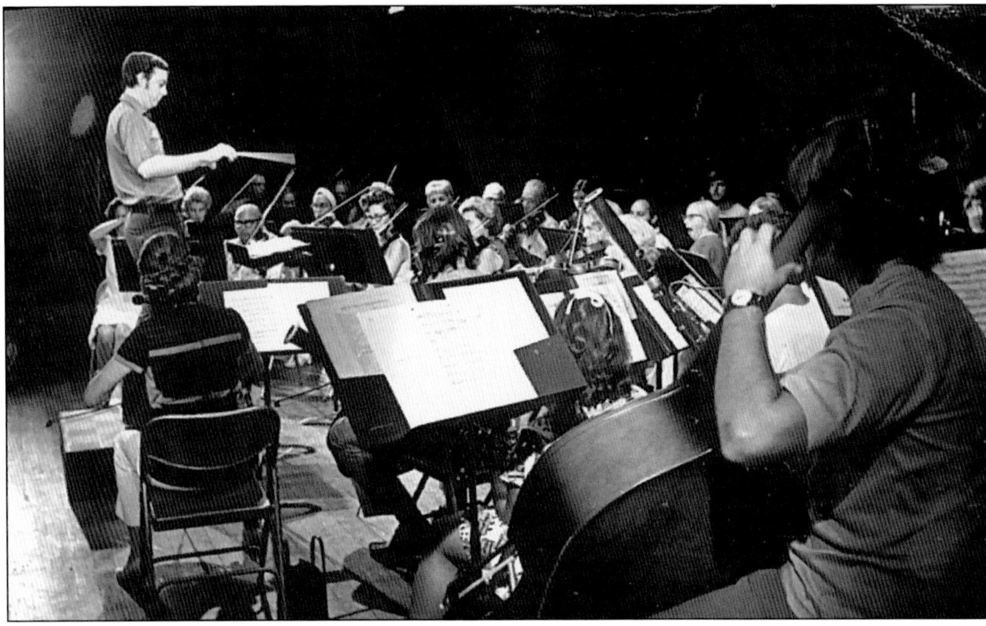

Prof. Jimmy Woodle leads the college orchestra in practice.

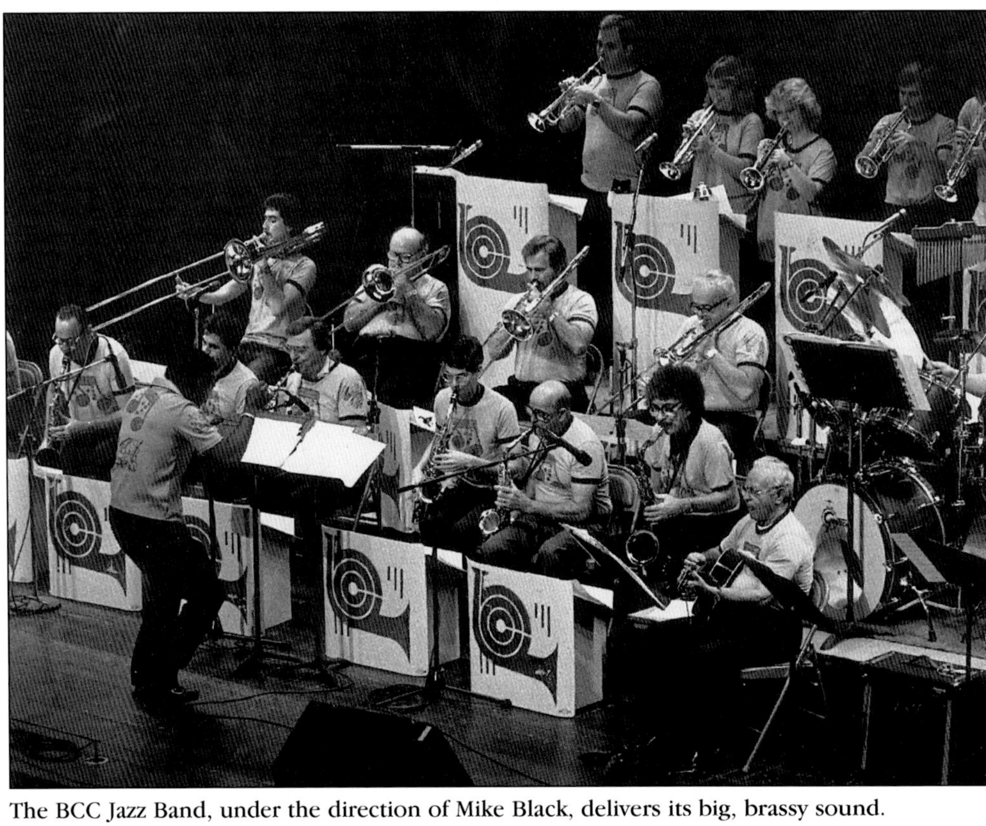

The BCC Jazz Band, under the direction of Mike Black, delivers its big, brassy sound.

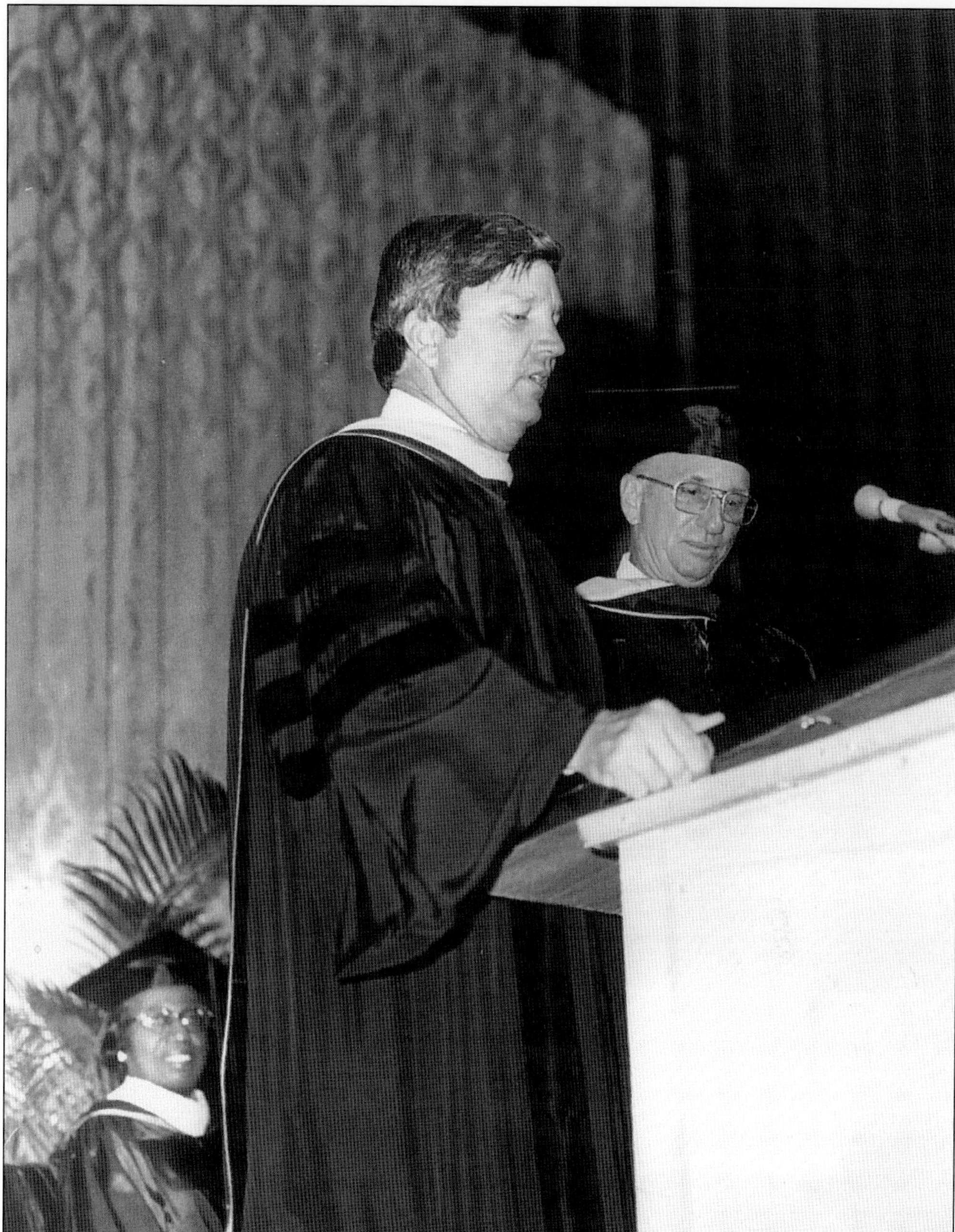

Dr. Adams presents Broward Judge James Minnet with a Distinguished Service Award in 1978.

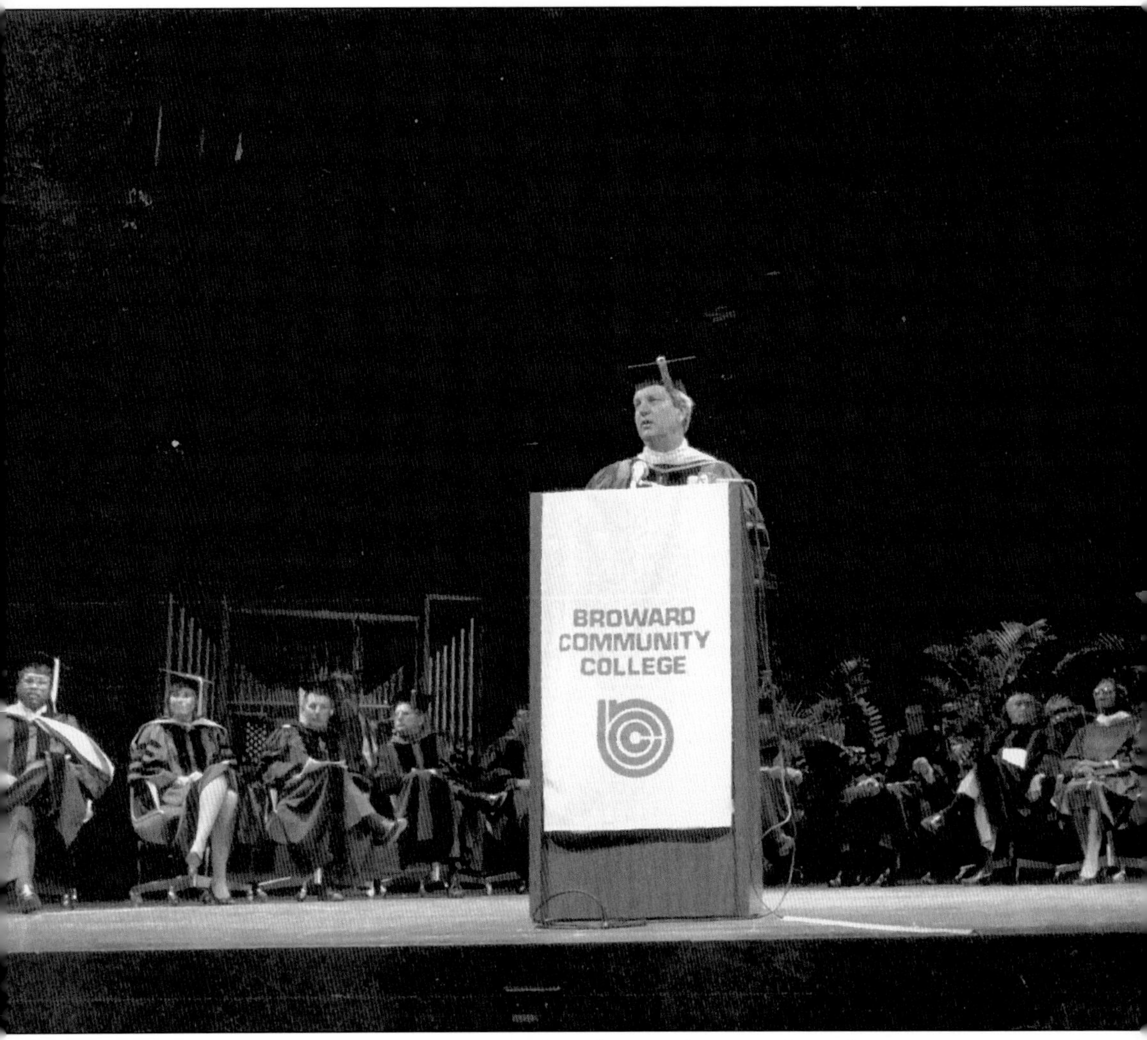


Dr. Adams served Broward Community College from 1968 to 1986, guiding its rise in size and prestige among the nation's two-year colleges. To honor his accomplishments and service to the college, Central Campus was renamed A. Hugh Adams Central Campus in December 1986.

# *Four*

# The Holcombe Era

## To the Millennium and Beyond

*Willis Holcombe, a protégé of Dr. James Wattenbarger, offered BCC a perfect mix of youth, preparation, and experience when the college began its search for a president after Dr. Adams announced his intent to retire.*

*As the fourth president of the college, Dr. Holcombe initiated an expansion effort that led to significant growth in enrollment, facility expansion, and new instructional programs. Libraries were his first priority with the needs of student affairs second. He recognized that the demand for technical education would grow rapidly, but made sure that the mission of preparing students for transfer to upper-division colleges and universities would not be compromised as a result.*

*The college prospered in many other ways. The BCC Foundation flourished. The Honors Institute grew and diversified, as did the International Education Institute. The Downtown Center in Fort Lauderdale became an instructional center as well as the administrative headquarters for the college; still, no matter how much growth took place, the emphasis on excellence remained.*

*What might come to be Dr. Holcombe's greatest legacy is his effort to create community partnerships that allow students to gain greater choice and flexibility in career choices and taxpayers to get more value for their dollars. "We can't exist alone if we are going to meet the higher education needs of Broward County," he says.*

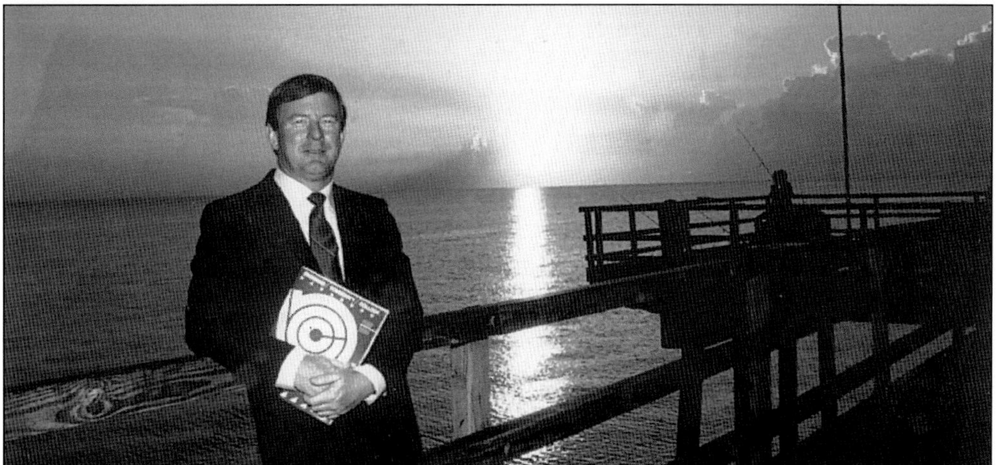

Willis Holcombe became the fourth president of BCC on January 1, 1987. A native of Iron Mountain, Michigan, he earned his undergraduate degree at Baldwin-Wallace College where he was an all-America sprinter. He earned his graduate degrees at the University of Florida.

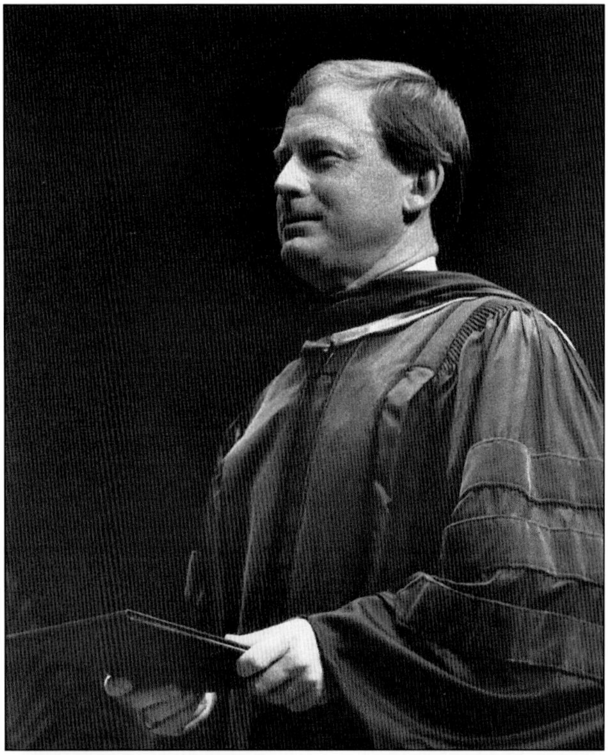

Under Dr. Holcombe's leadership, the campuses resumed growing to meet current and future needs.

The transition from Dr. Adams to Dr. Holcombe was smooth and orderly because of Holcombe's history at the college. He had served as an English professor, Dr. Adams's assistant, academic dean, and Central Campus provost before leaving for Brevard Community College.

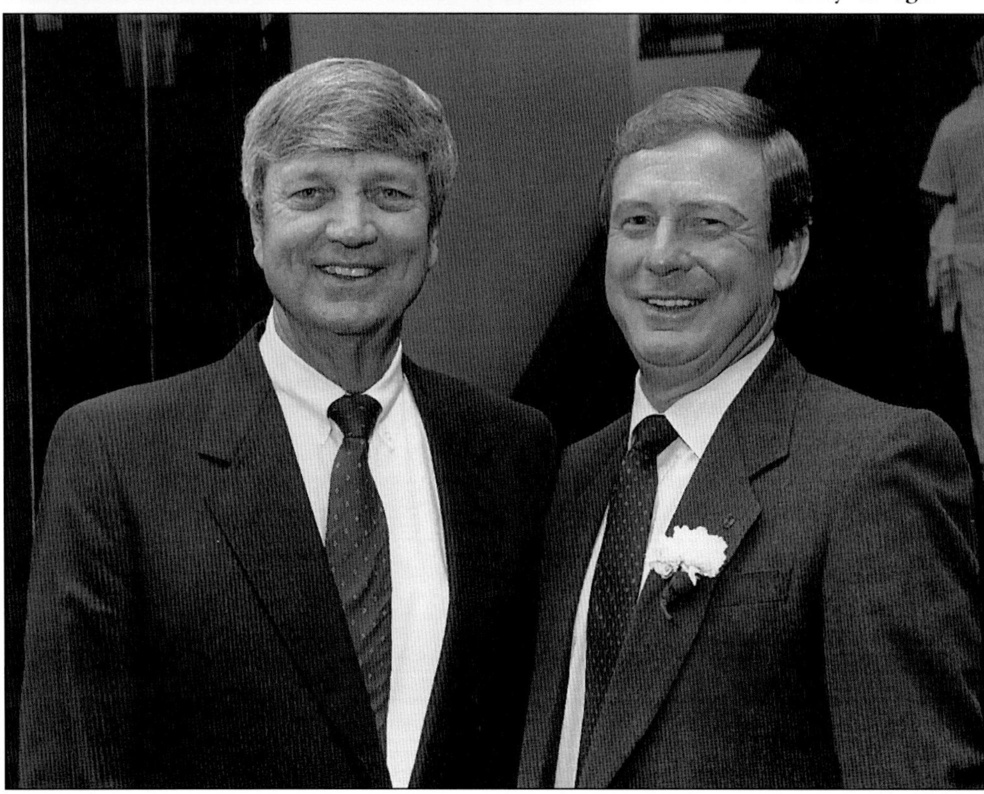

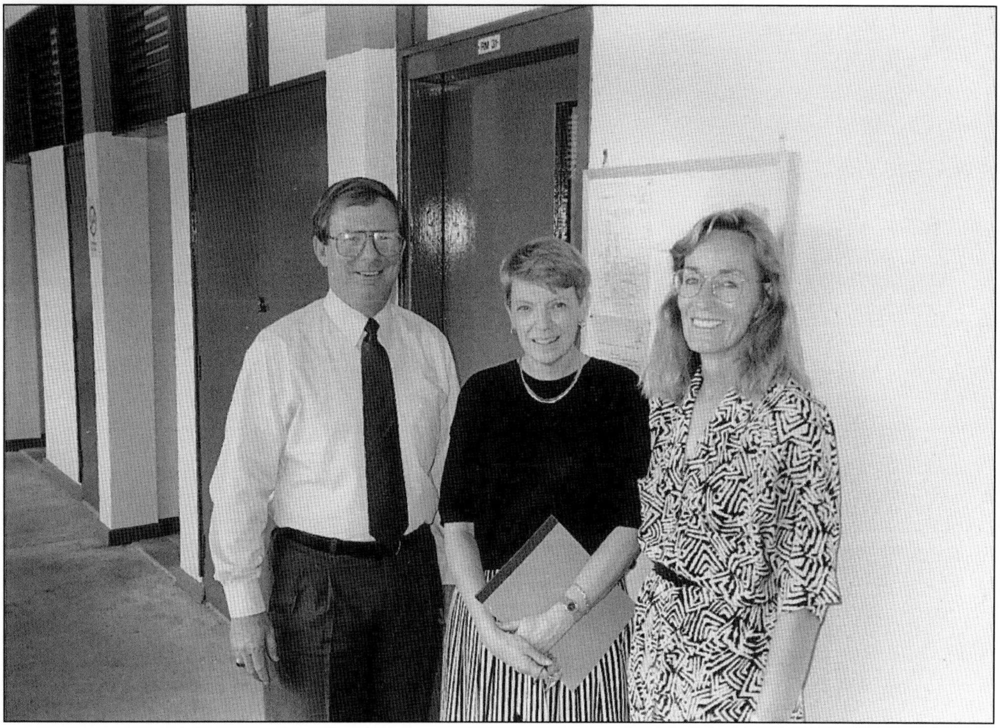

Dr. Holcombe expanded the college's participation in international education. In this picture, he joins with Ellen Cangi and trustee Joyce Cross at the Center for American Education in Singapore.

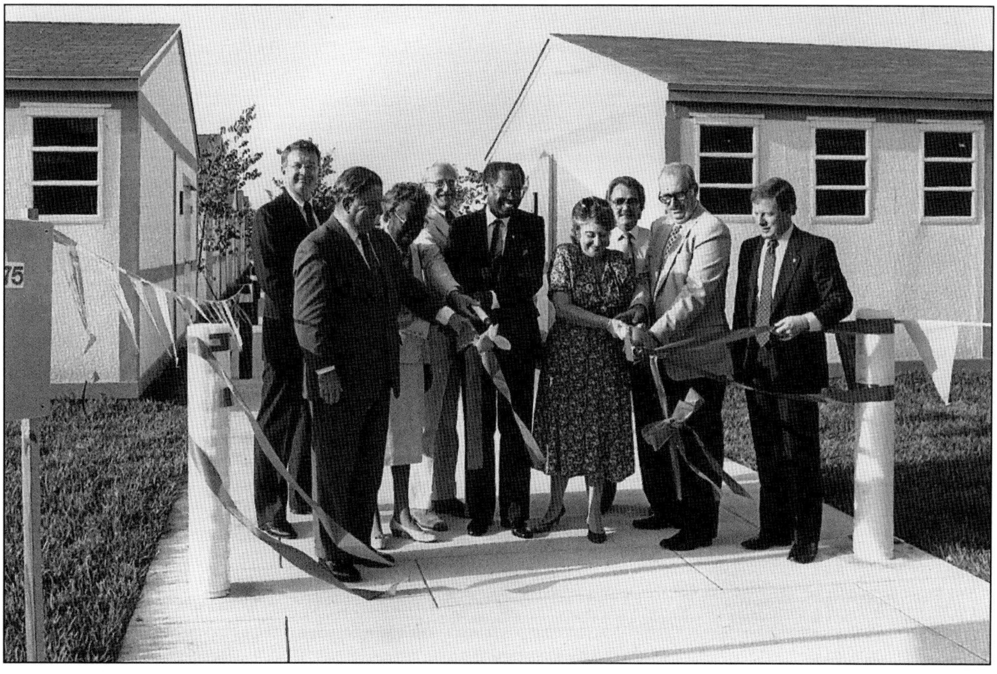

The rapid growth of the South Campus necessitated installation of modular classroom buildings. The modular buildings help give South Campus a warm, cozy atmosphere.

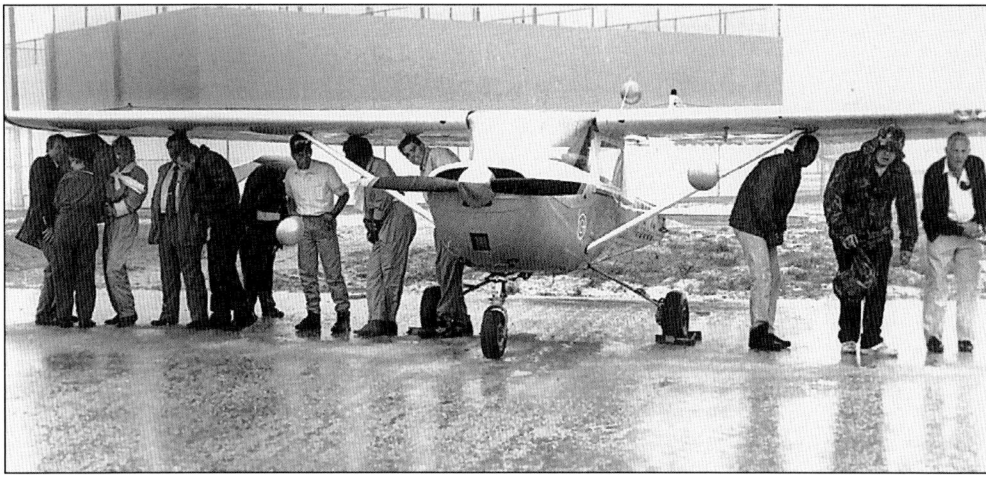

Rain canceled some of the outdoor activities at the opening of the Aviation Institute in February 1993, but the hangar, the spacious new complex, and the airplanes kept participants sheltered from the elements.

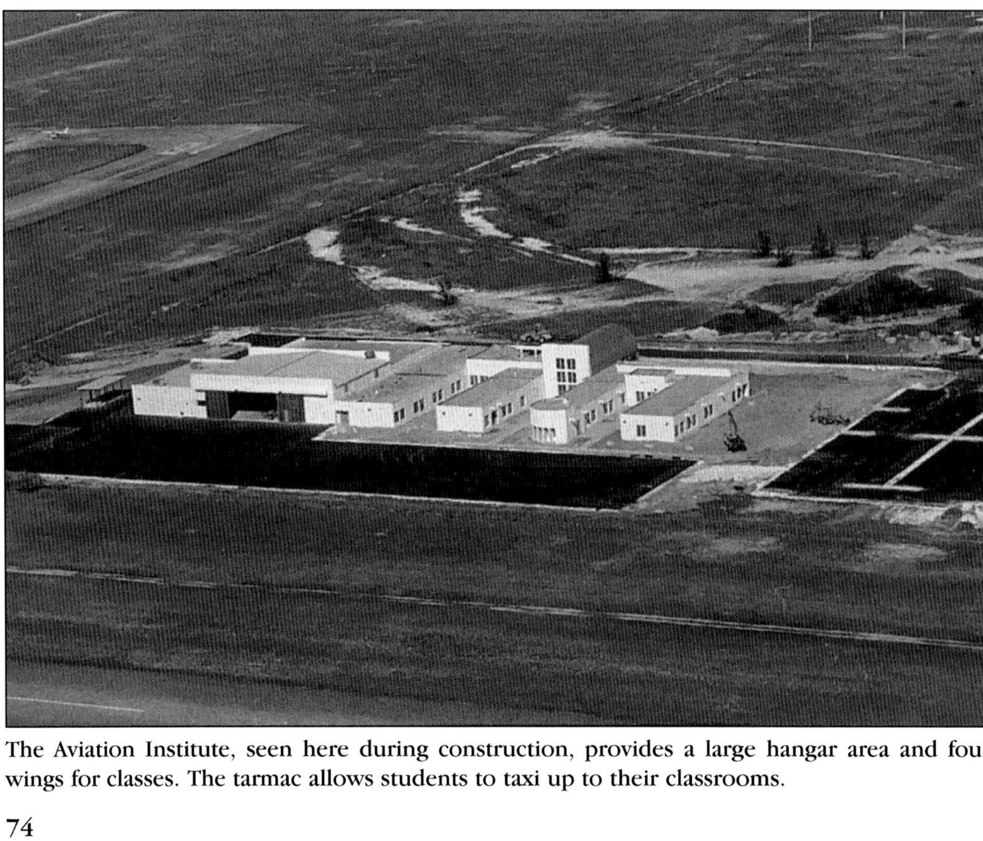

The Aviation Institute, seen here during construction, provides a large hangar area and four wings for classes. The tarmac allows students to taxi up to their classrooms.

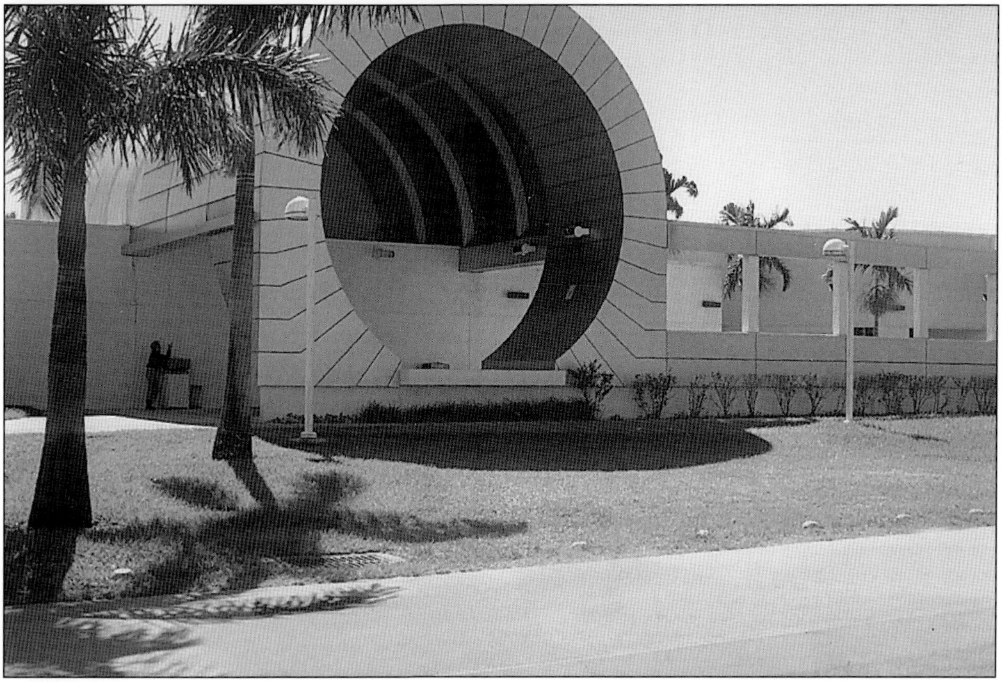

The focal points of the Aviation Institute are the dramatic cross-sectioned fuselage facade and the clean, aerodynamic lines of the building.

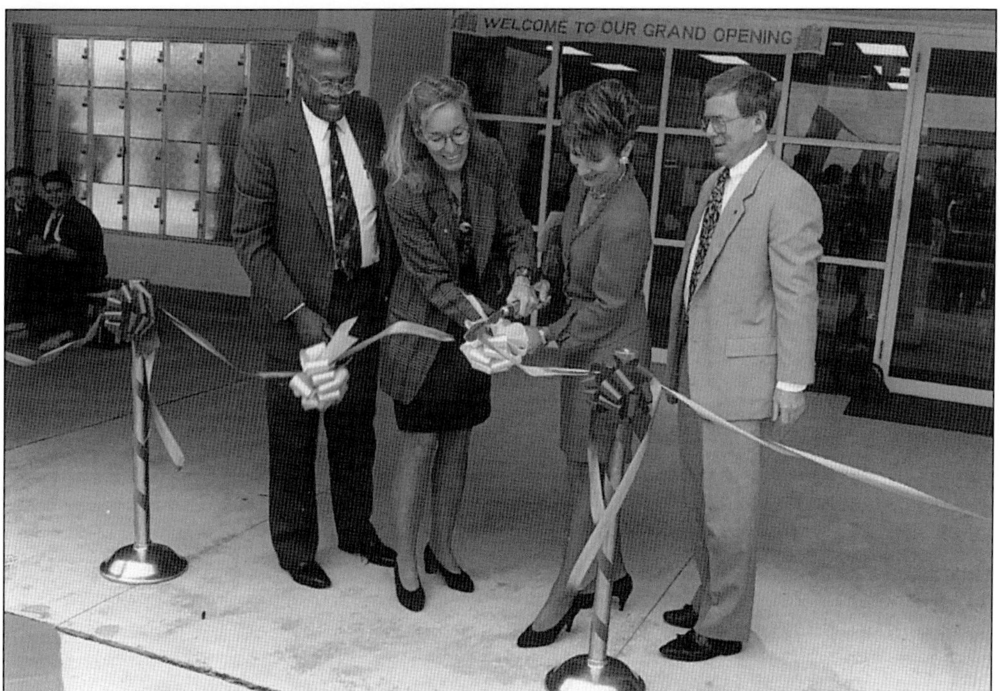


South Campus Provost Dr. Carl Crawford and Dr. Holcombe look on as trustees Joyce Cross and Katharine Barry cut the ribbon to open the South Campus bookstore.

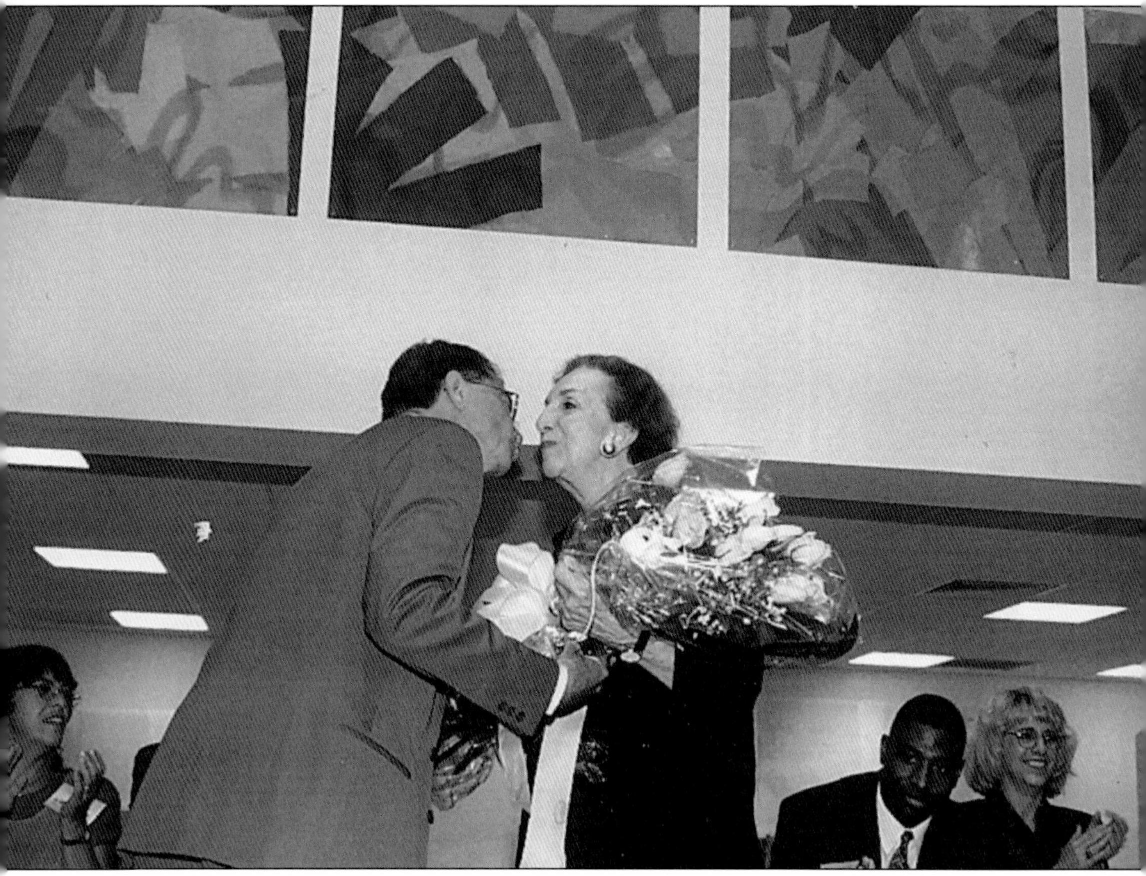

Acclaimed artist Dorothy Gillespie receives a bouquet of yellow roses and a kiss from South Campus Provost Dr. Mont Smith at the dedication of the Student Services Building. Visible above their heads is part of Gillespie's 32-panel 1998 work *Symphony in Color*, one of several of her works on South Campus. Others include *Royal Crest*, which is inside building 69; *Colored Clouds and Ribboned Currents*, located outside the teleconference center; and *Celestial Arrangement*, also found inside the Student Services Building.

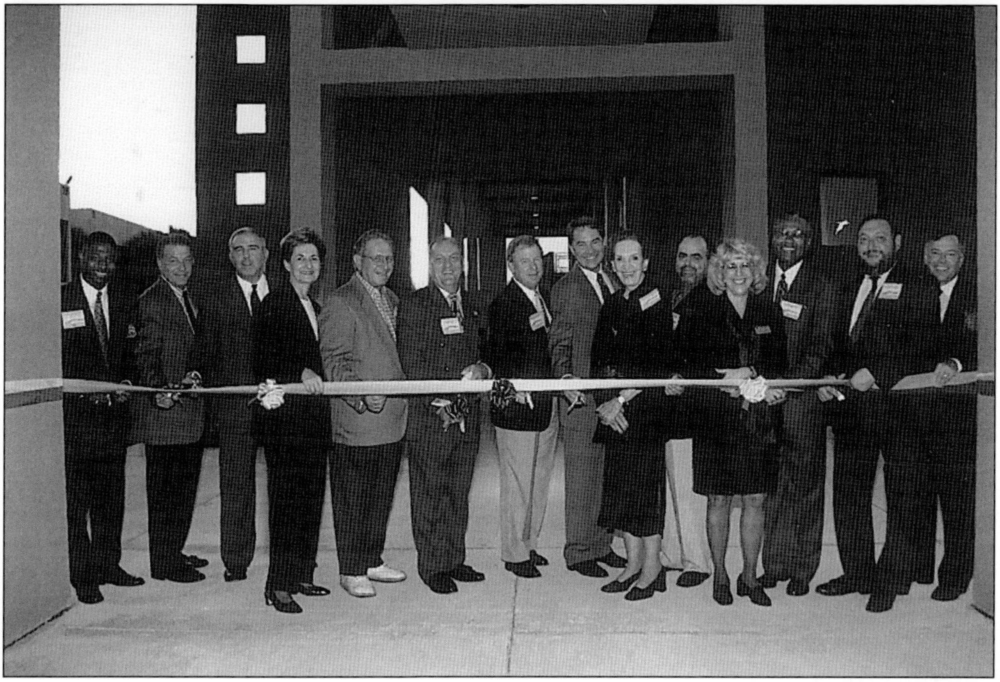

Trustees, Dr. Holcombe, Provost Dr. Mont Smith, former provost Dr. Carl Crawford, and state senator Howard Forman join with foundation officials, Pembroke Pines city officials, and other dignitaries to cut the ribbon on the South Campus Student Services Building in October of 1998.

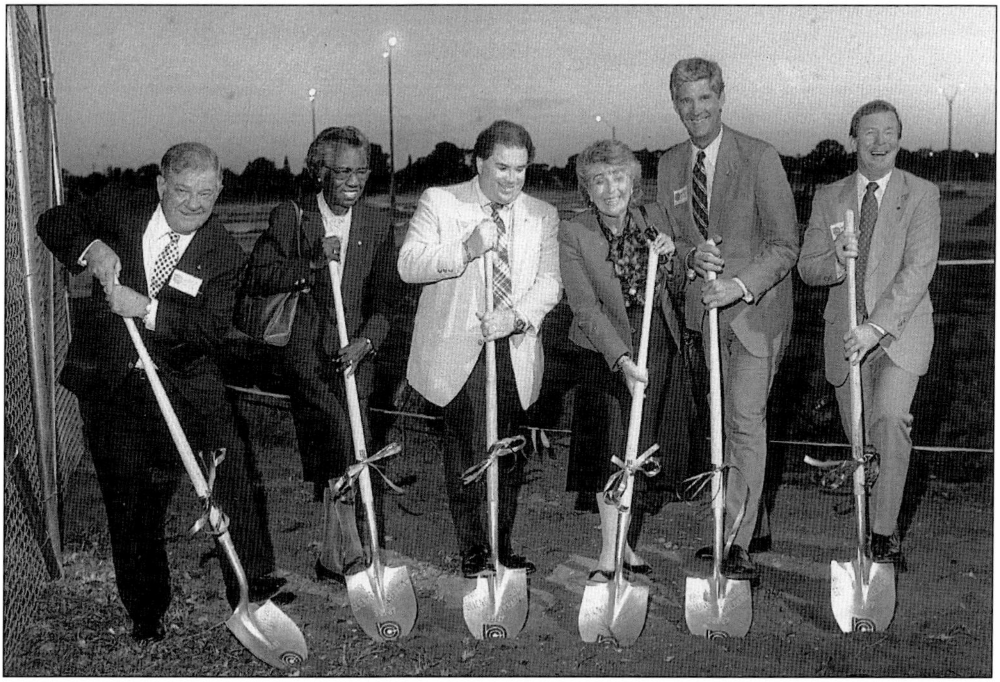

Pictured from left to right, Bill Duke, Margaret Roach, Rep. Jack Tobin, Elinor Wilkov, Mike Curran, and Will Holcombe break ground for the North Campus mathematics and science building in March of 1989.

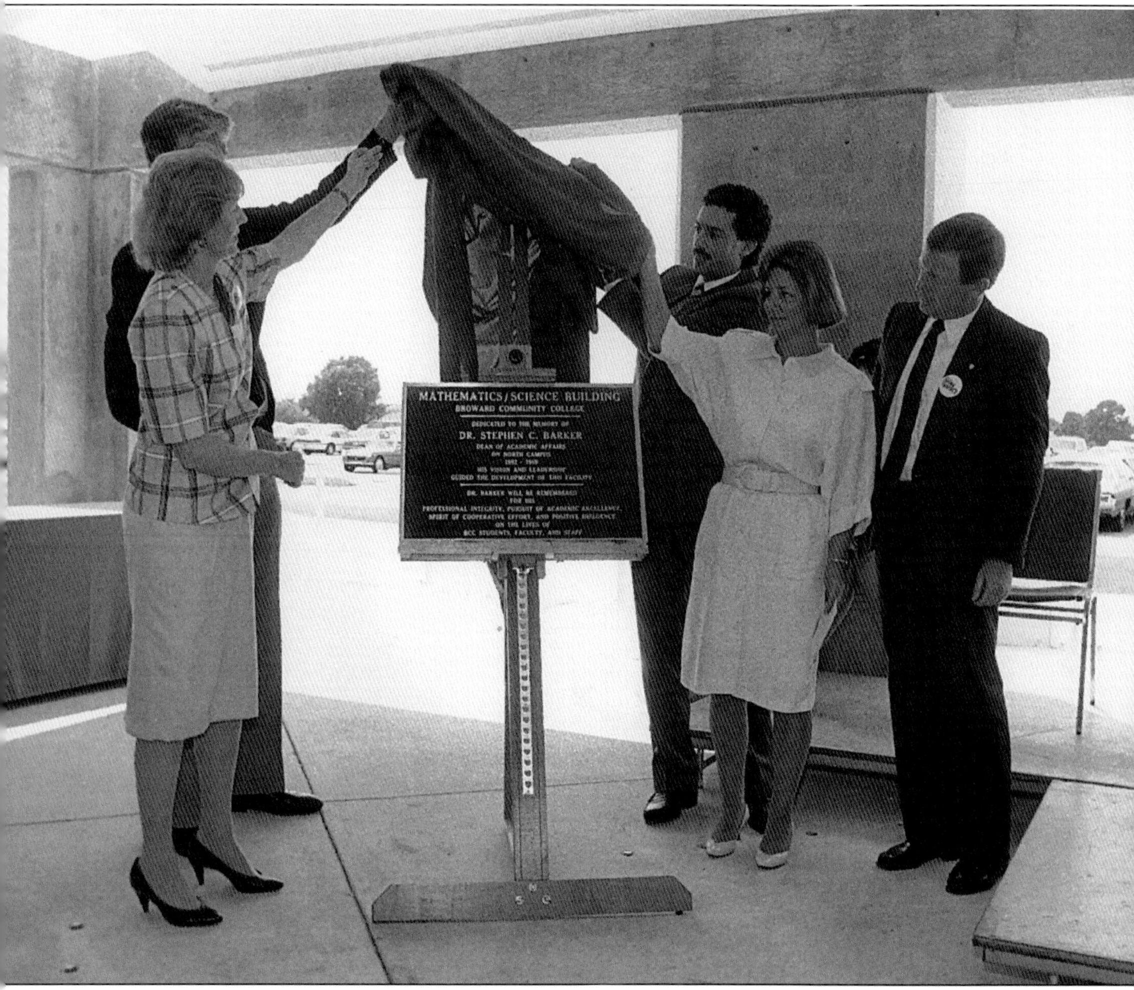


From left to right, Prof. Peggy Green, trustee Michael Curran, Prof. Carey Witkov, and Prof. Karen Walsh unveil the dedication plaque for the North Campus mathematics and science building on September 27, 1990. The building is dedicated to the memory of Stephen C. Barker, dean of academic affairs on North Campus until his tragic death in a 1989 boating accident.

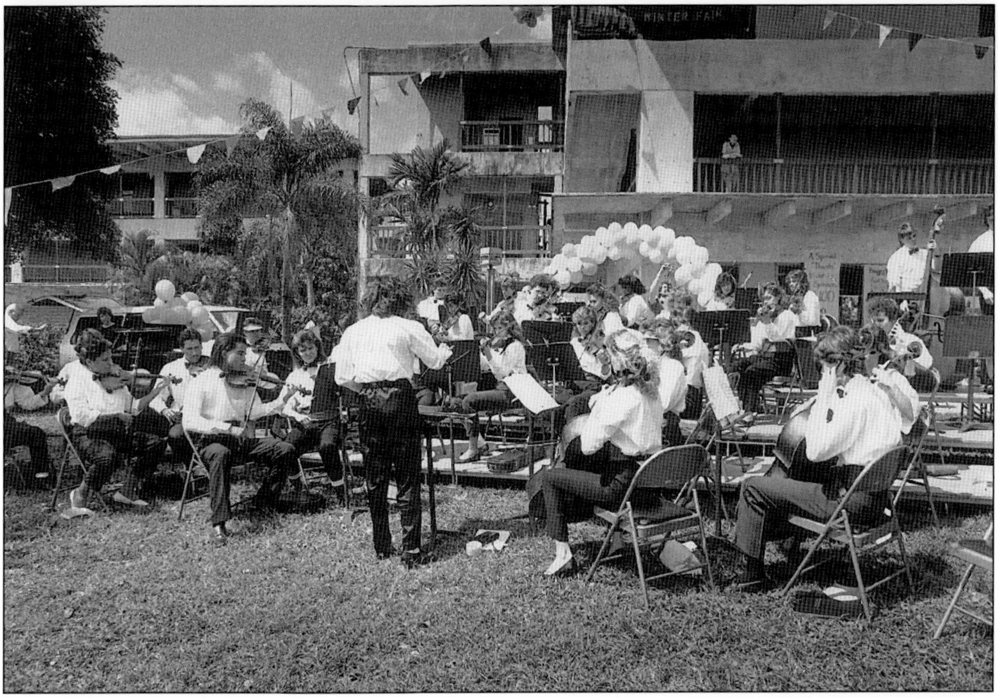


The student orchestra performs the classics al fresco on the North Campus at the annual winter fair.

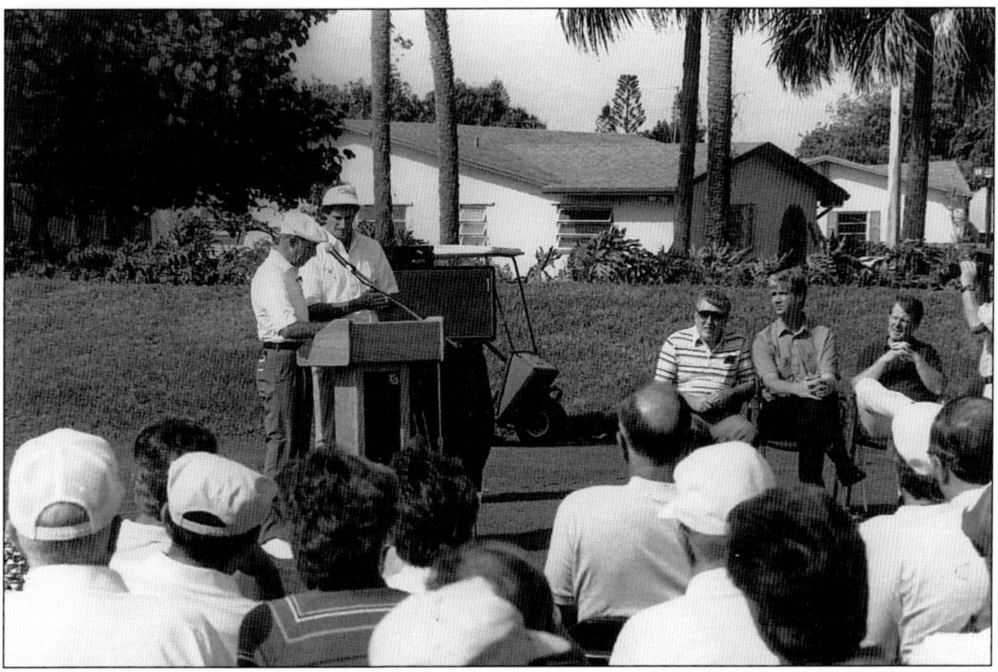

Former golf professional and famed instructor Bob Toski (left at podium) is pictured here with Gary Battersby as they address the audience at dedication ceremonies for the Toski-Battersby Golf Training Center at North Campus. Seated, from left to right, are Provost Dr. Larry McFarlane, trustee Michael Curran, and Dr. Holcombe.

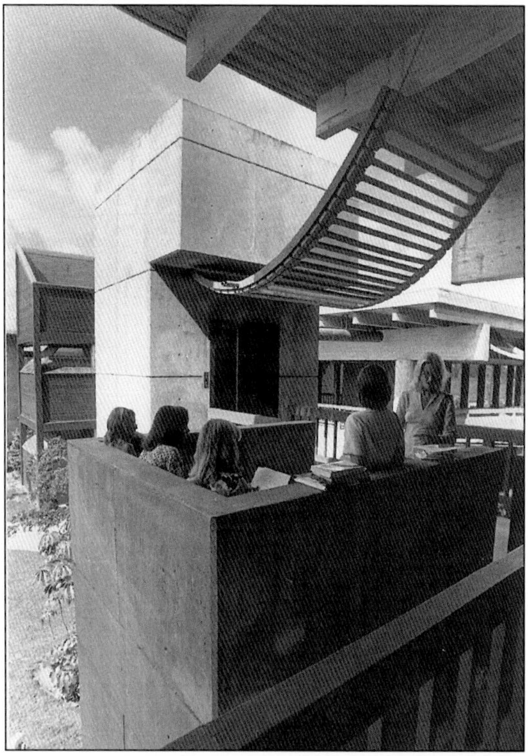

The distinctive architecture and landscape design give the campus flexibility. Students can enjoy being out in the fresh air and still have space to gather in cozy nooks to study or converse.

Tables dot the campus for students to eat, study, or relax with friends while black olive and umbrella trees provide shade.

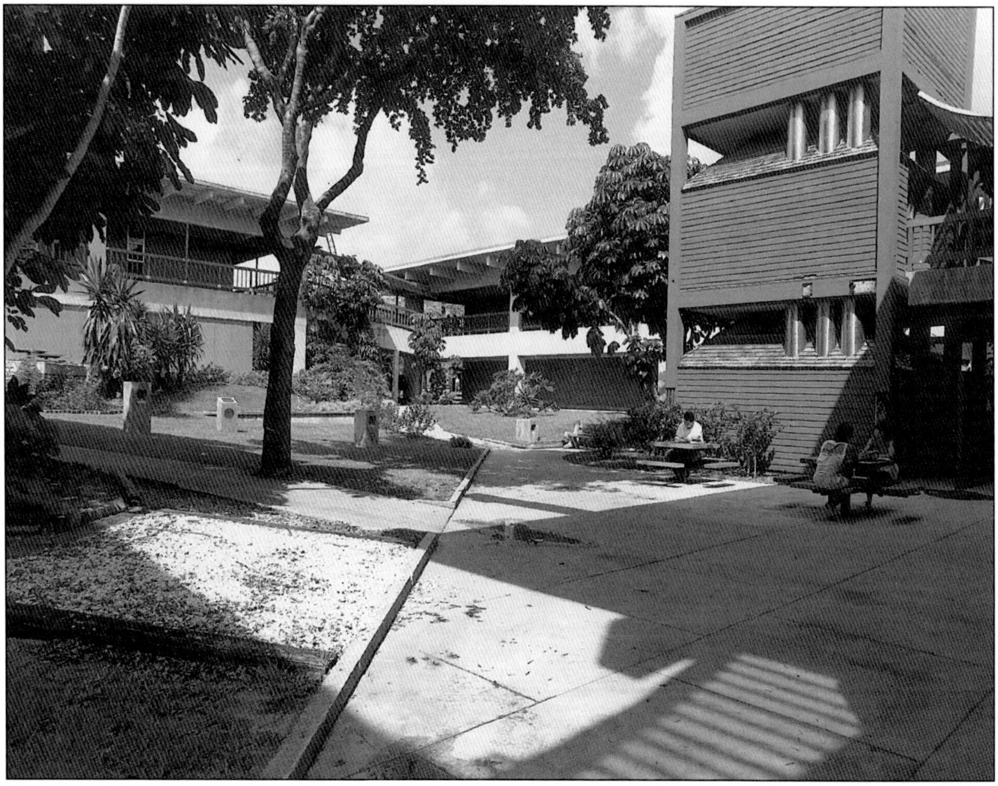

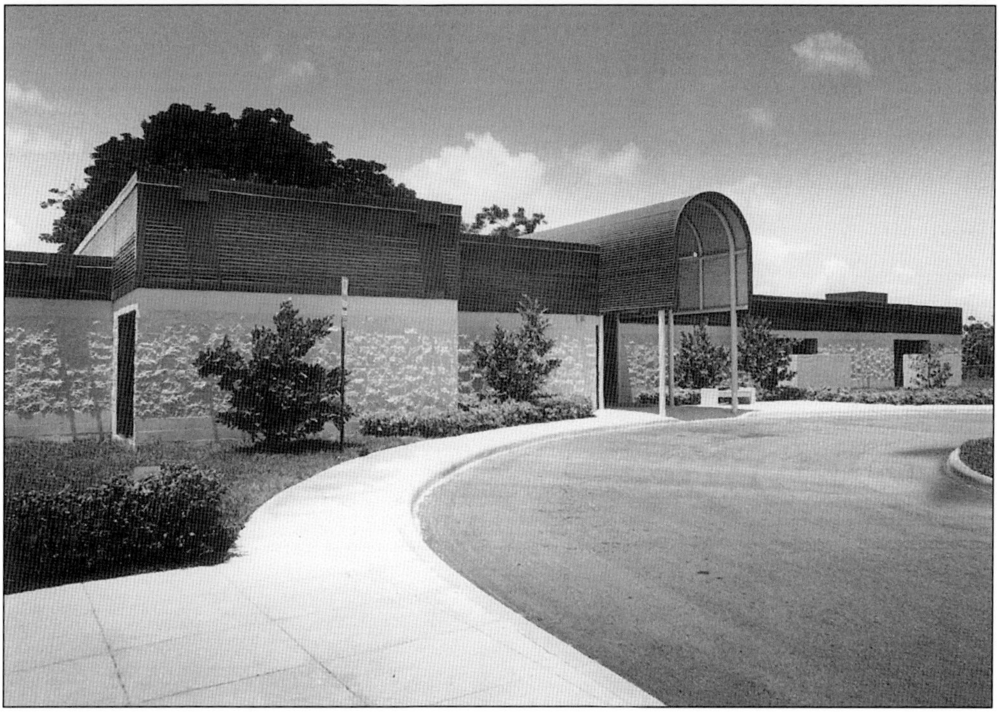

BCC and Broward County teamed up to open the North Campus Outreach Center in September of 1987. The college also opened the Carver Ranches Outreach Facility in Hollywood and a third facility on Sistrunk Boulevard in Fort Lauderdale. They were designed to provide access to college and social service agencies, but did not produce the results the partners had hoped to achieve.

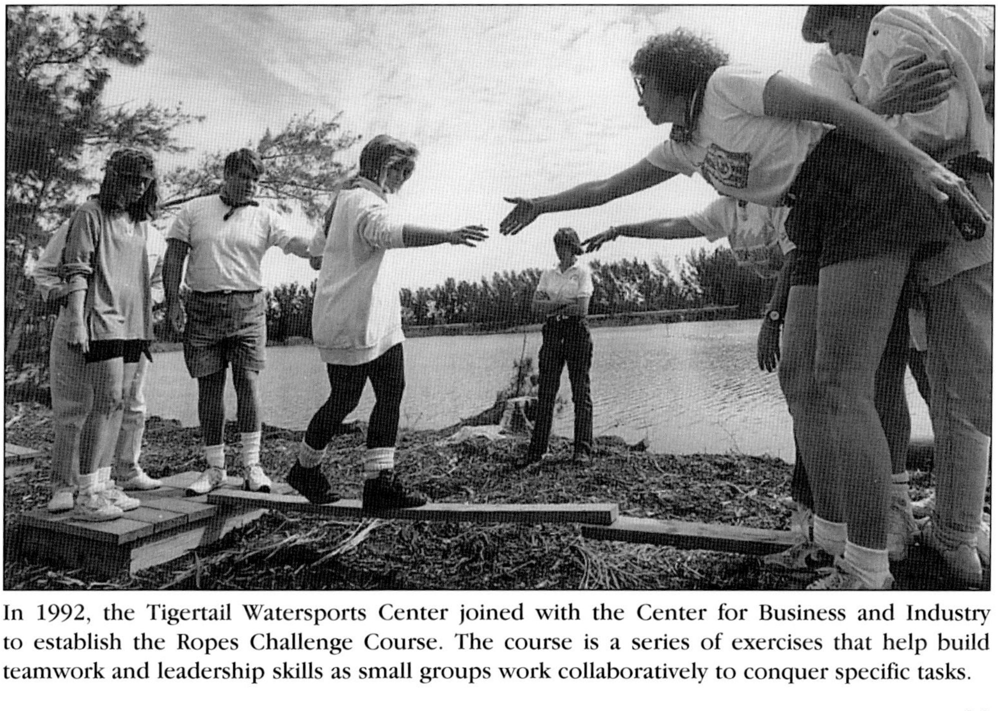

In 1992, the Tigertail Watersports Center joined with the Center for Business and Industry to establish the Ropes Challenge Course. The course is a series of exercises that help build teamwork and leadership skills as small groups work collaboratively to conquer specific tasks.

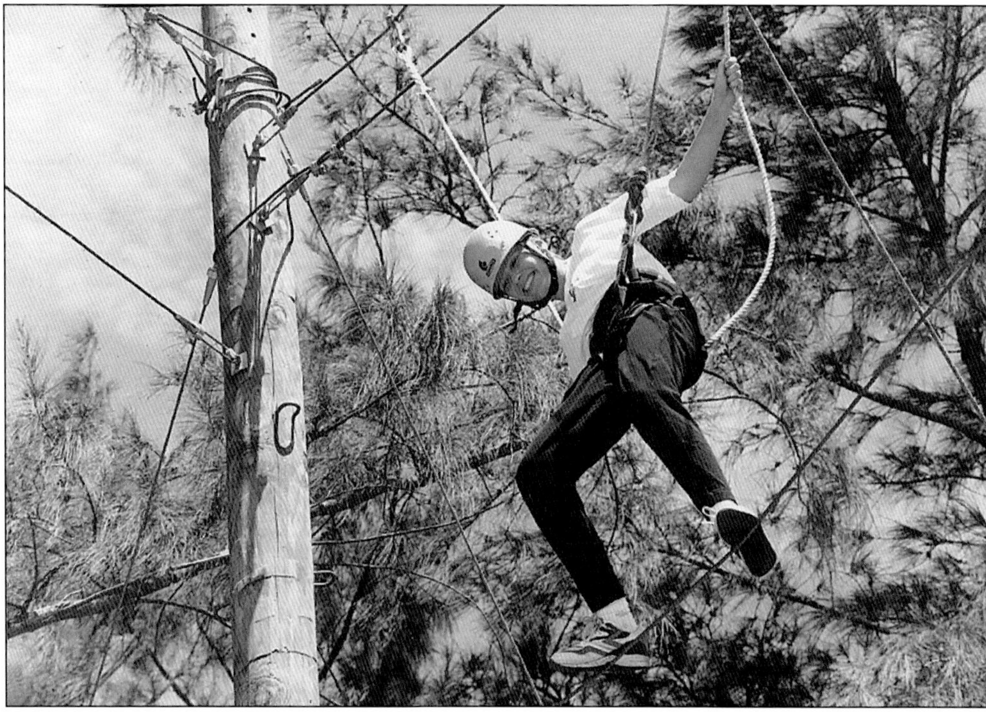

Although many of the high challenges seem dangerous, the risk is actually minimal. The Ropes Challenge Course is used by student groups and the staff development program as well as by corporations throughout Broward County.

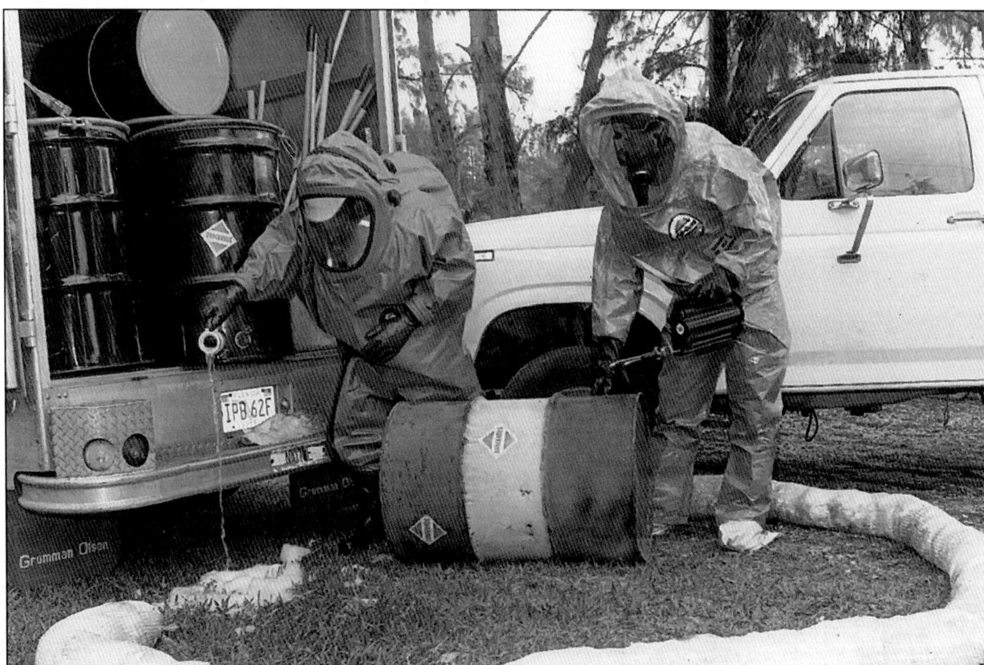


The Tigertail Center is utilized for other purposes, too. Here students practice safely handling hazardous waste materials.

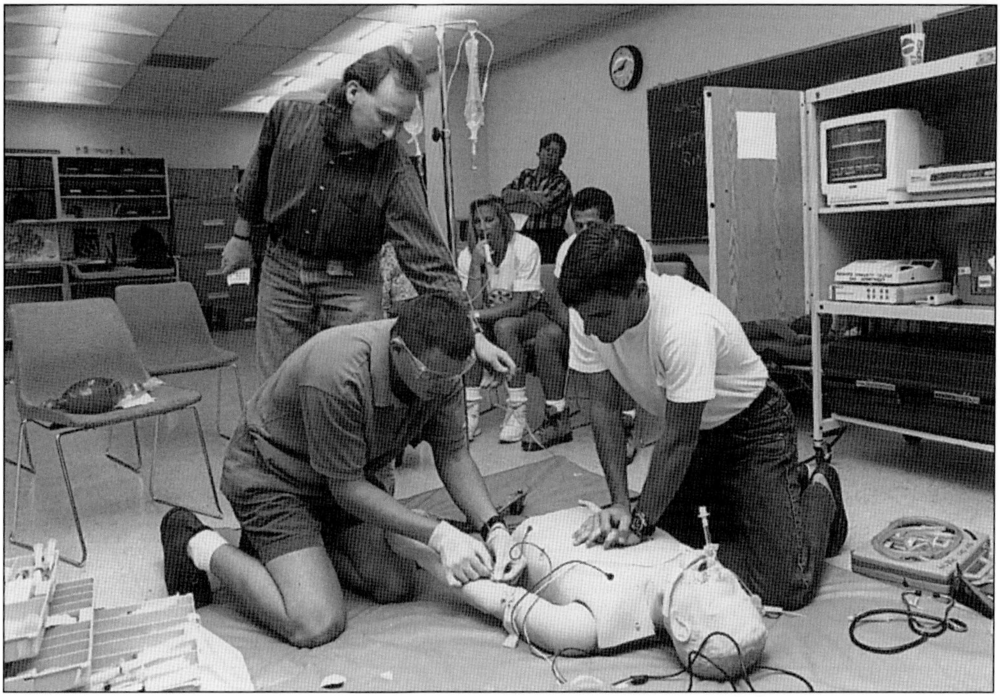

Prof. Joe Jones directs students in the paramedic and emergency medical technology programs as they treat a dummy programmed to exhibit symptoms of a heart attack.

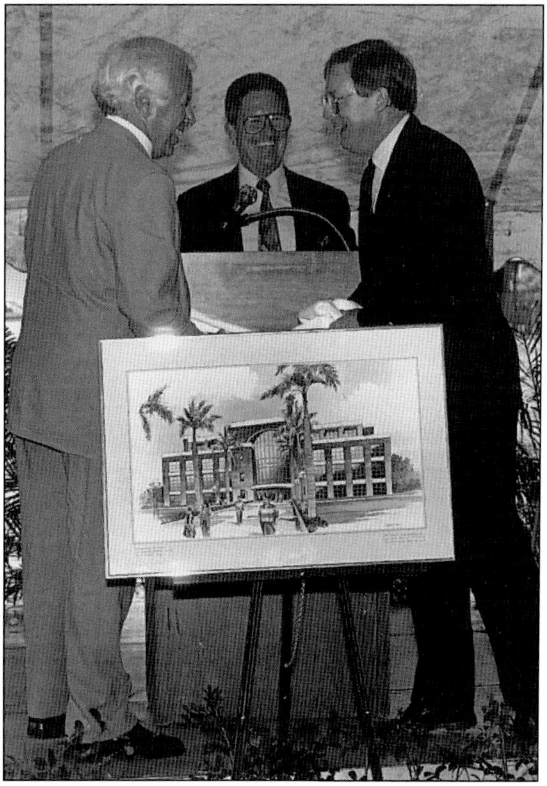

FAU Pres. Anthony Catanese (left), BCC Central Campus Provost Glen Rose, and BCC Pres. Willis Holcombe are all smiles at groundbreaking ceremonies for the joint library on Central Campus on April 26, 1994.

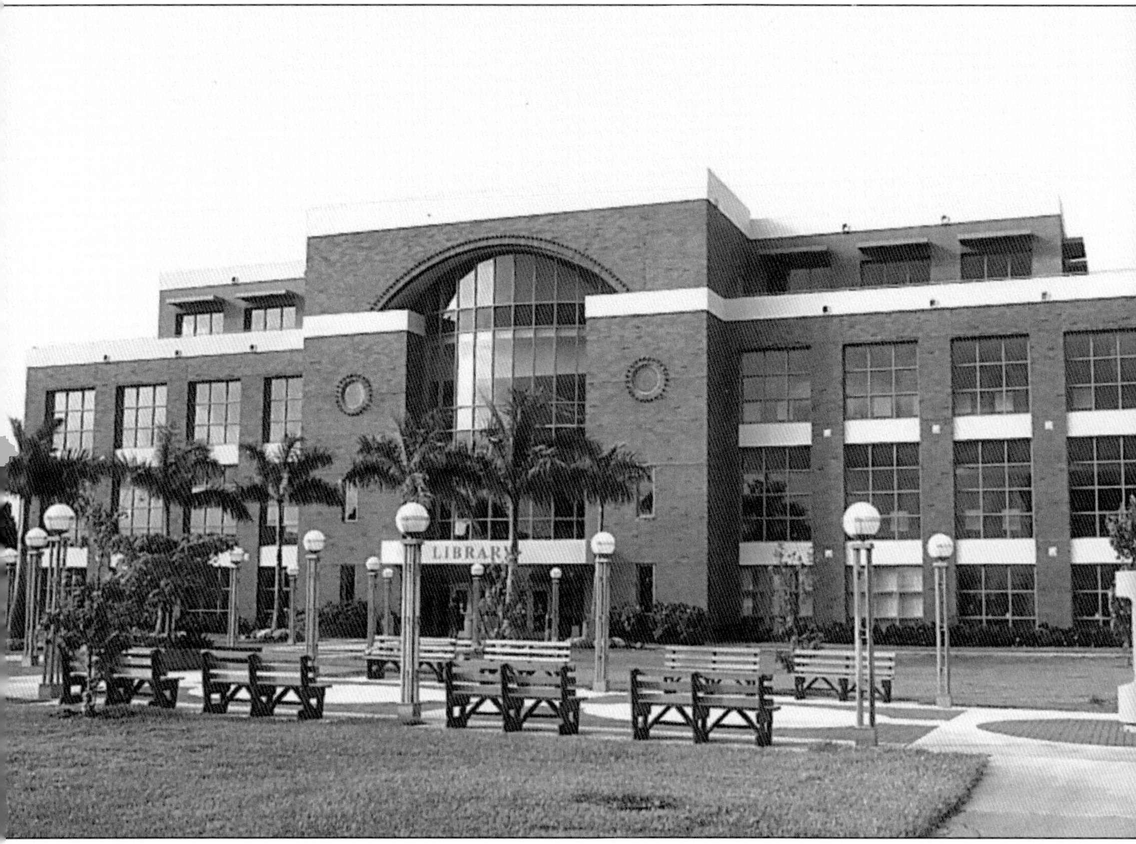


The $14.5 million FAU/BCC University/College Library expanded the old library's holdings by more than 100,000 volumes, expanded its physical size from 37,000 square feet to 112,000, and added sophisticated technological capabilities to benefit students.

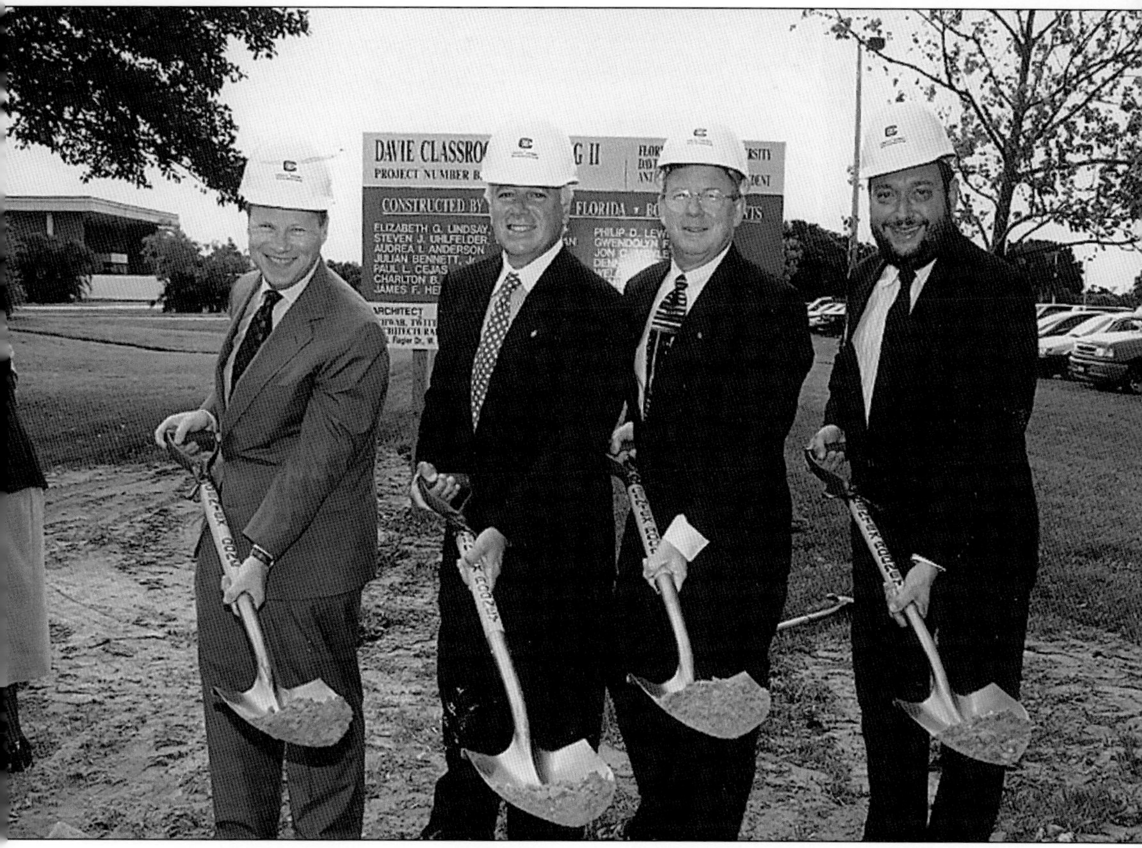


Not all of the constructions on BCC's campuses have been BCC buildings. Here, Dr. Holcombe helps with groundbreaking for Florida Atlantic University's Davie Classroom Building II on Central Campus. Joining him, from left to right, are state senator Ken Jenne, Dr. Catanese, and state senator Howard Forman. The FAU Liberal Arts building is another example of the university's presence on Central Campus.

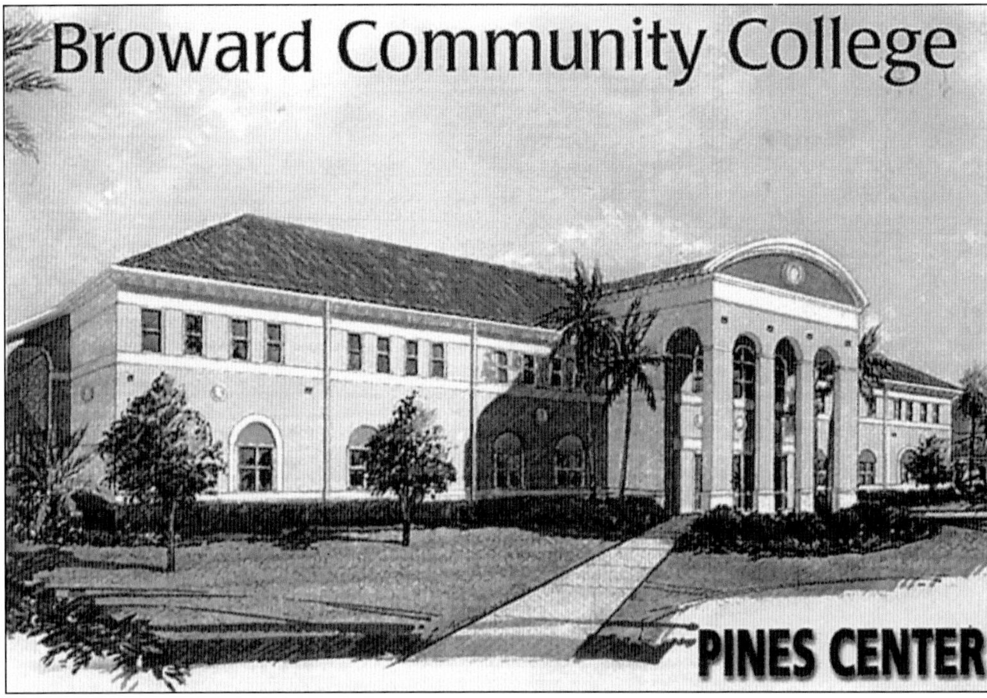


The $3.5-million Pines Center, part of the Pembroke Pines Academic Village, provides a charter high school, a branch of the county library, and athletic fields for city residents. The two-story Pines Center, at Sheridan Street and 172nd Avenue, is of Mediterranean architectural style and serves up to 5,000 students.

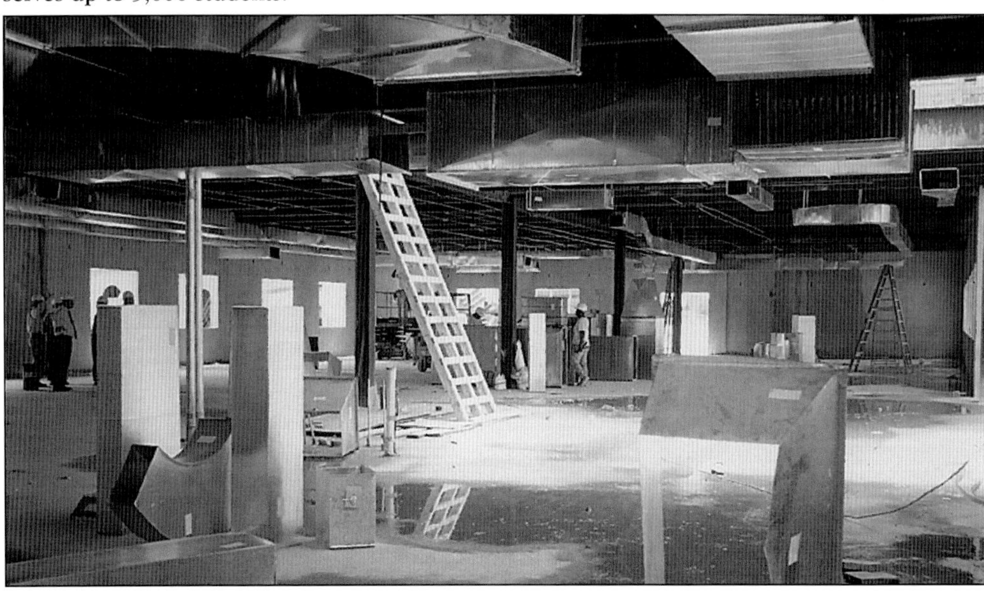

This is a photo of the 26,000 square-foot interior of the Pines Center under construction. The building was designed to provide state-of-the-art technological instructional opportunities to students. It contains two completely computerized multimedia classrooms and teleconference facilities. The Academic Village is constructed on a 77-acre campus built in the Jeffersonian quadrangle mode of the University of Virginia.

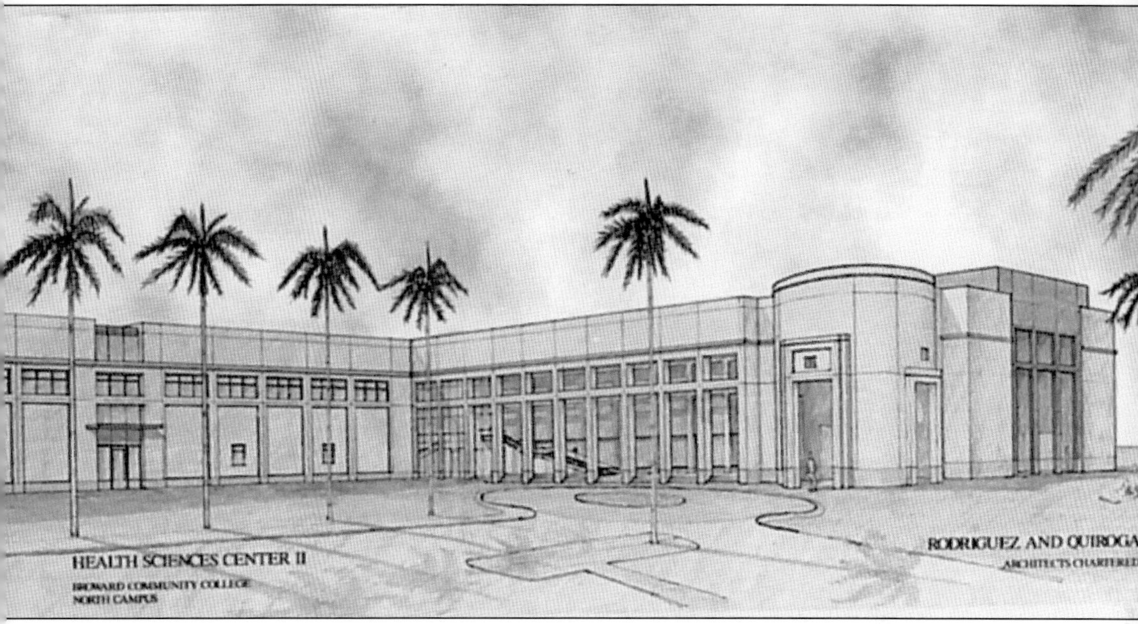


On North Campus, the two-story, L-shaped Health Science Center II occupies the space where the original campus building stood. The building was designed by the architectural firm of Rodriguez and Quiroga.

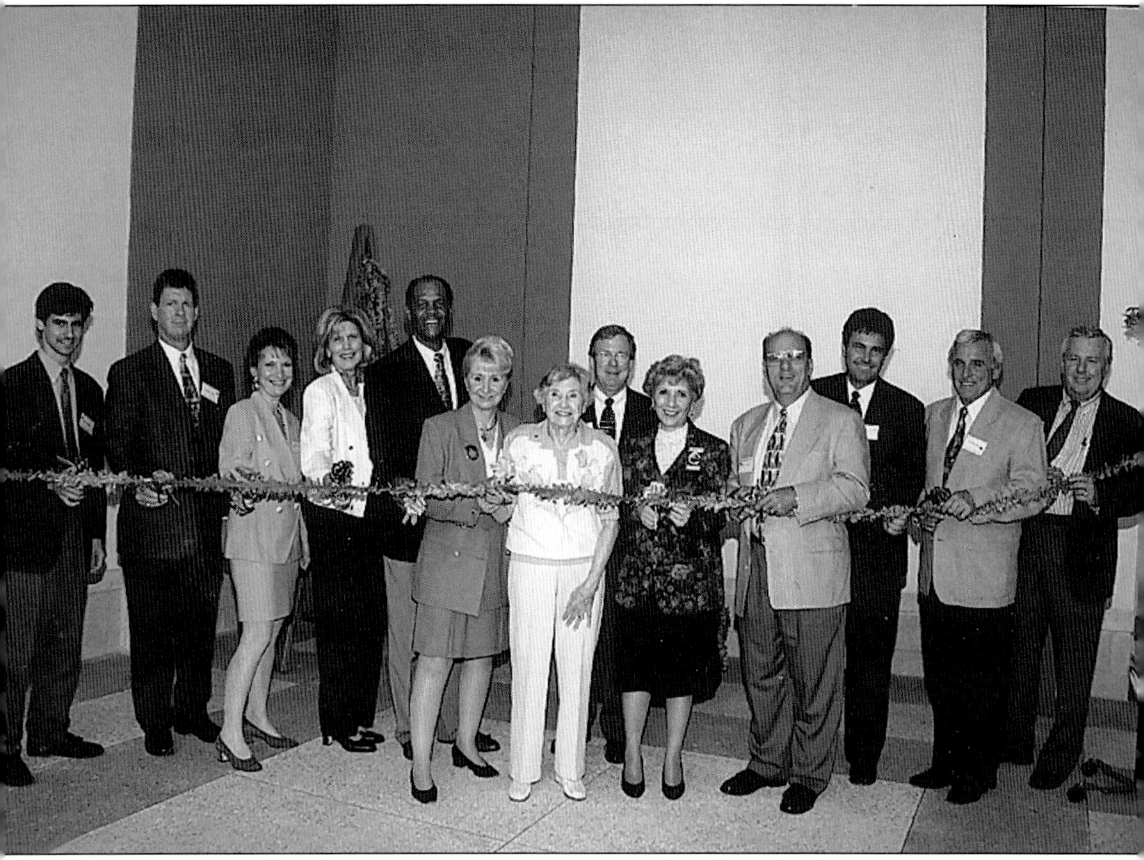

Irene Fischley, benefactor for BCC's health sciences programs, proudly stands at dedication ceremonies for the Health Science Center II in February 1997. Also pictured are trustees Katharine Barry, Jan Cummings, Leon Watts, Frank Ortis, Mario Cartaya, Dr. Holcombe, North Campus Provost Dr. Larry McFarlane, and Dr. Wanda Thomas.

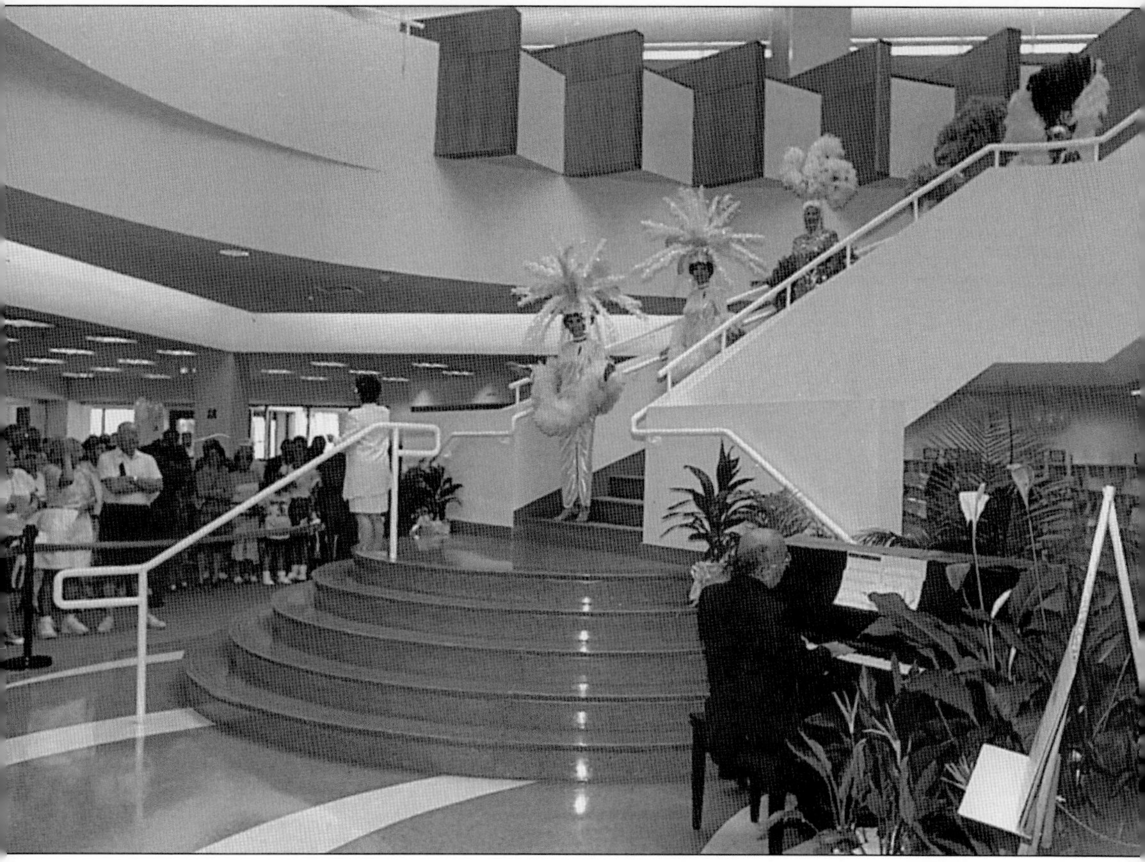

Members of the Zigfeld Girls of Florida added a touch of glamour to dedication ceremonies of the BCC/North Regional Library in June 1994.

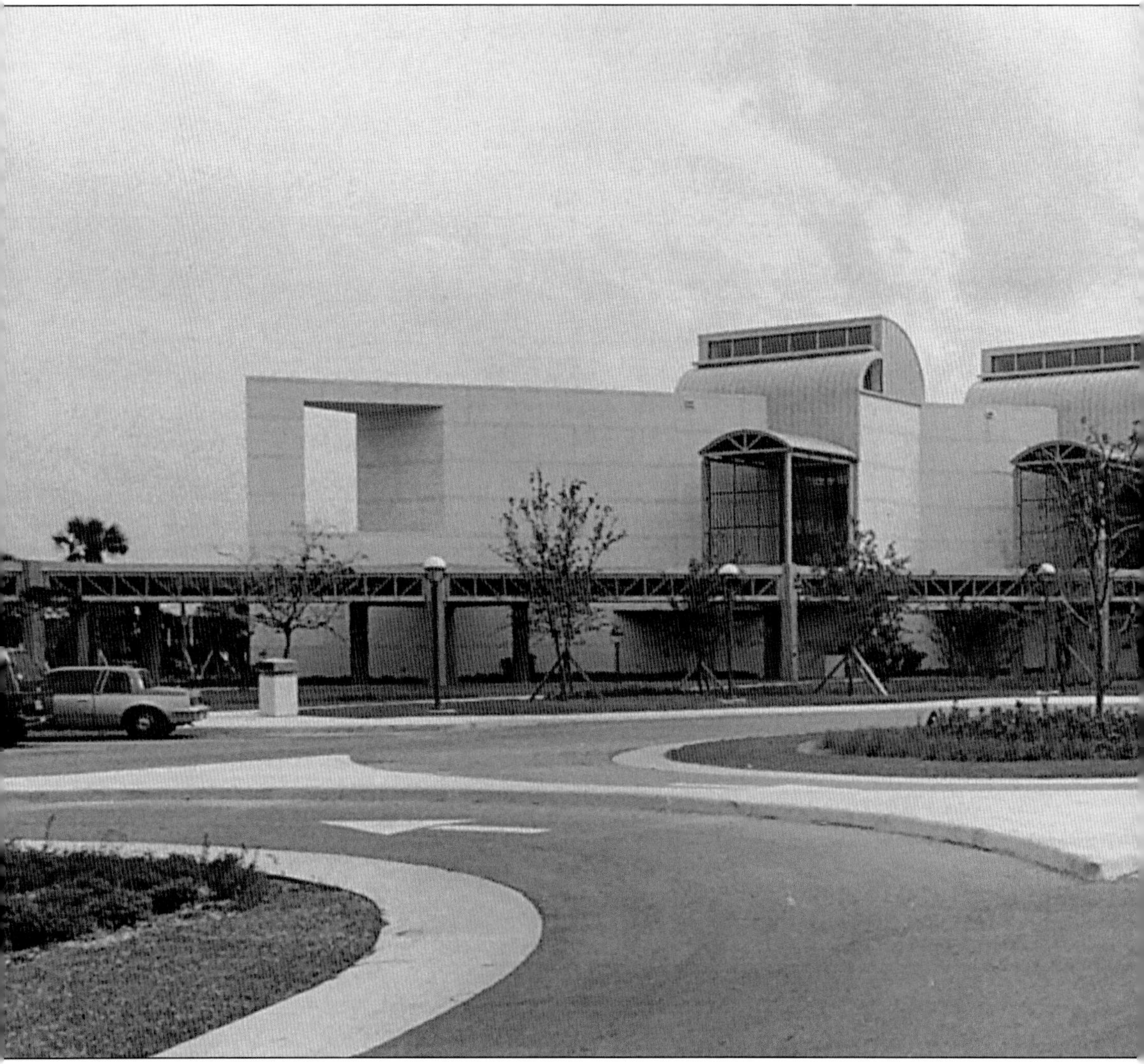

The BCC/North Regional Library marked the second partnership between the Broward County

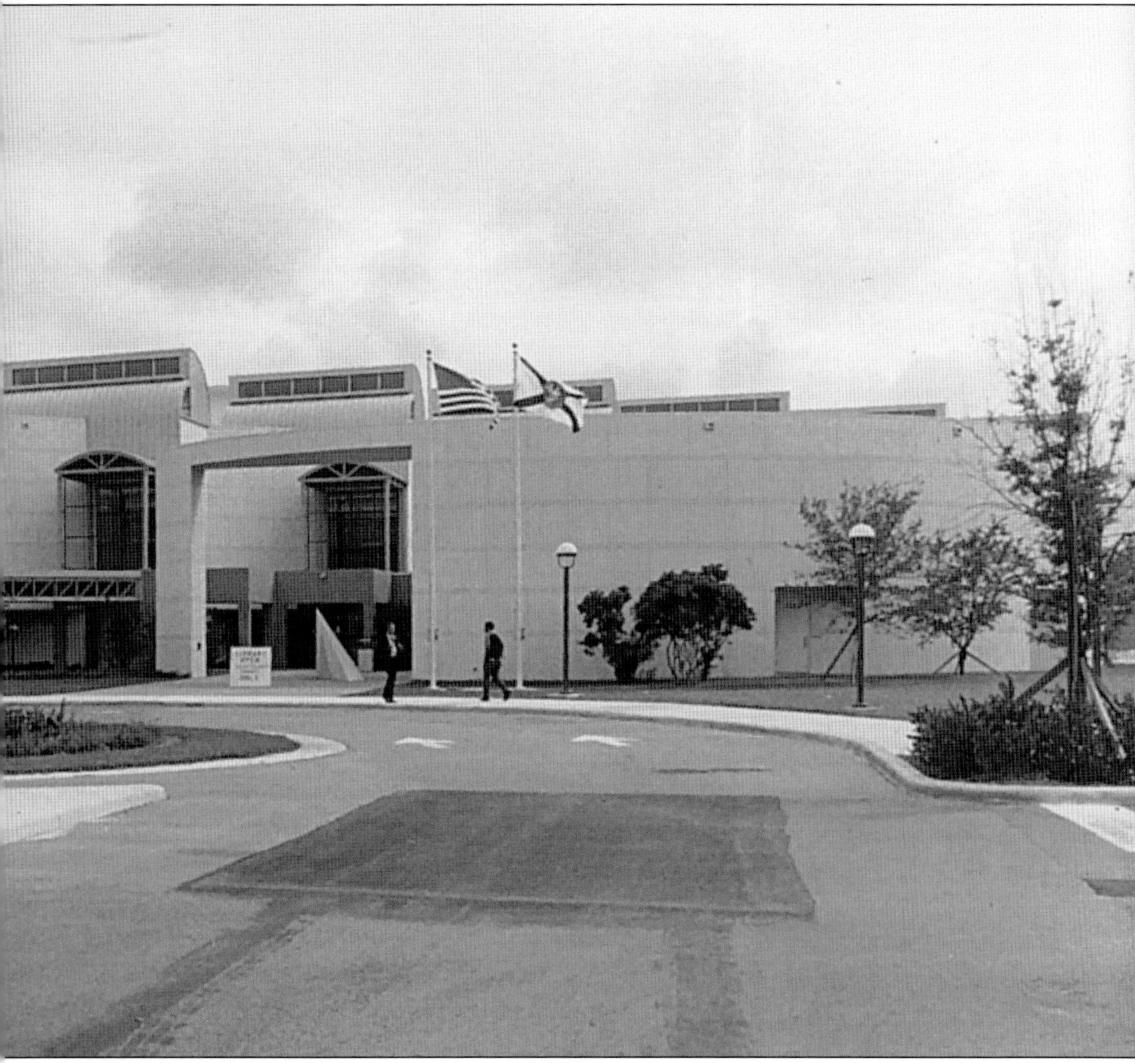

Library and BCC and is widely used by BCC students and county residents.

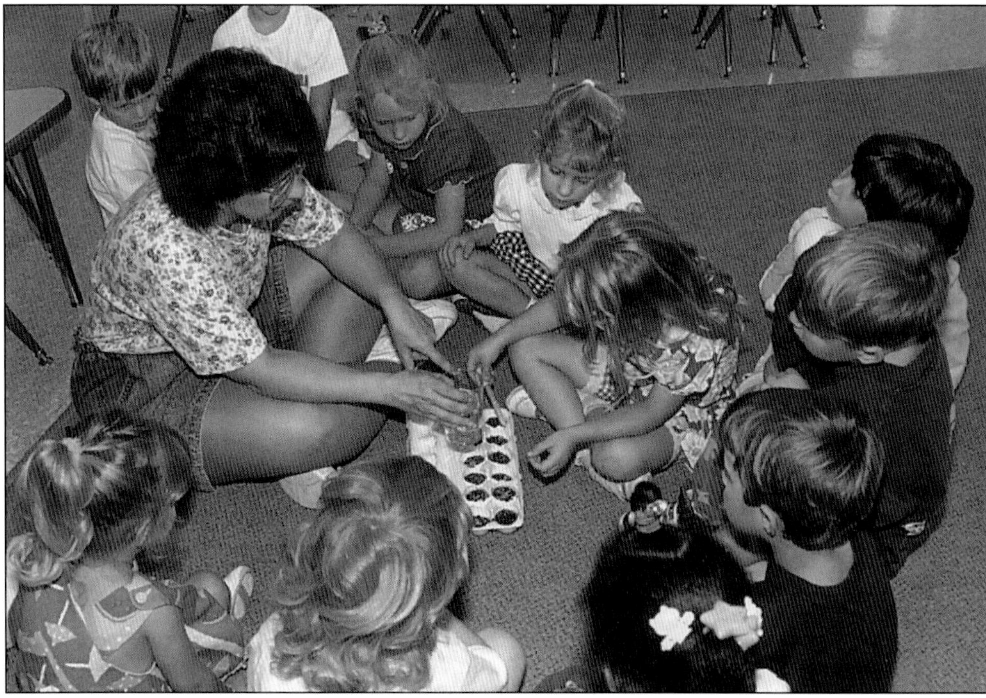

Constructed as part of the library project, the Little Learners College is a daycare center for the young children of students, faculty, and staff. The center is also used as a training facility for students in the early childhood education programs.

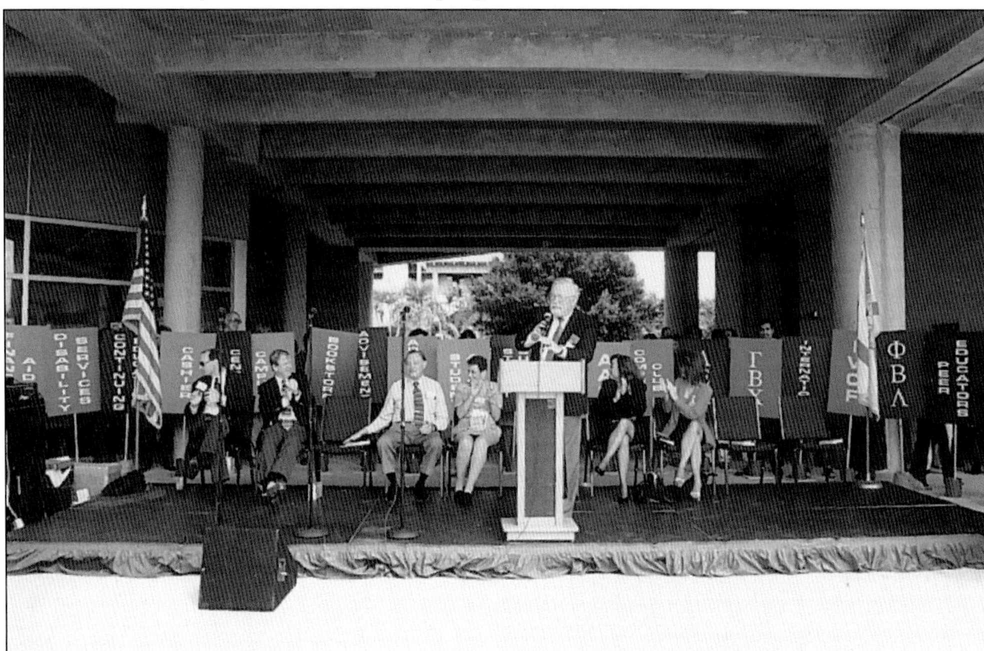


North Campus Provost Dr. Larry McFarlane addresses guests at dedication ceremonies for the North Campus Admissions and Student Services Center in February 2001. The 65,000 square-foot building is the 14th building constructed on North Campus.

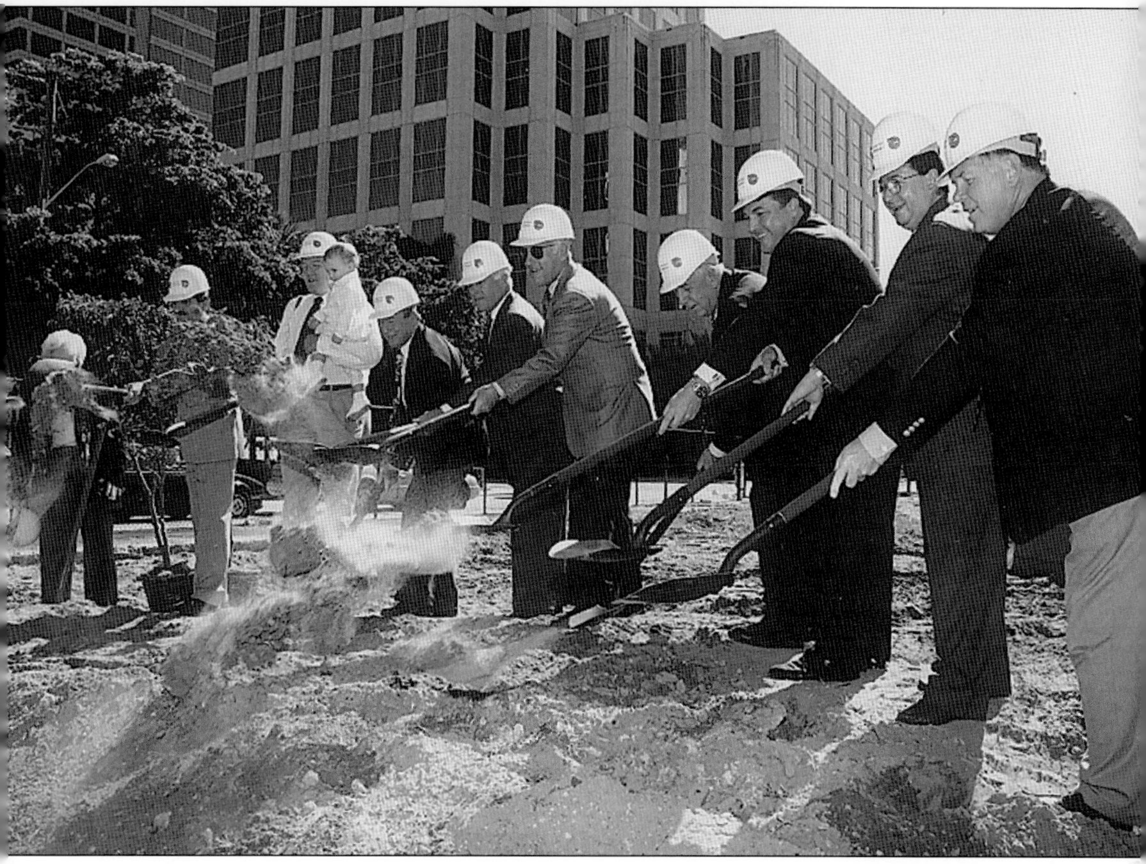

Dr. Holcombe and Dr. Catanese, along with local and state dignitaries, pitch the ceremonial shovels of dirt in groundbreaking ceremonies for the BCC/FAU Higher Education Center in November 1999.

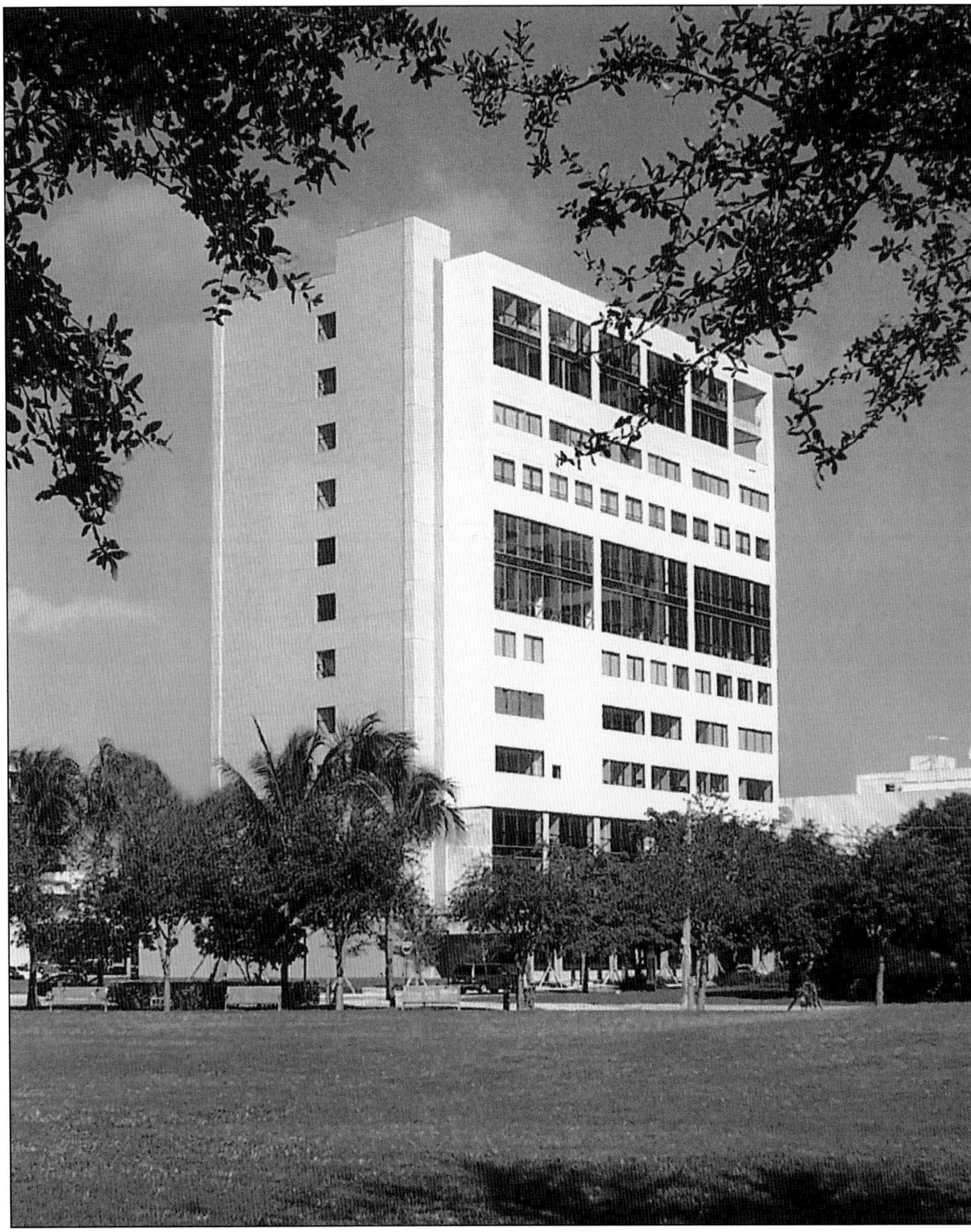

The 12-story, $18-million Higher Education Center was designed by Singer Architects of Fort Lauderdale and constructed on the former site of the historic Governor's Club Hotel. The building covers 147,000 square feet.

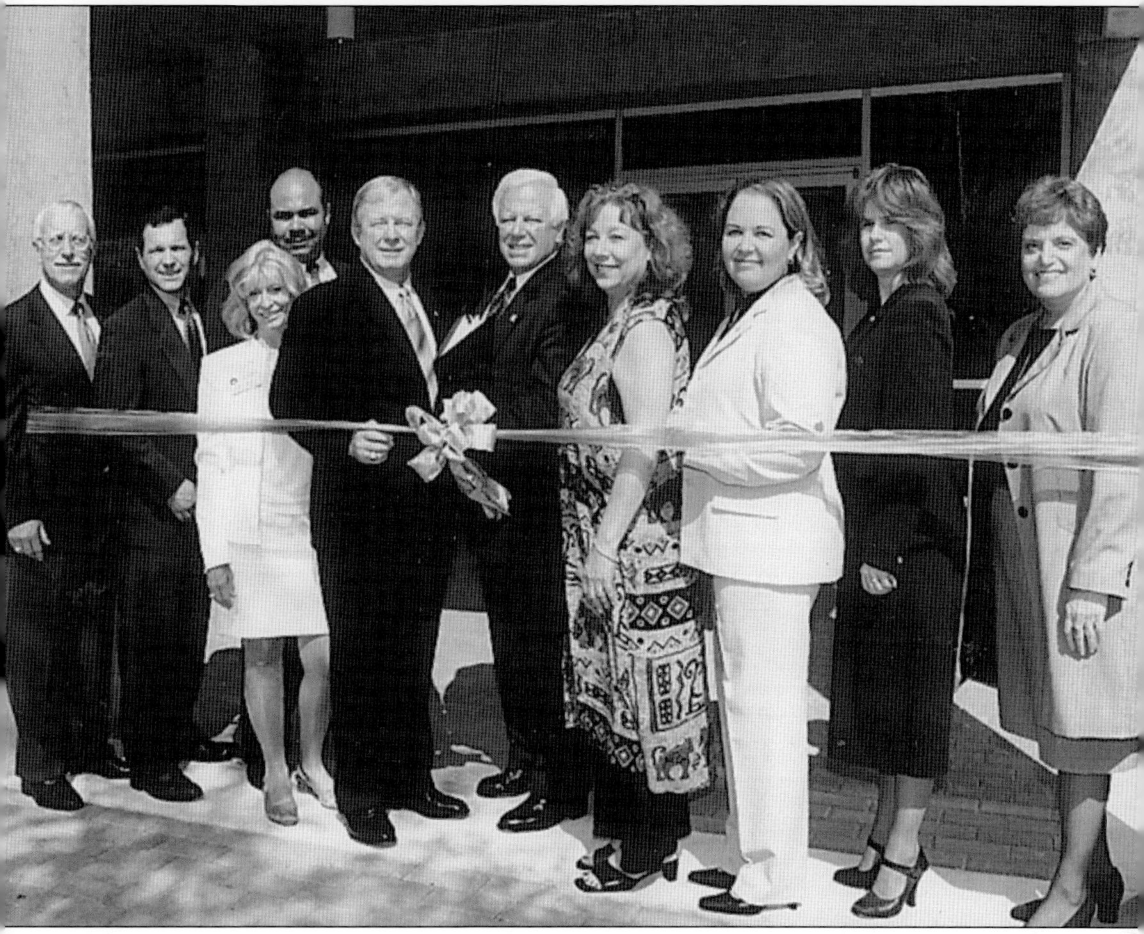

Members of BCC's boards of trustees and administrators are all smiles at the October 2001 dedication ceremonies of the Higher Education Center in downtown Fort Lauderdale. From left to right are Norman Tripp, Dr. Ken Wiant, Ginny Miller, Levi Williams, Dr. Holcombe, Dr. Catanese, Georgette Sosa Douglass, Lourdes Garrido, Cheryl Krause, and Dr. Linda Liberman.

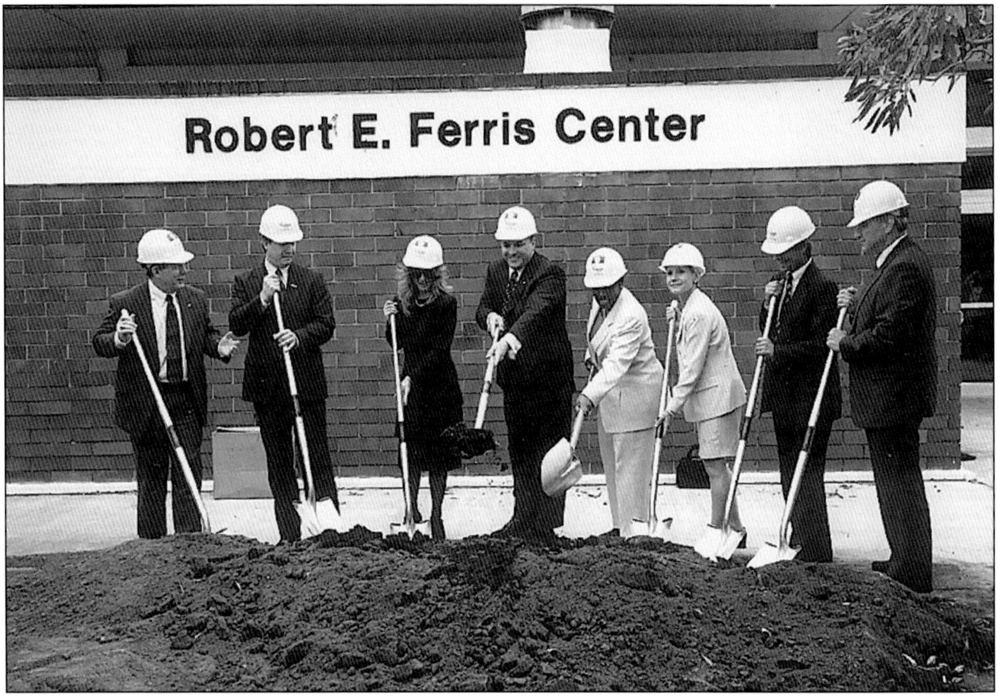


Dignitaries join trustees Paul Anderson and Cheryl Krause, Dr. Holcombe, Central Campus Provost Dr. Patricia Caldwell, and Dean of Student Affairs Dr. Carol Ross-Black in turning the earth for reconstruction of the Robert E. Ferris Center in 2000.

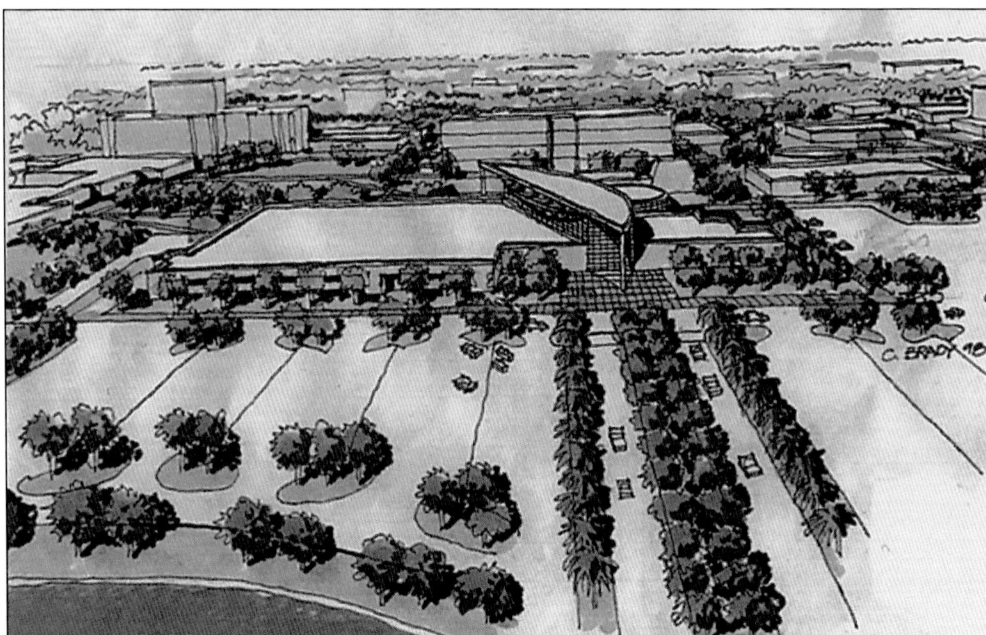

The new Ferris Center, dedicated in March 2002, is architecturally distinctive and offers a greater variety of Student Affairs functions.

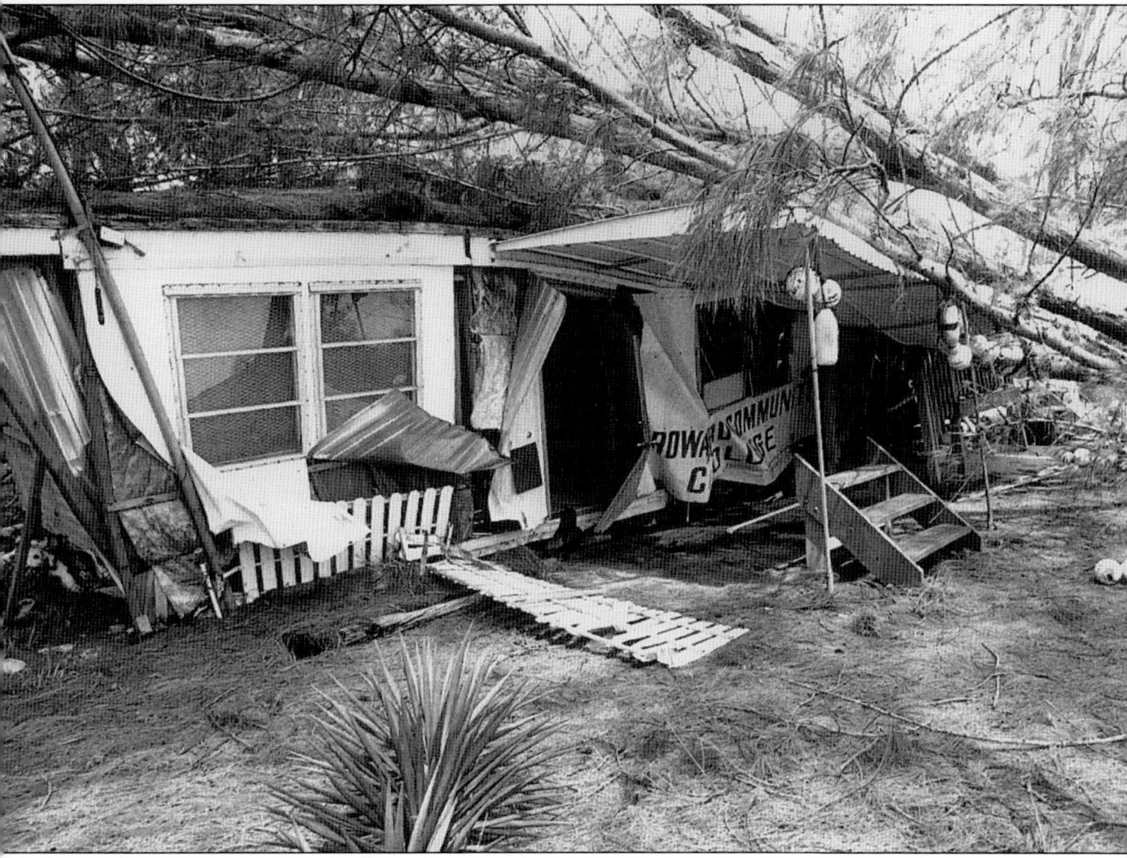

Hurricane Andrew came aground in South Florida on August 24, 1992. While much of southern Miami-Dade County was leveled, Broward County damage was moderate. BCC's most dramatic damage was at the Tigertail Watersports Complex, where Australian pines crashed onto a trailer.

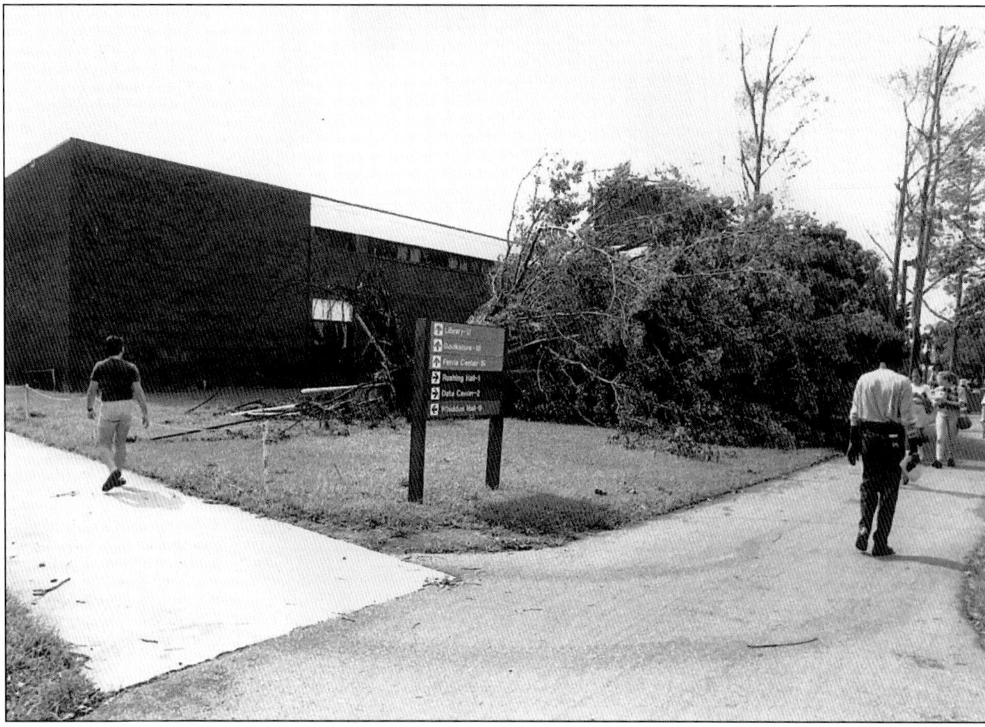

Hurricane Andrew's damage to Central Campus was largely confined to signs and trees, as shown in this view of the west side of the campus.

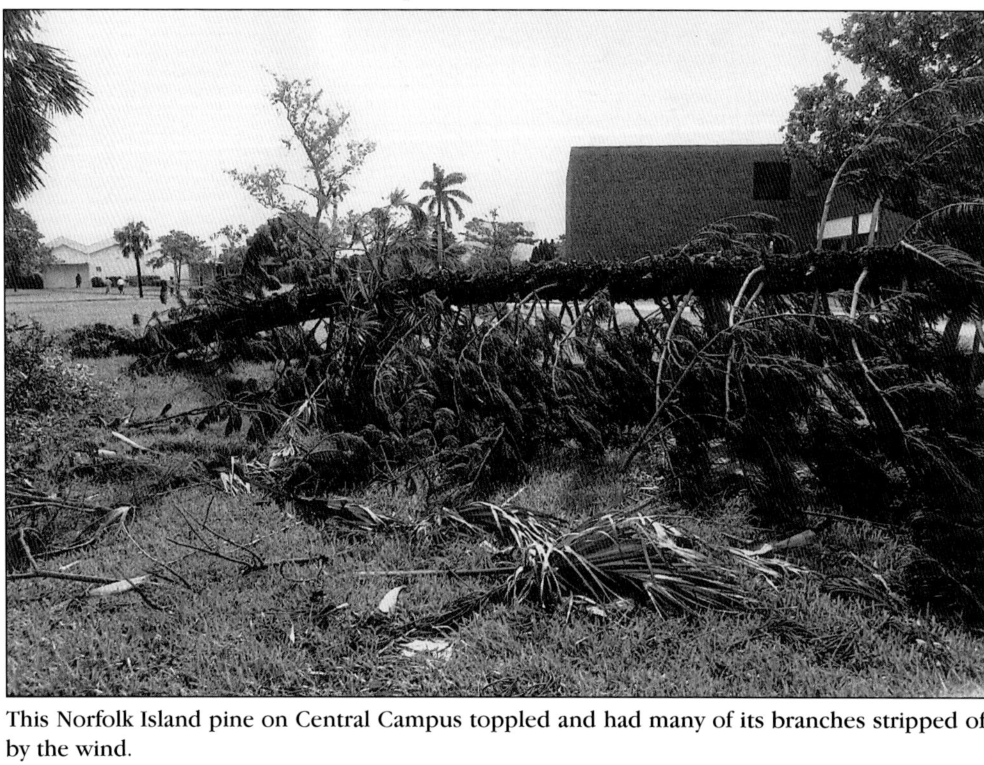

This Norfolk Island pine on Central Campus toppled and had many of its branches stripped off by the wind.

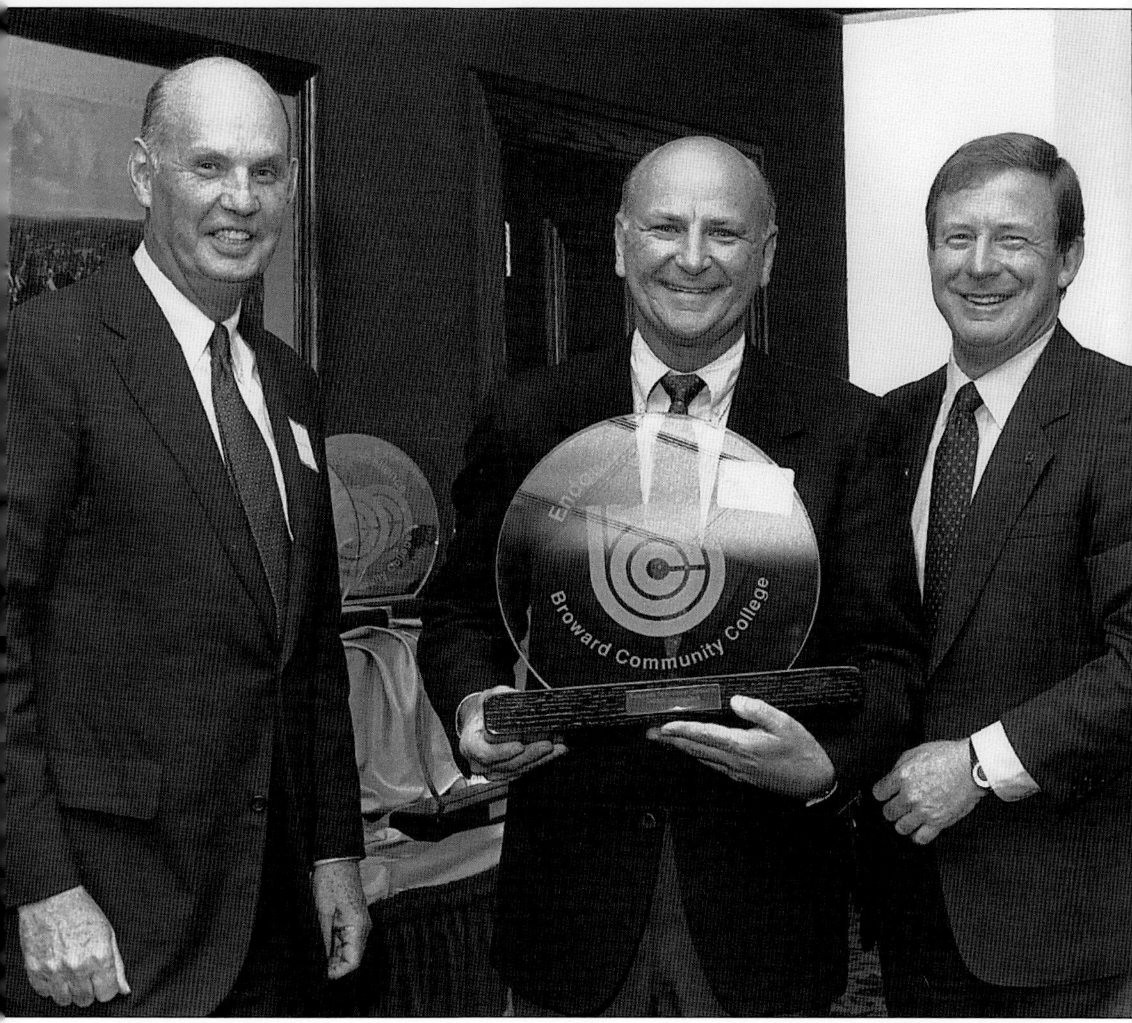


The Junior College of Broward County Foundation Corporation was incorporated in 1966, but never completed its organizational activities. In 1971, the Broward Community College Foundation was incorporated and took root. Today the BCC Foundation is one of the nation's top community college foundations, with total assets of more than $55 million. The BCC Foundation was the nation's first community college foundation to complete an endowed teaching chairs campaign. In this 1990 picture, Hudson Whitley of C&S Bank (left) joins with Dr. Holcombe to present a memento to H. Wayne Huizenga for establishing the Blockbuster Entertainment Group Endowed Teaching Chair.

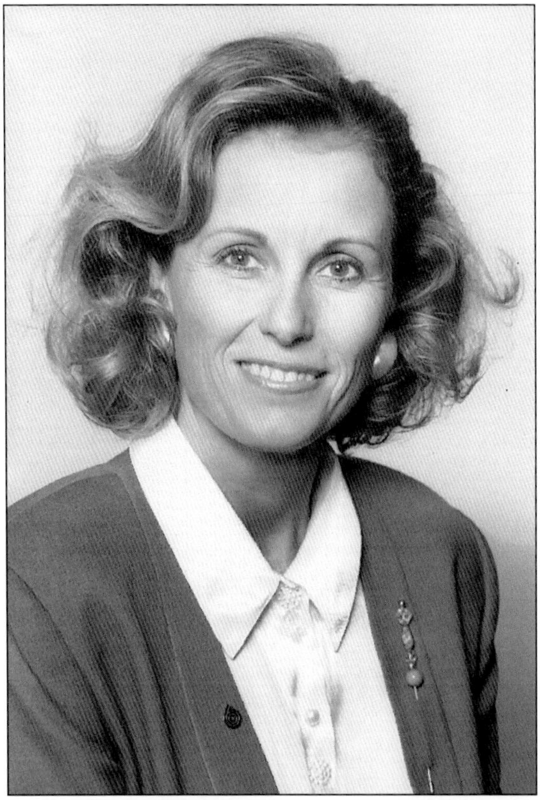

After serving as provost of South Campus for three years, Dr. E. Ann McGee was named vice president for development and executive director of the BCC Foundation in December 1985. Under her direction, the foundation grew to over $12 million in assets and ranked third in the nation for size of endowment and sixth nationally for cash raised. In November 1995, she left BCC to become president of Seminole Community College in Sanford.

The BCC Madrigals entertained at the "Home for the Holidays" fund-raiser at the Design Center of the Americas, which benefited the BCC and Cleveland Clinic Florida foundations.

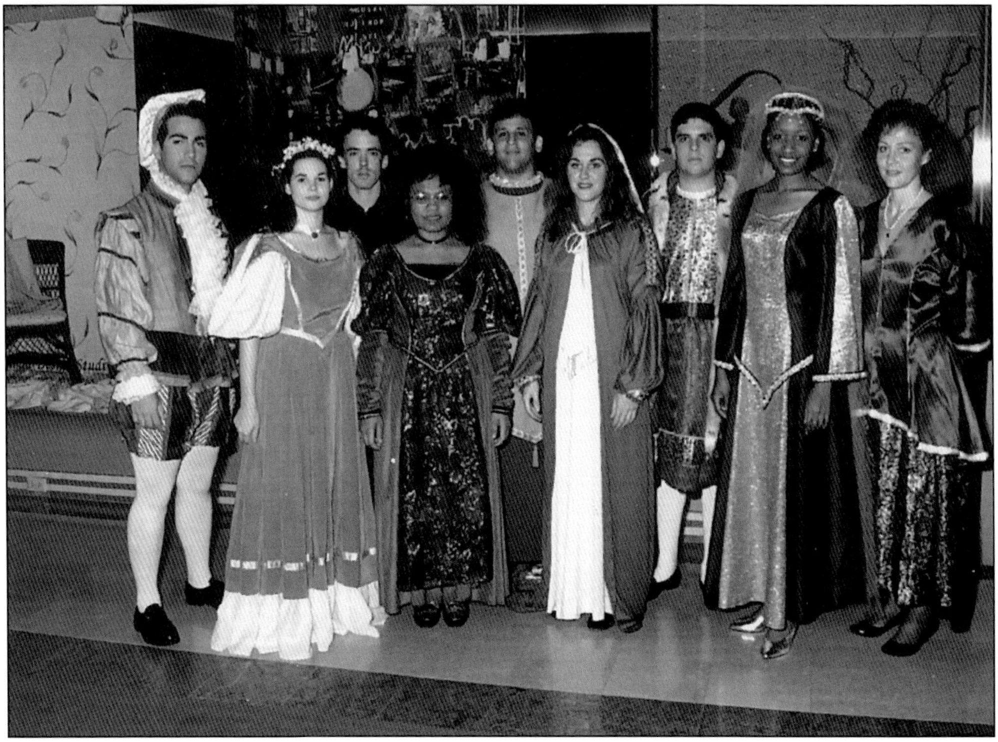

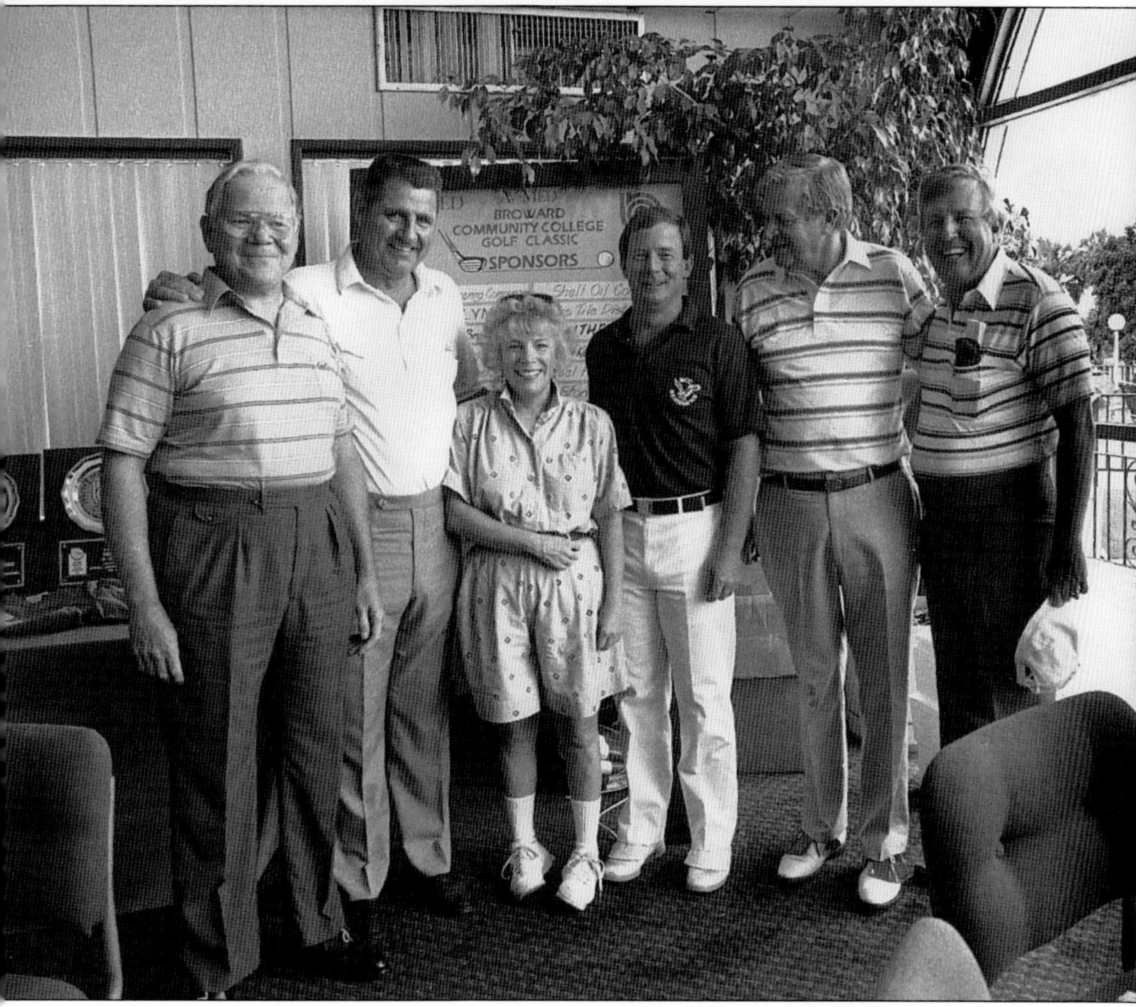


The foundation's annual fund-raising activity is a golf classic. The second tournament was held in 1989 at Earl Morrall's Arrowhead Golf Club in Davie. Pictured from left to right are Fred Millsaps, Earl Morrall, Dr. Holcombe, Av-Med's Ludy Price, Broward schools superintendent Sam Morgan, and Dr. Larry McFarlane, who first envisioned the idea of a fund-raising golf tournament for the college. Dr. McFarlane conducted the event for its first few years. The 1989 tournament raised more than $15,000 for scholarships and instructional aids. The tournament has also been held at Crystal Lake Country Club, the historic Fort Lauderdale Country Club, and Lago Mar Country Club.

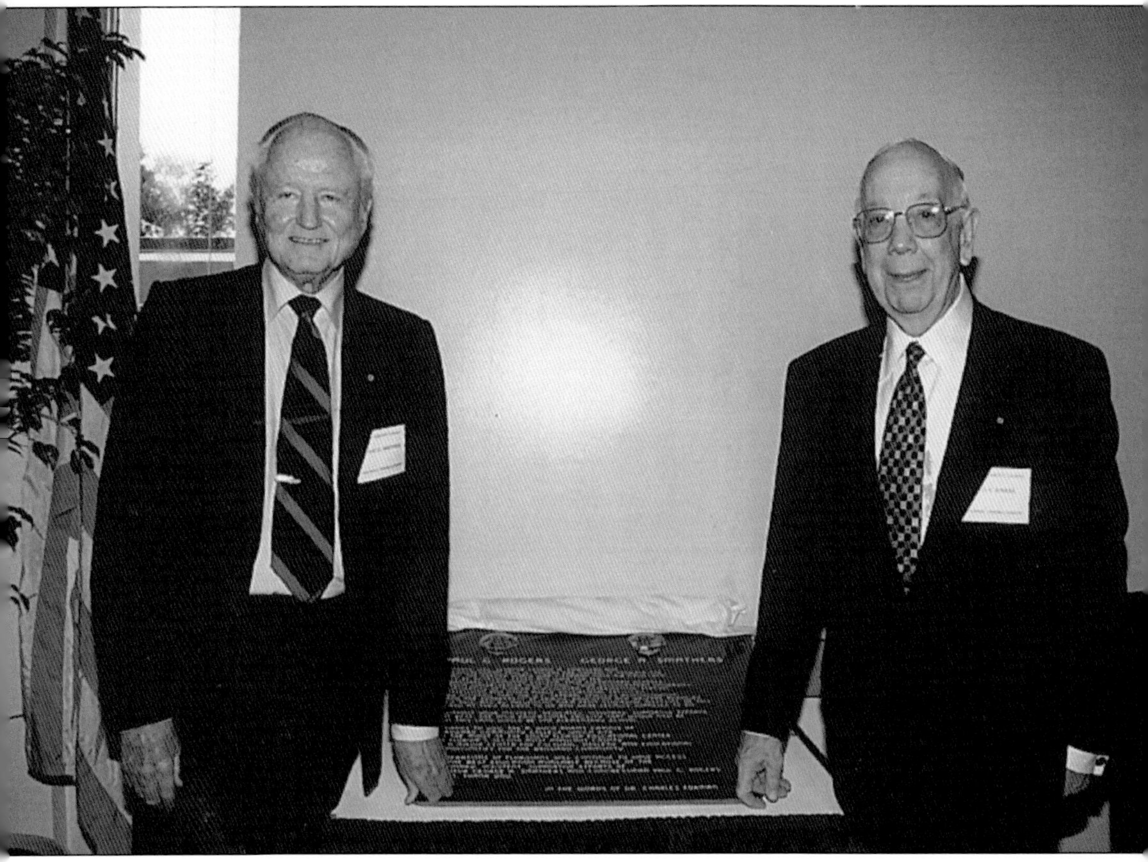

In November 1997, the BCC Foundation honored former United States Sen. George Smathers, left, and Rep. Paul Rogers with a plaque commemorating their efforts in obtaining land on which to build Central Campus. The plaque is permanently mounted on a pedestal in the garden at Joe B. Rushing Hall.

Judy Bowen became vice president for development and executive director of the BCC Foundation as it began its $12 million Campaign 2000 in 1996, but helped reach its goal two years before the anticipated completion date. Under her guidance, the foundation's assets have reached $55 million.

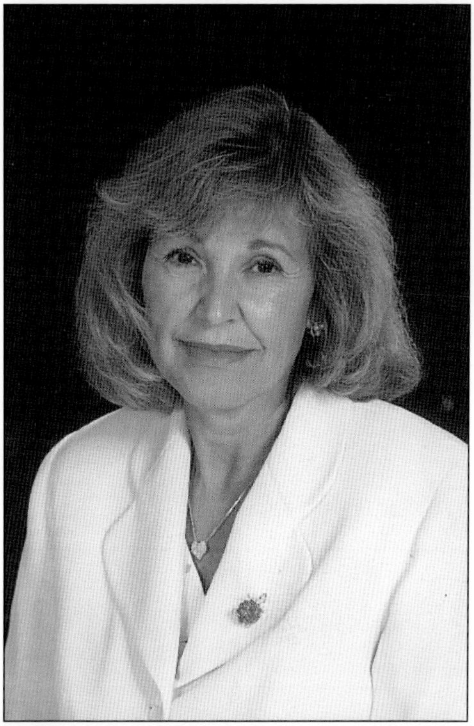

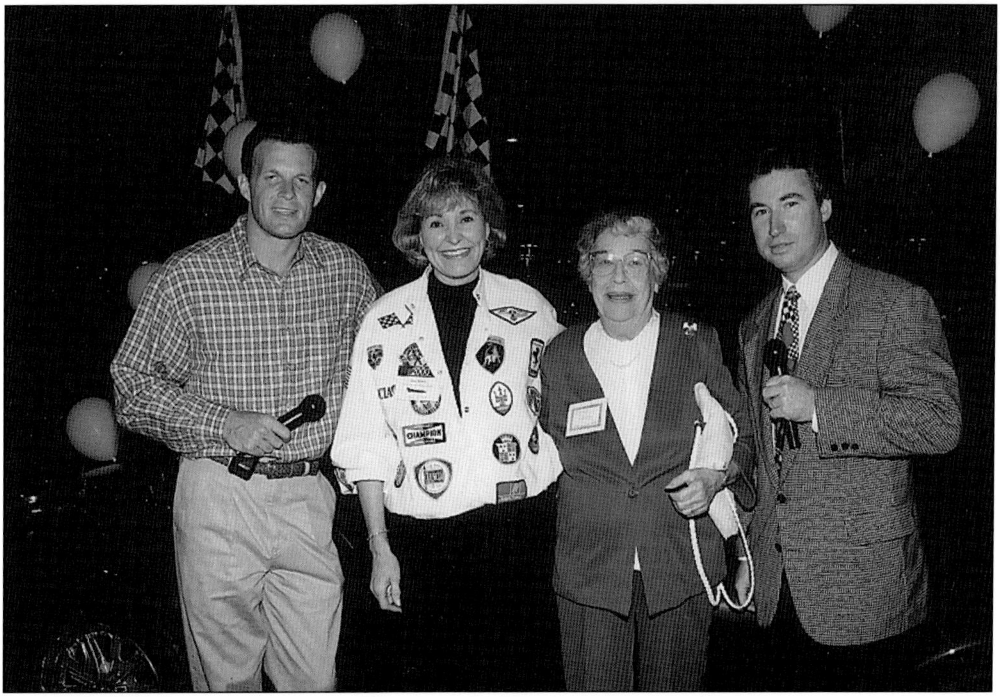

The kickoff event for Campaign 2000 was the Rally for BCC at Auto Nation in Coconut Creek. WPLG–TV personality Doug Dunbar (left) and Scott Whiddon (right) greeted and interviewed Judy Bowen and donor Elsie Davie as they arrived for the festivities. The evening's entertainment included races, videos, demonstrations of pit changes, and a pit crew change.

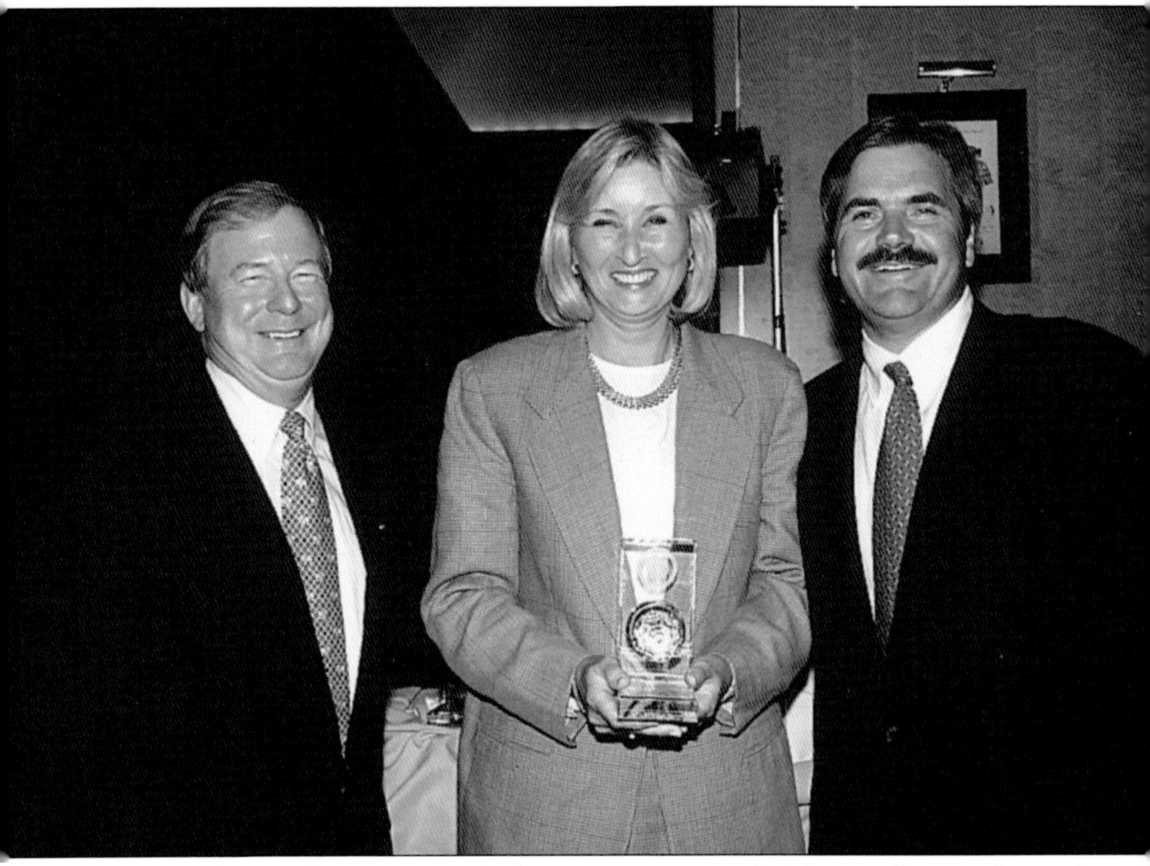

At the conclusion of Campaign 2000, donors were presented with specially created crystal doorknobs because their donations helped open doors to brighter futures for students. In this picture, Auto Nation's Gale Butler accepts a memento on behalf of Wayne and Marti Huizenga from Dr. Holcombe and campaign chairman Steve Berrard.

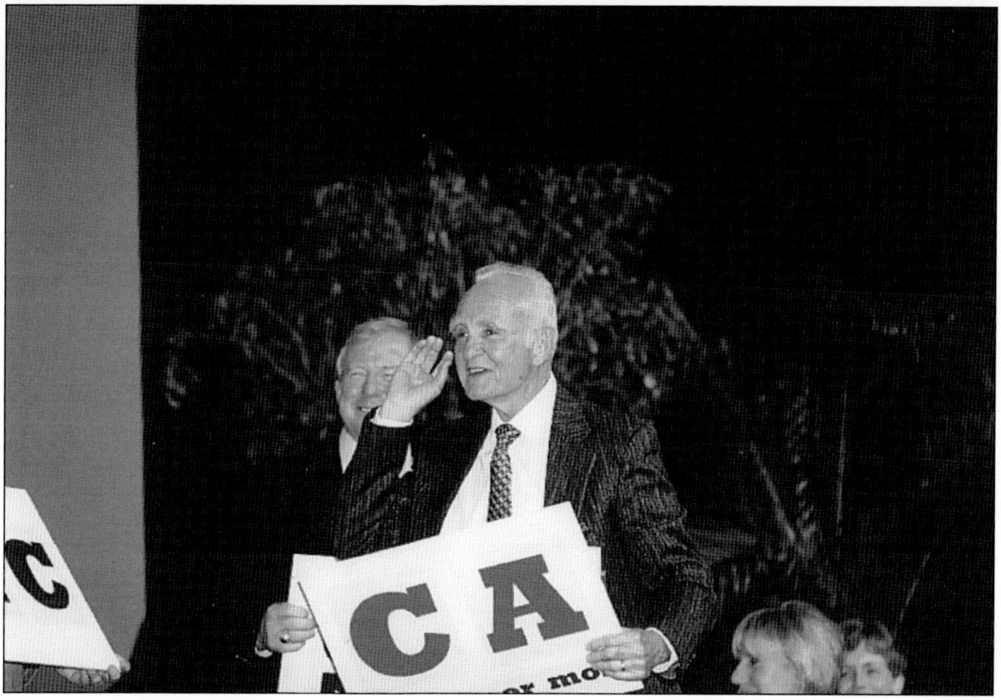

Some foundation board members continued or renewed ties with the college when they joined the board. Retired architect F. Louis Wolff designed the North Campus Omni Auditorium.

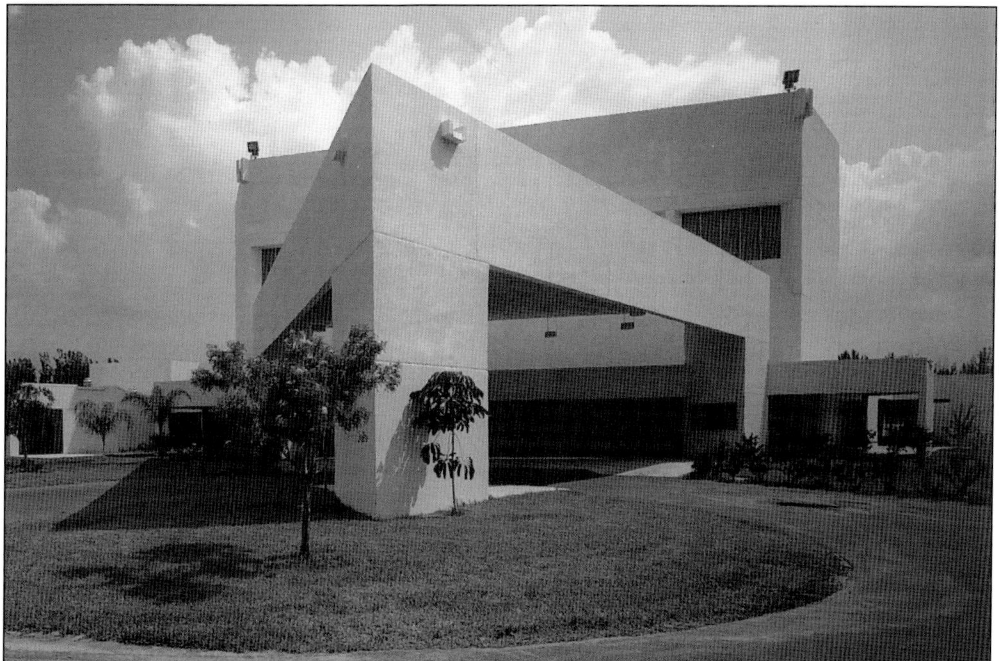

The Omni, shown just after its completion in 1980, is home to the BCC men's basketball team and the women's volleyball team and is used for theatrical productions, graduations, and cultural events. The facility seats 2,000.

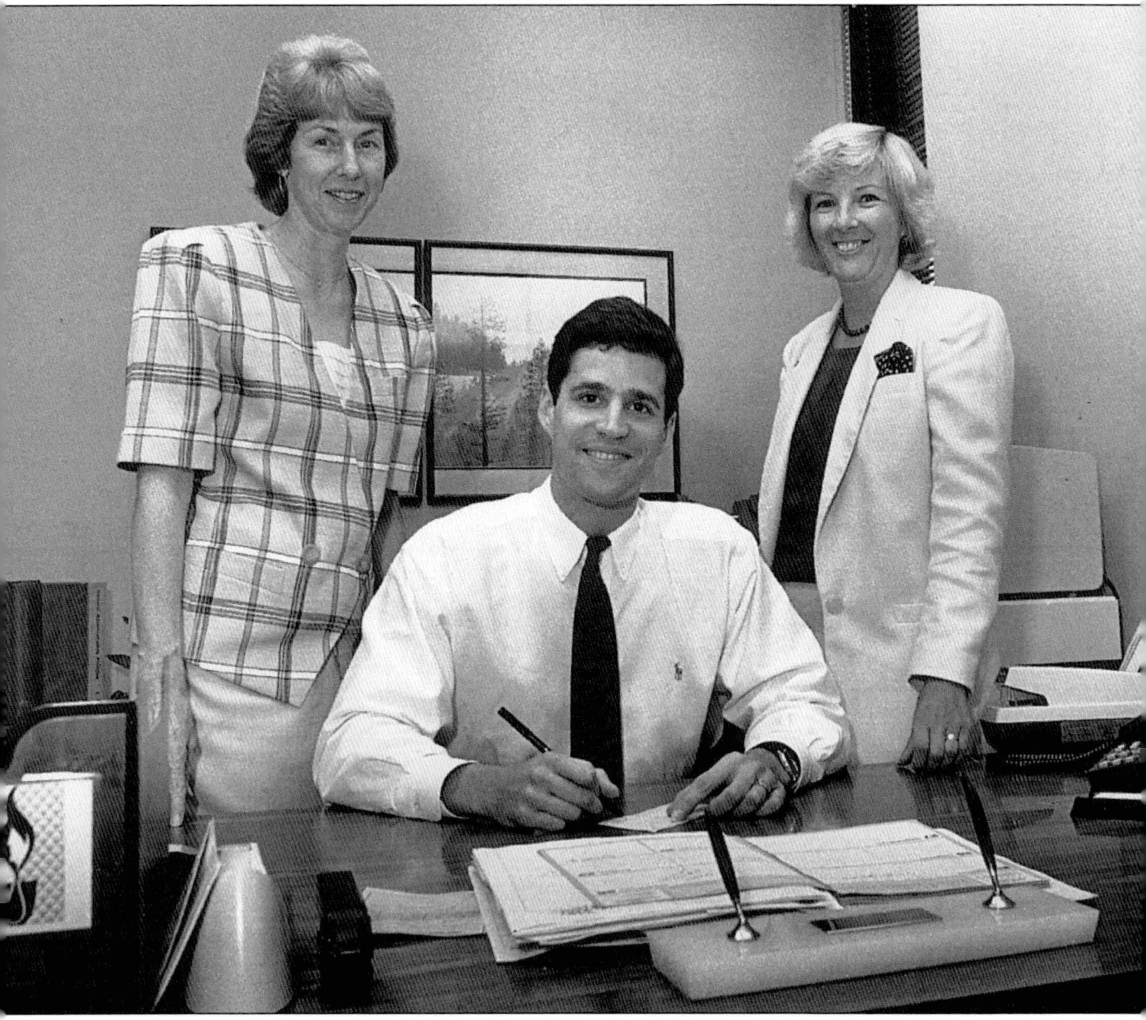

Professors Peggy Green (left) and Jeanette Madea (right) receive a donation from Richard Rowe, employee relations administrator for Allied Signal, the "Science 4 Kids" program. Started in 1981, the program incorporates hands-on experiments for Broward County elementary students at the North and South campuses.

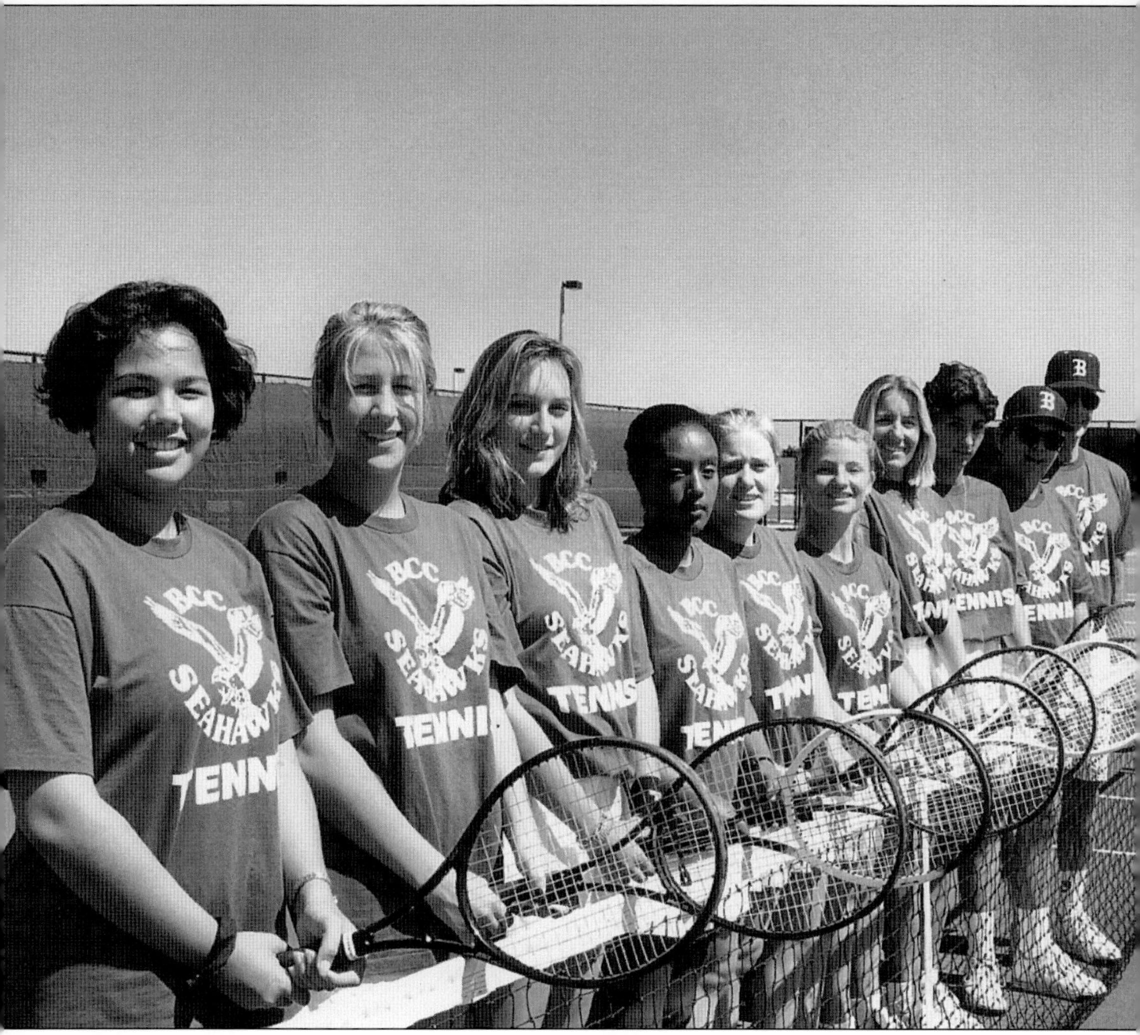


After many top-four finishes, the women's tennis team won the 1996 National Junior College Athletic Association Championship. The players and coaches are, from left to right, Rosa Pons-Nunez, Tracy Hollinger, Edith Tieber, Azeb Kidane, Tiffany Odlum, Ella Ionescu, Vesna McKenna, Adolfina Hadamofsky, head coach Tom Burke, and assistant coach Wil Gifford.

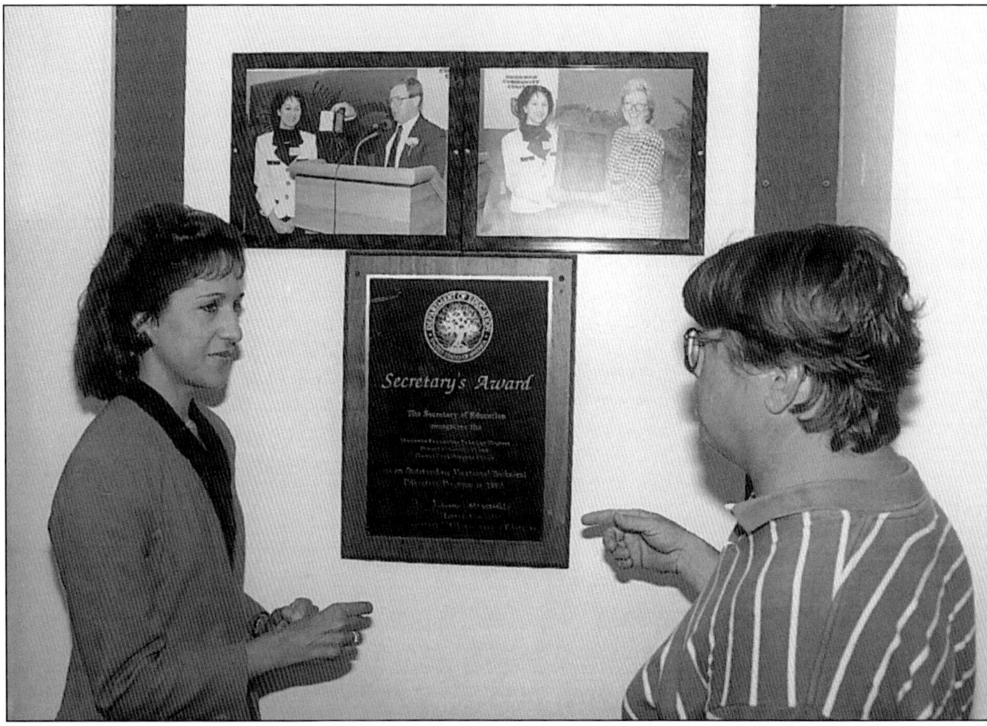


Electronic Engineering Technology Program Director Sandra Sanders, left, shows off the Secretary of Education's Award for Outstanding Vocational/Technical Education Programs, awarded to the college in 1992.

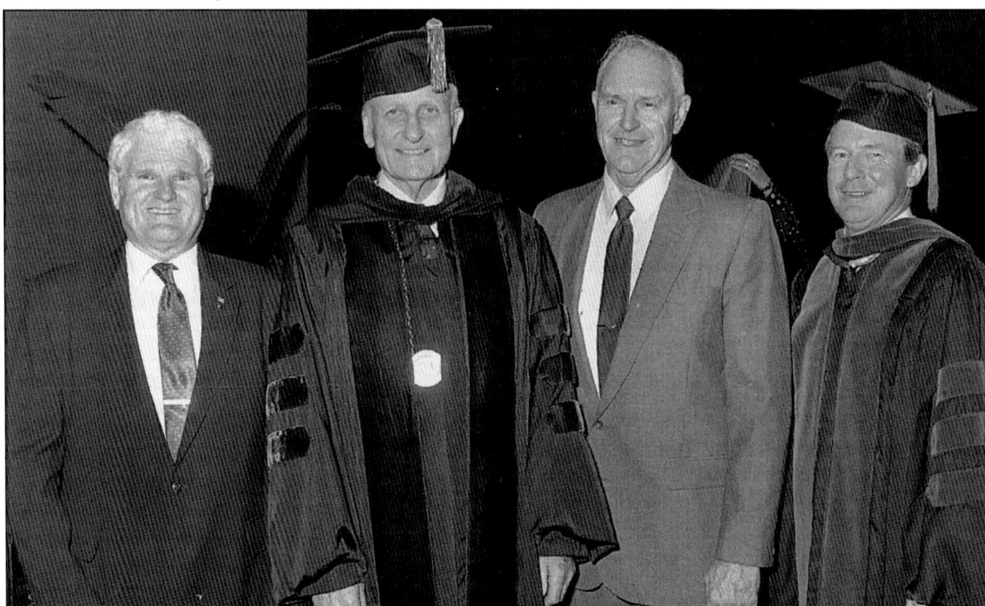

Dr. Joe Rushing returned to BCC as the commencement speaker. There, he was reunited with two physical education professors who had served on his faculty. From left to right are Rex Brumley, Dr. Rushing, Alton "Andy" Andrews, and Dr. Holcombe.

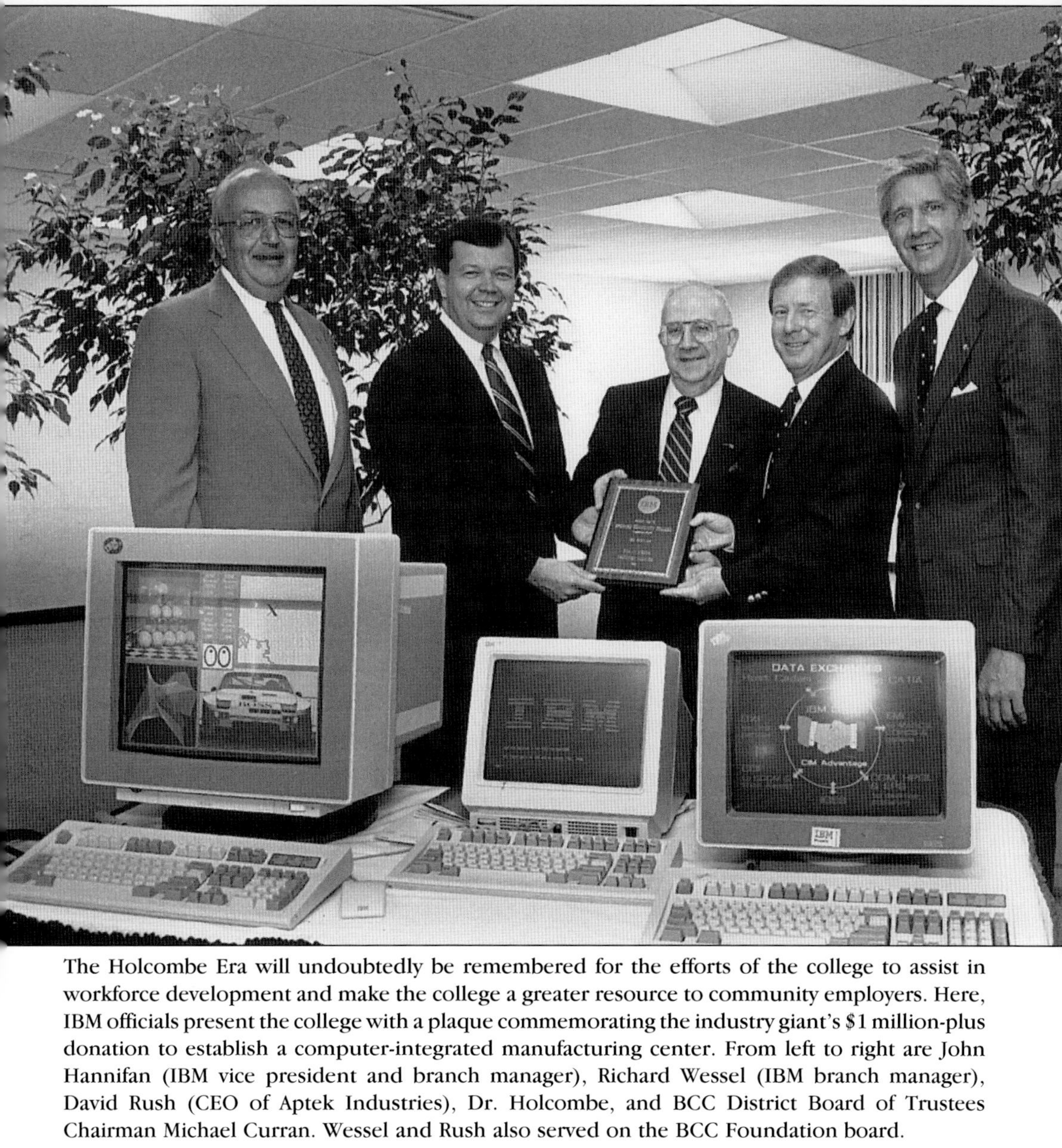

The Holcombe Era will undoubtedly be remembered for the efforts of the college to assist in workforce development and make the college a greater resource to community employers. Here, IBM officials present the college with a plaque commemorating the industry giant's $1 million-plus donation to establish a computer-integrated manufacturing center. From left to right are John Hannifan (IBM vice president and branch manager), Richard Wessel (IBM branch manager), David Rush (CEO of Aptek Industries), Dr. Holcombe, and BCC District Board of Trustees Chairman Michael Curran. Wessel and Rush also served on the BCC Foundation board.

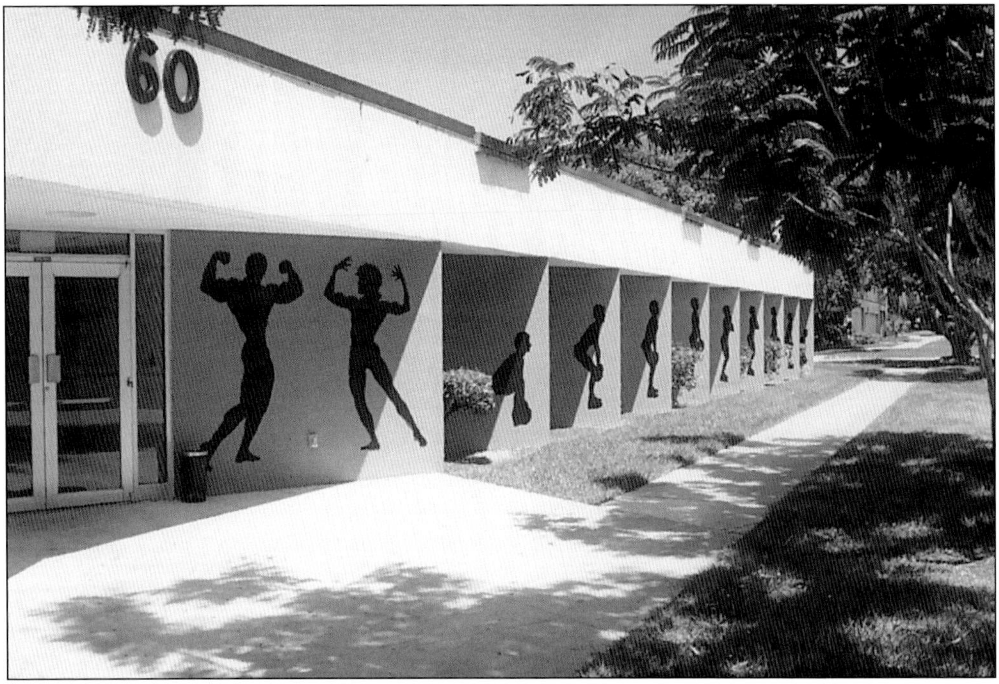


Student artists took a novel approach in decorating the wing walls on building 60 on North Campus.

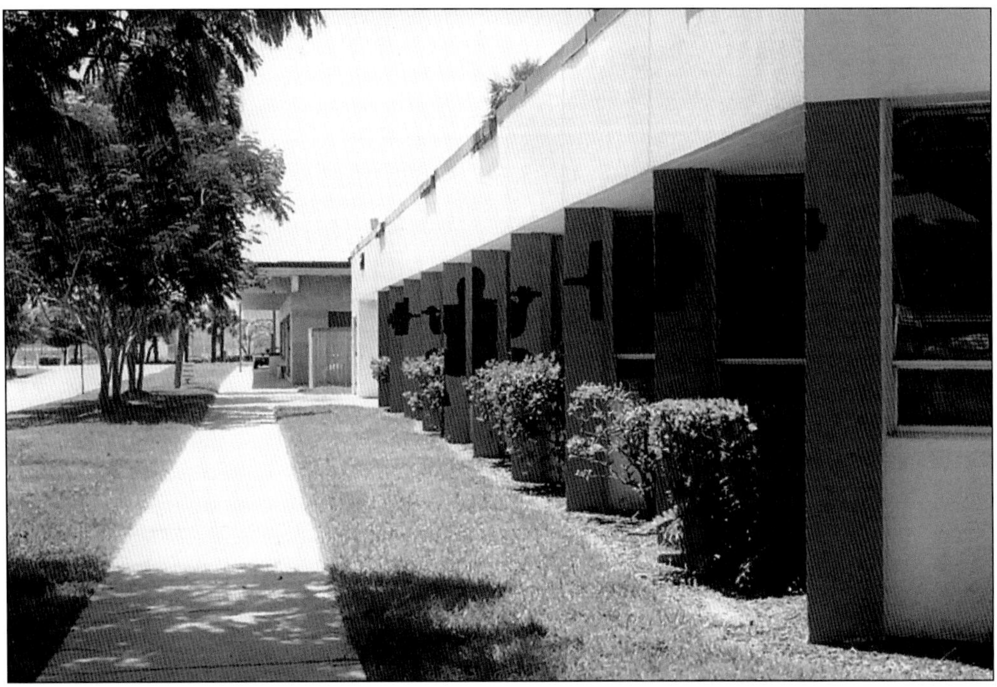

The works of art depicting power lifters and body builders are part of the campus "Gallery without Walls" program.

Mime Darby Hayes spent a two-month residence at BCC in 1993, giving performances to student and community groups and teaching about the art of acting without words.

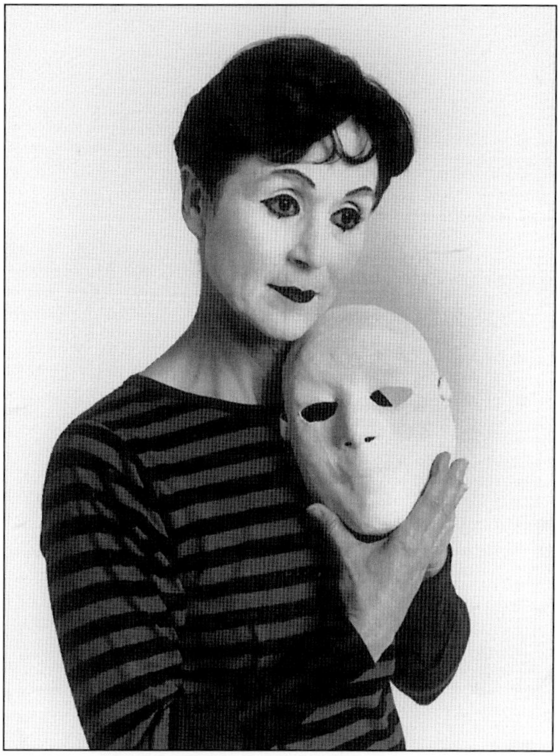

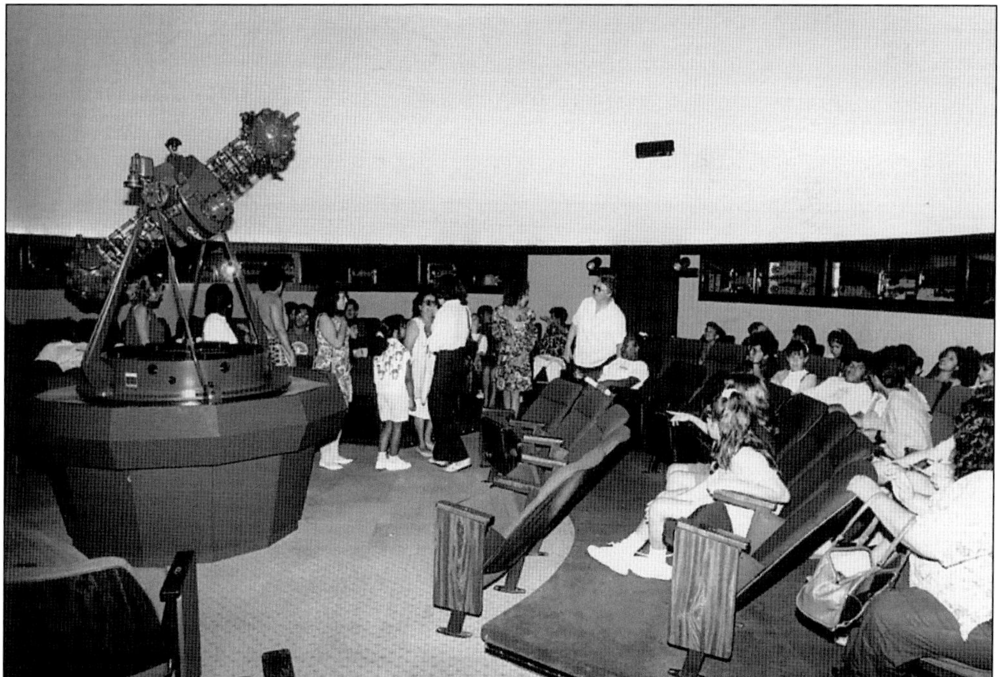

The Buehler Planetarium is home to the world's fourth Zeiss M1015 Star Projector, making it one of nation's most sophisticated planetariums. Thousands of school children and community members visit the planetarium annually.

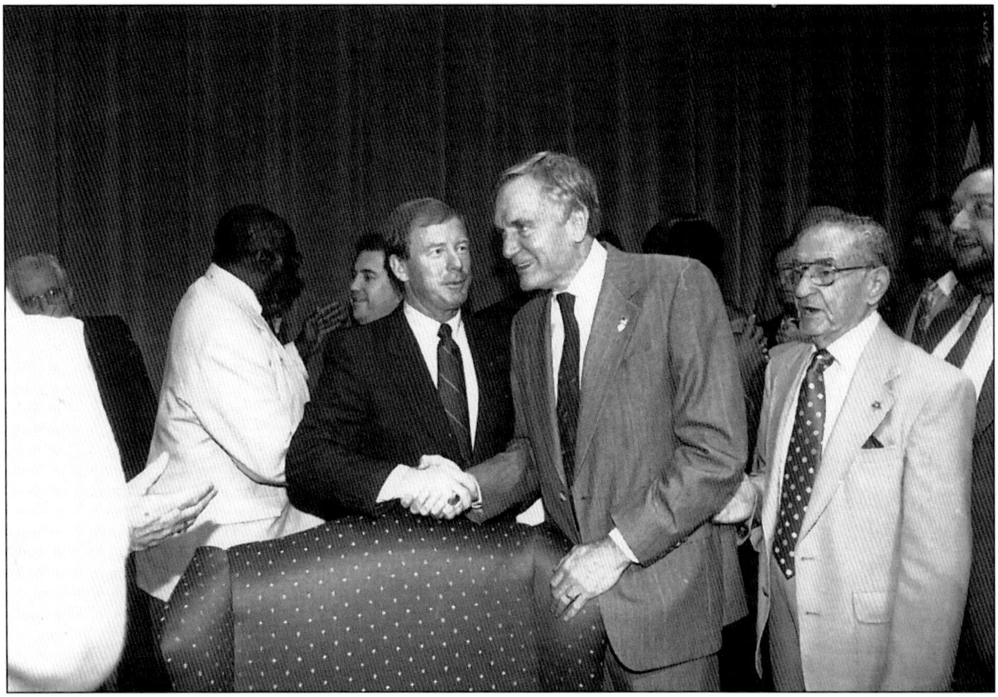

An expert on educational policy, Dr. Holcombe is sought after for advice by community college officials and lawmakers alike. Here, he greets former governor Lawton Chiles.

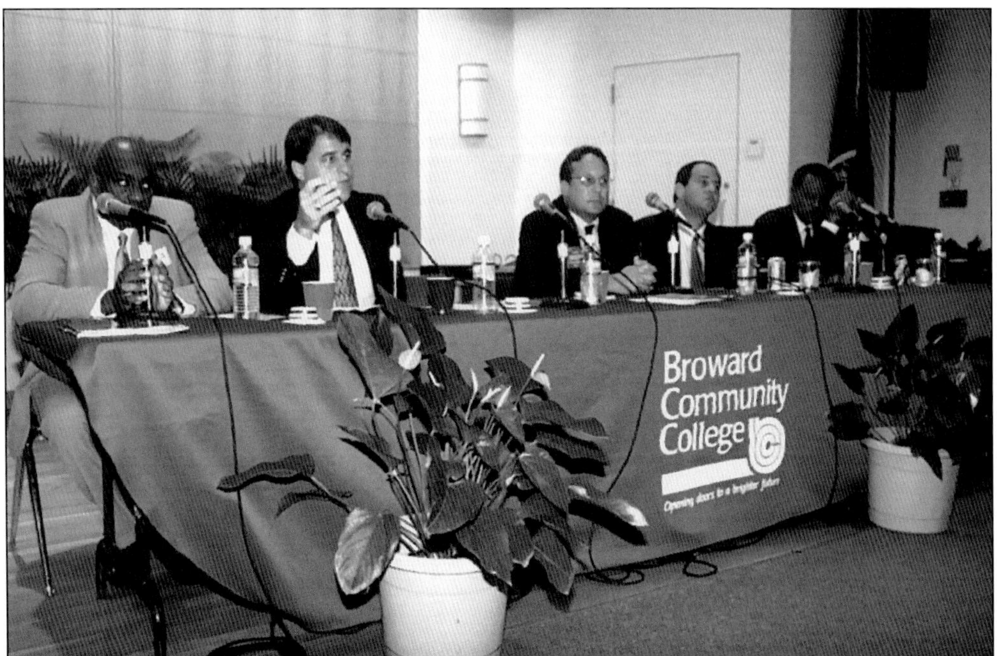


In recent years, the college has invited candidates and lawmakers onto BCC's campuses so they can learn about the college and its role in the community. In this picture, Rep. Jack Seiler of Wilton Manors (second from left) responds to a question during a candidate's forum.

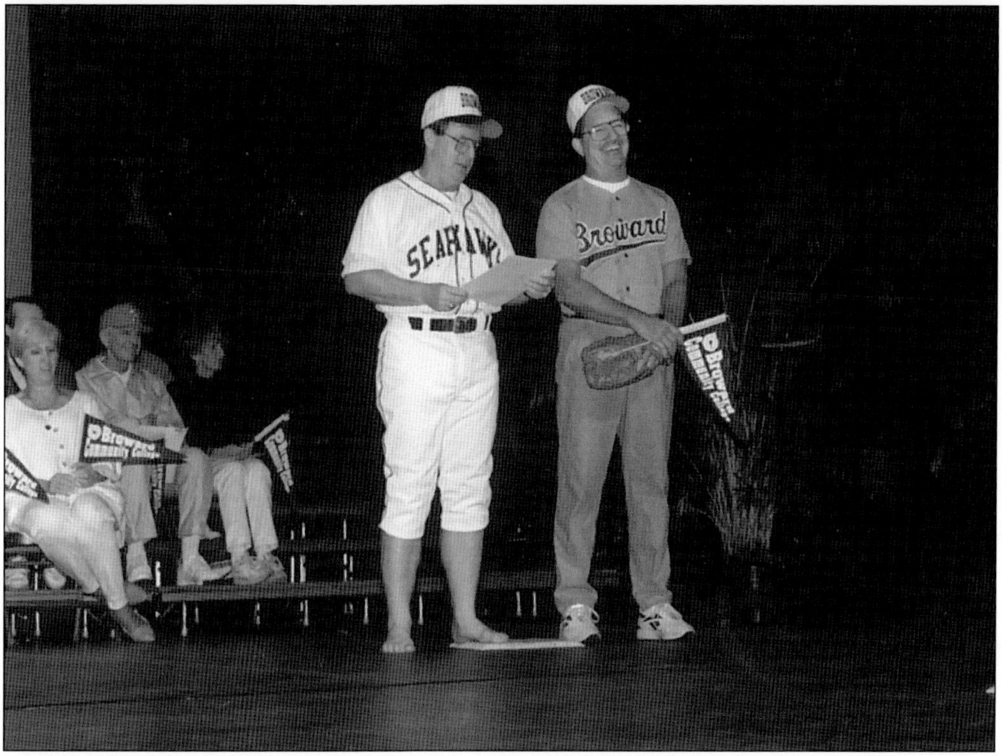

Each year's Colleague Recognition Day gives Dr. Holcombe a chance to demonstrate his acting ability. Among the characters he has portrayed are Elvis, James Bond, Gerald Ford, and Shoeless Willie Holcombe, along with Central Campus Provost Glen Rose.

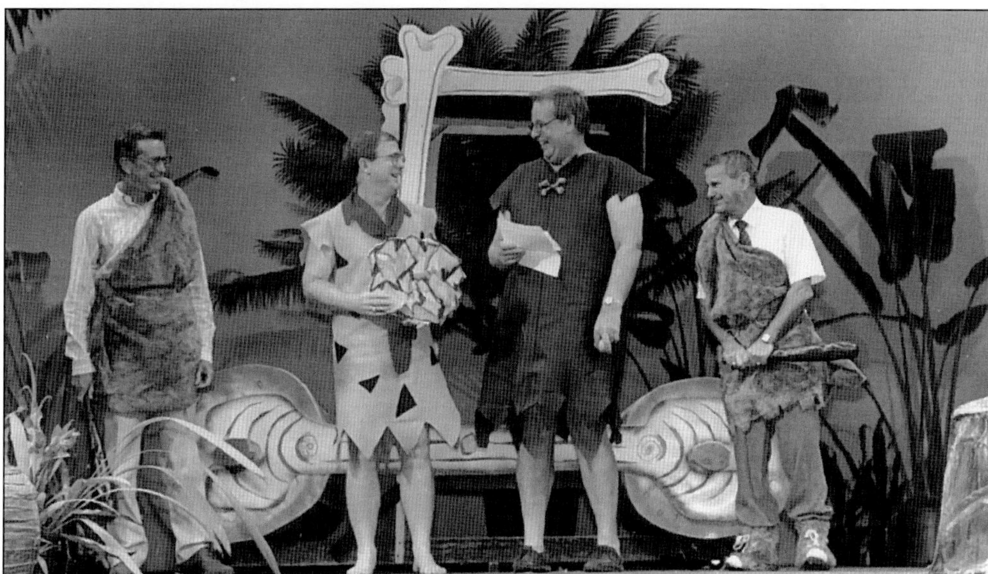

"Fred Flintstone" Holcombe and "Barney Rubble" George Young laughed it up with 30-year honorees Dr. John Pawlowski (left) and Dr. Bill Porterfield in the 1993 Colleague Recognition Day skit "Two Million Years BCC."

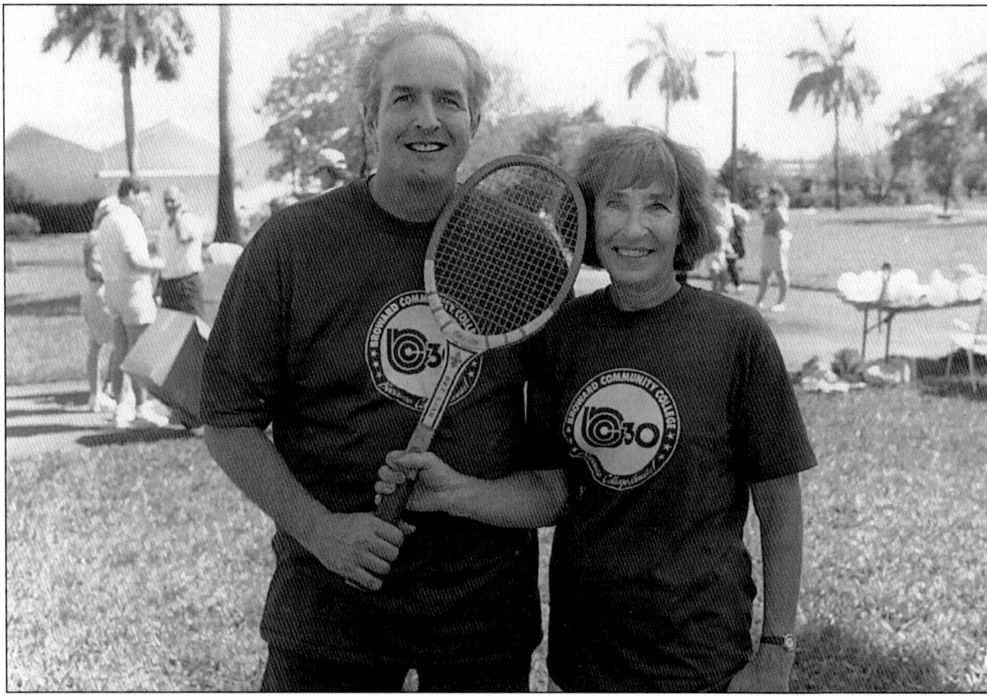

Among the events celebrating the 30th anniversary of the college in 1990 was a picnic and field day for the college family.

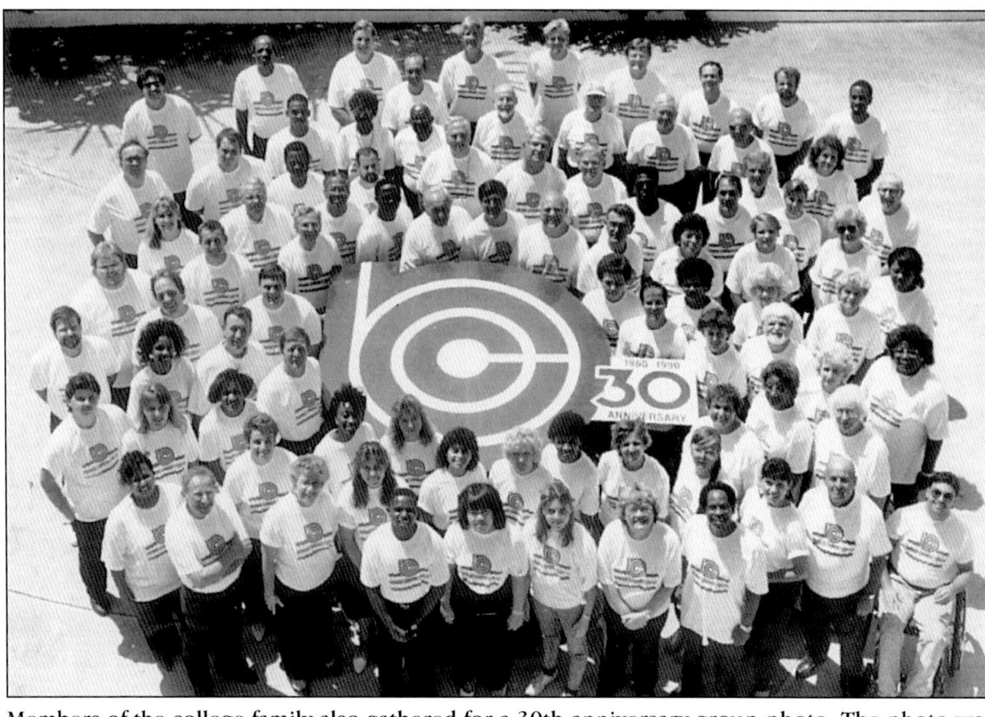

Members of the college family also gathered for a 30th anniversary group photo. The photo was used on the cover of the Fort Lauderdale phone book.

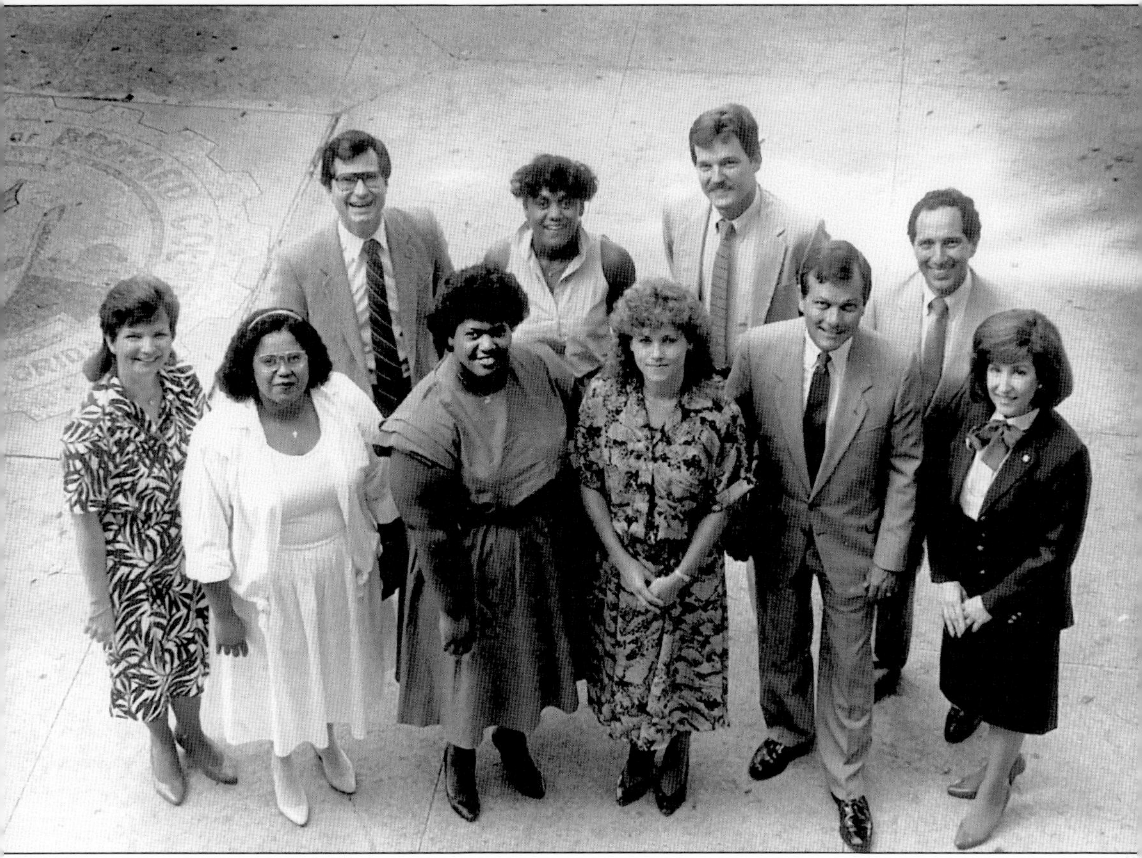

The things that make BCC faculty and administrators most proud are the accomplishments of the students, and there have been many students to be proud of in the college's 40-plus years. A 1987 edition of *CHOICES*, a college newsletter, featured 10 students who had gone on to achieve distinction in a variety of fields. From left to right they are (front row) journalist Linda Billeter, Urban League administrative assistant Barbara McDuffie-Edwards, music teacher Janice Wilkes, art director Sheila Trank, Broward General Medical Center administrator Wil Trower, Plantation High principal William Milano, and state representative Debby Sanderson; (back row) attorney Stephen McDonald, child-care worker Sheila Jenkins, and Fort Lauderdale Commissioner Jim Naugle. Naugle has since gone on to become the mayor of Fort Lauderdale, Sanderson now serves in the Florida Senate, Milano is principal at Taravella High, and Trower is the CEO of the North Broward Hospital District.

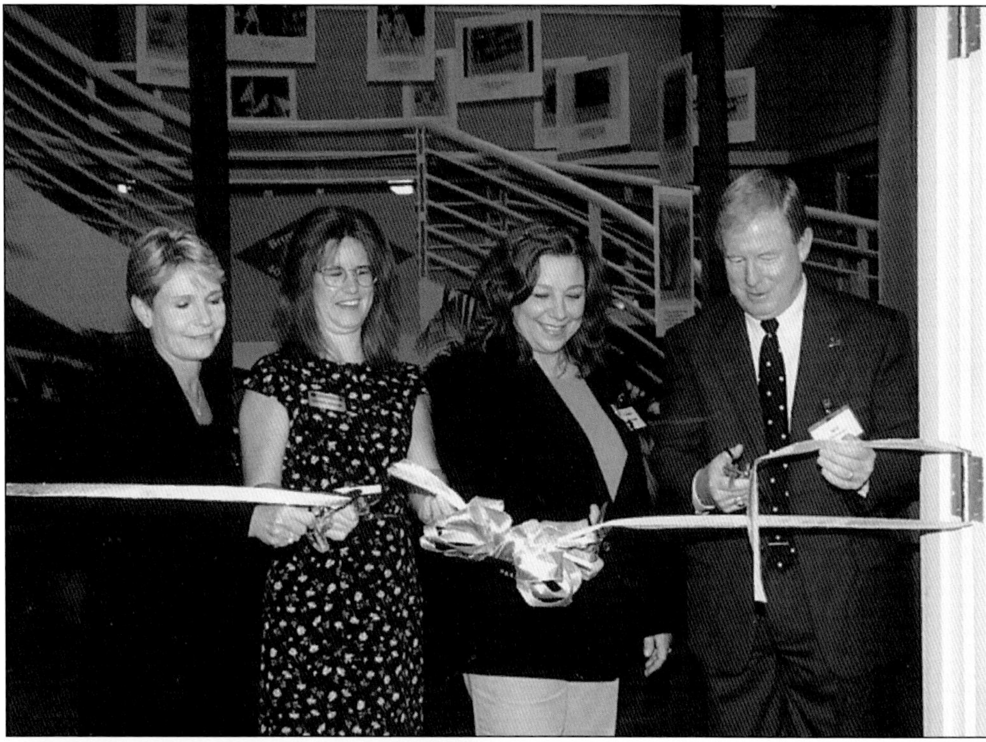

Central Campus Provost Dr. Patricia Caldwell, Trustees Cheryl Krause and Georgette Sosa Douglass, and Dr. Holcombe cut the ribbon opening a 40-year photographic retrospective at Central Campus for the 40th anniversary of the college.

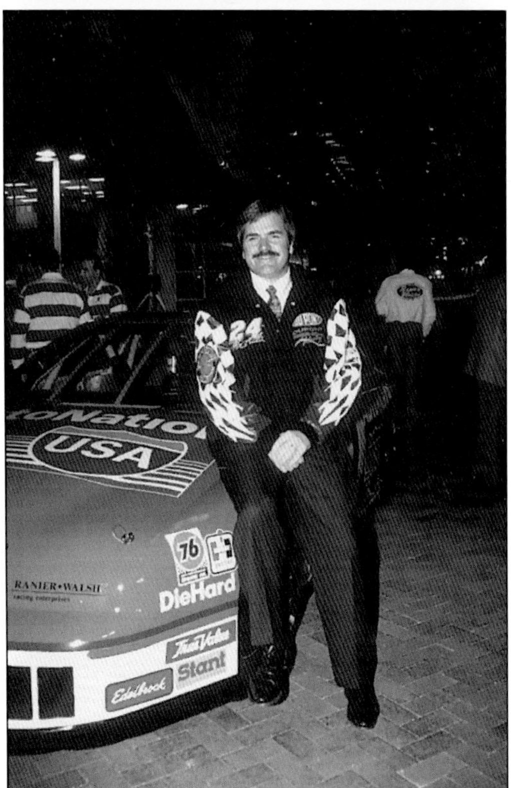


BCC graduates are local, state, and national leaders. One of the business giants of Broward County, Steve Berrard has served as the president and chief executive officer of a variety of local and national companies, including Blockbuster Entertainment Group and Republic Industries. He currently is one of the founders of New River Capital Partners. He was named winner of the Sun-Sentinel's Excalibur Award in 1995 and recipient of the LeRoy Collins Distinguished Alumni Award in 1996.

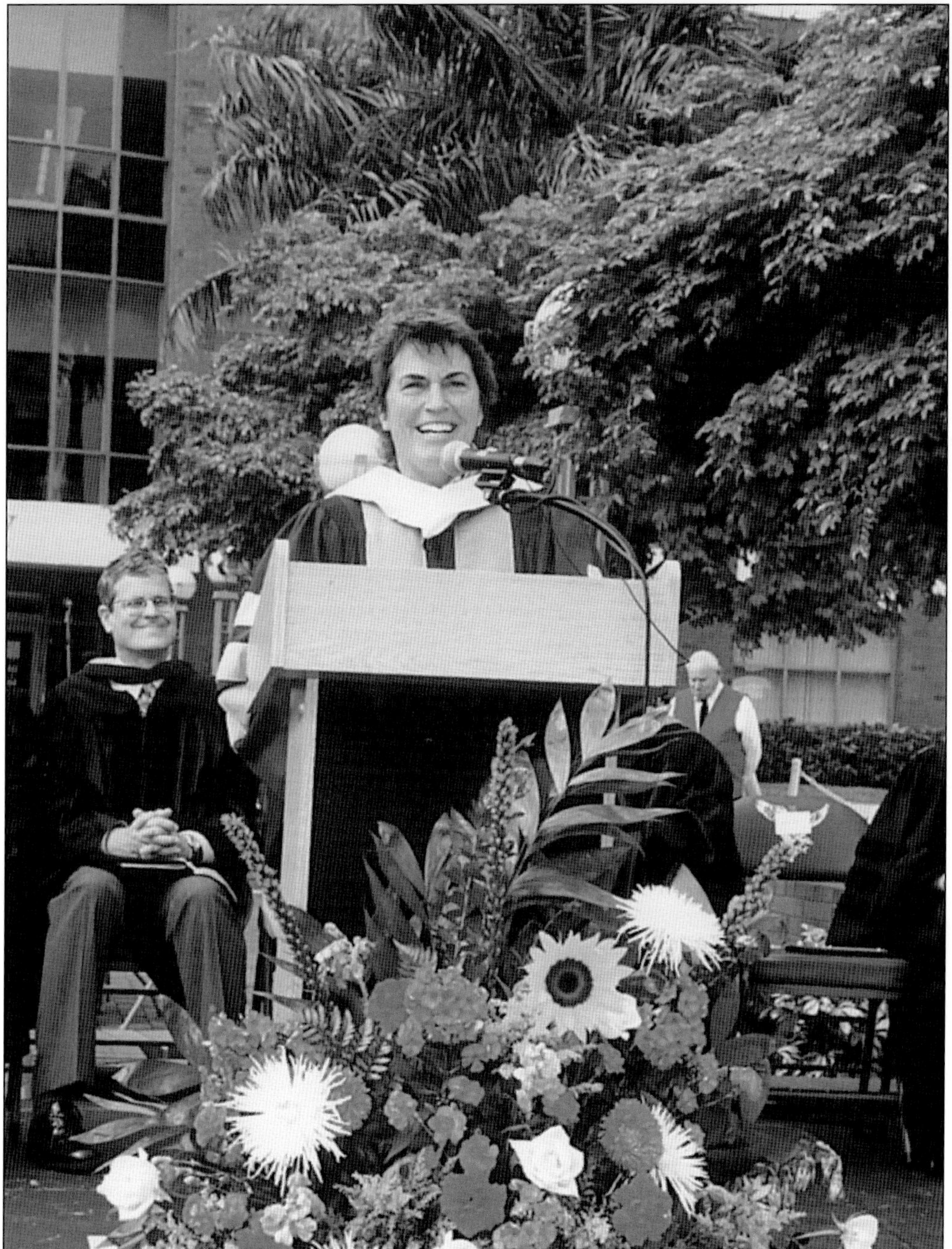

Author and screenwriter Rita Mae Brown, a member of the Class of 1965 and a 1999 recipient of the American Association of Community College's Outstanding Alumni Award, addressed the graduates at the May 2001 commencement exercises as Dr. Steve Obenauf, Central Campus Professor of the Year, listened. Four months before the September 11 tragedy, Brown told the graduates that many of America's problems stemmed from the county's wealth and power. "Sisters and brothers, pick up an oar and row," she told them. "We are all in the same boat together."

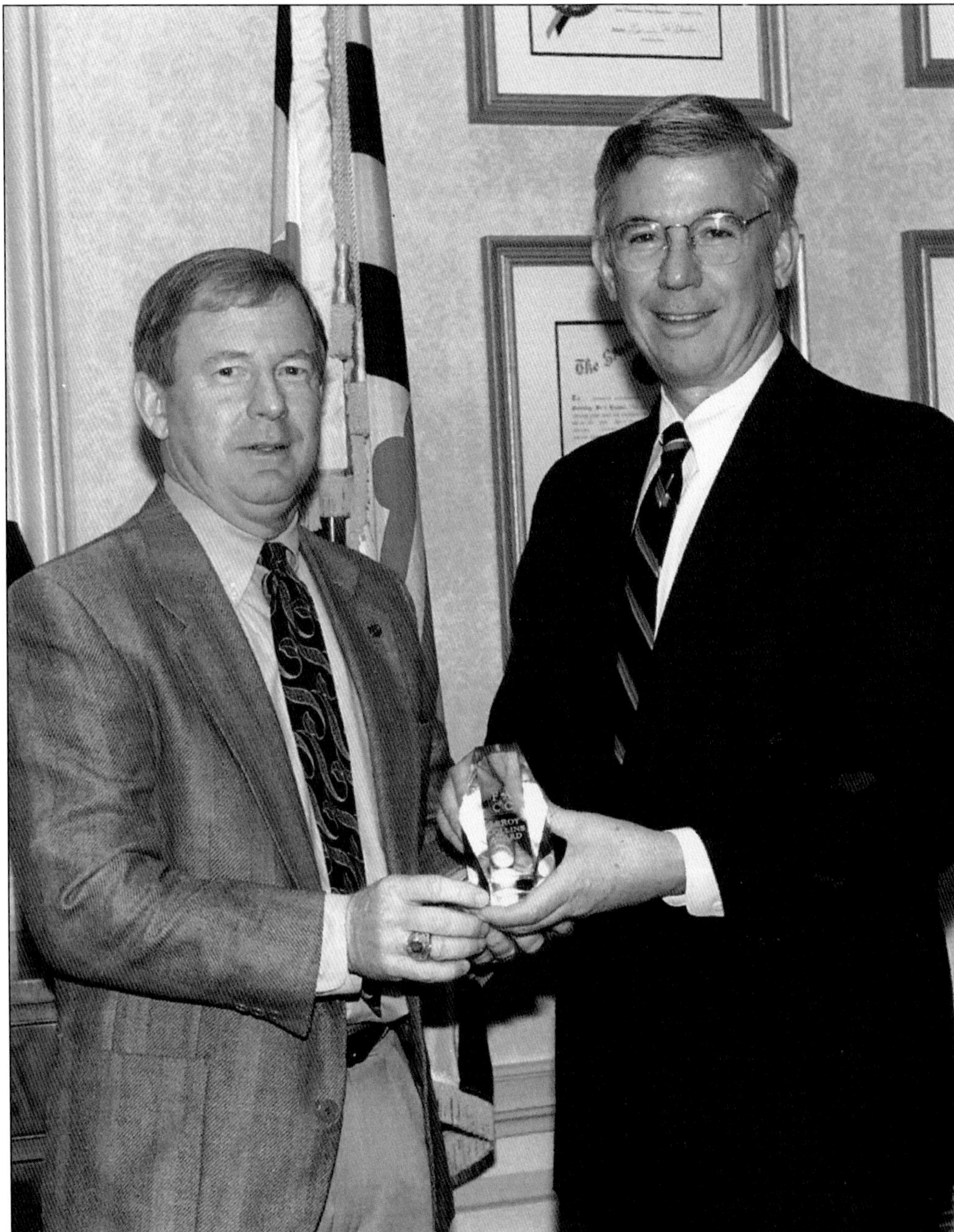

Two-term Maryland governor Parris Glendening was named one of the AACC's Outstanding Alumni Award winners for 1997. Glendening was a member of BCC's first graduating class and the youngest student in Florida State history to receive a doctorate in political science. In this picture, he receives his AACC award from Dr. Holcombe in Maryland.

A high school dropout, Gary Farmer came to realize the importance of higher education while serving in the Marines. After his discharge, he worked nights as a desk clerk and auditor at a beach motel to support his family while he attended classes at BCC. Today he serves as one of 12 appellate judges on Florida's Fourth District Court of Appeal in West Palm Beach.

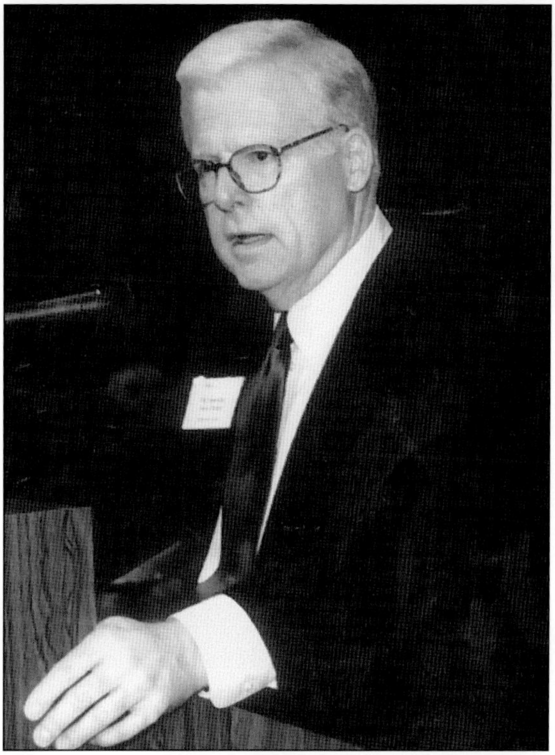

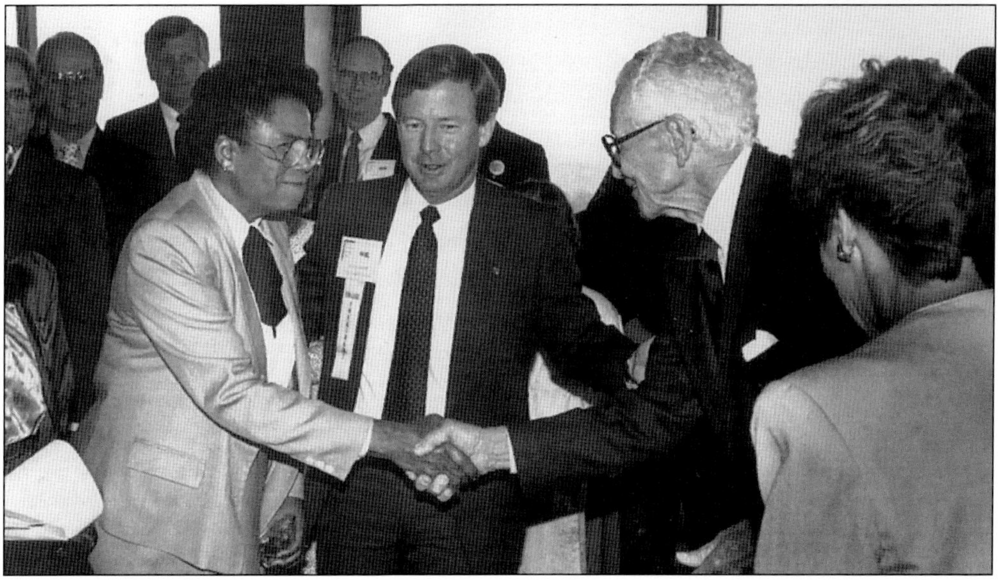

Evelyn Hardy, born in poverty in rural Alabama, used BCC as a stepping stone to higher education. After bearing 10 children and then becoming a widow, she decided her life needed a new direction. She got her General Equivalency Diploma (GED) and went to BCC, where she attained honors. She went on to receive her bachelor's and master's degrees and was named recipient of a LeRoy Collins Distinguished Alumni Award in 1990. Hardy returned to BCC to work as a counselor on North Campus. She is shown meeting former governor Collins at the first Collins Awards ceremony. Collins was the guiding force behind community colleges in Florida.

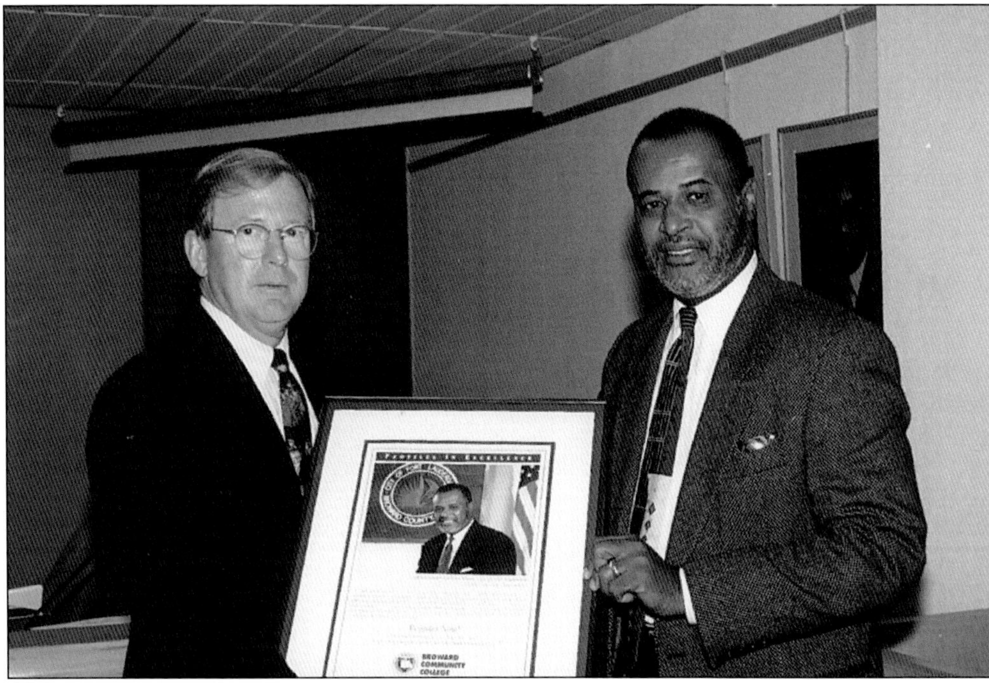

Carlton Moore, a Fort Lauderdale city commissioner, is also among BCC's Distinguished Award winners, as is his wife, Jasmine Shirley-Moore. Carlton Moore was named a recipient in 1988 and Jasmine Shirley-Moore, an epidemiologist, was named a recipient in 1989.

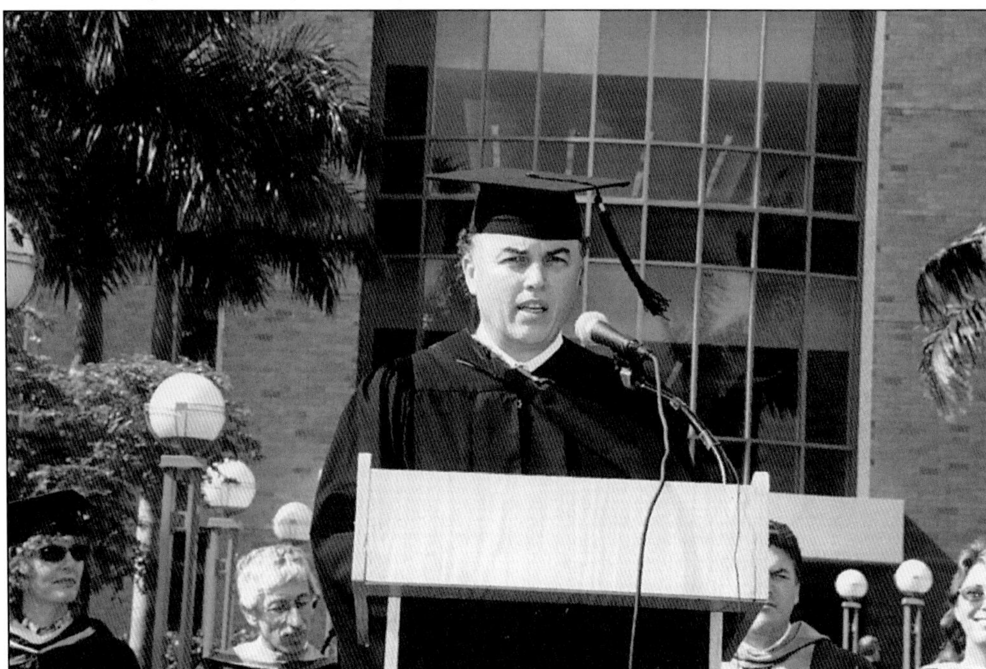

Arden Dickey, assistant vice president for circulation and call centers for Knight-Ridder Newspapers, is another recipient of a Distinguished Alumni Award. He also serves on the BCC Foundation board of directors.

Kimara March, who had been home-schooled until she began classes at BCC, was named Florida Community College Student of the Year by *Florida Leader* magazine in 1997. Also a member of the *USA Today* All-America Academic Team, March went on to the University of Florida, then to medical school at Georgetown University.

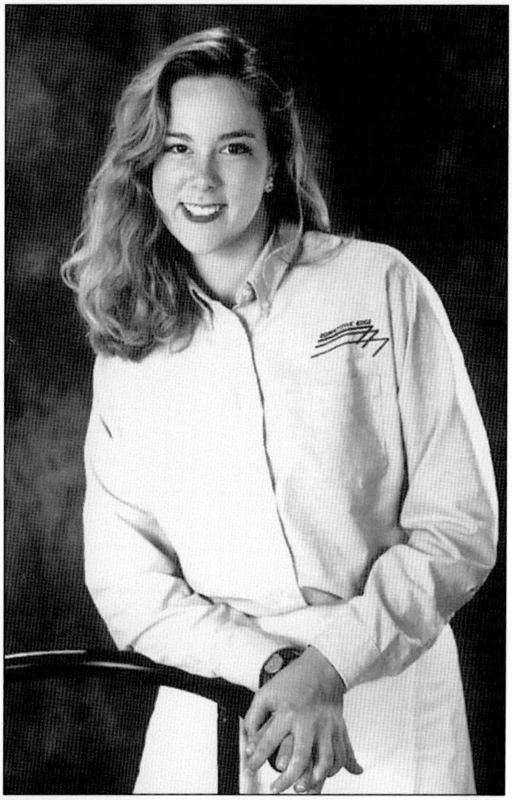

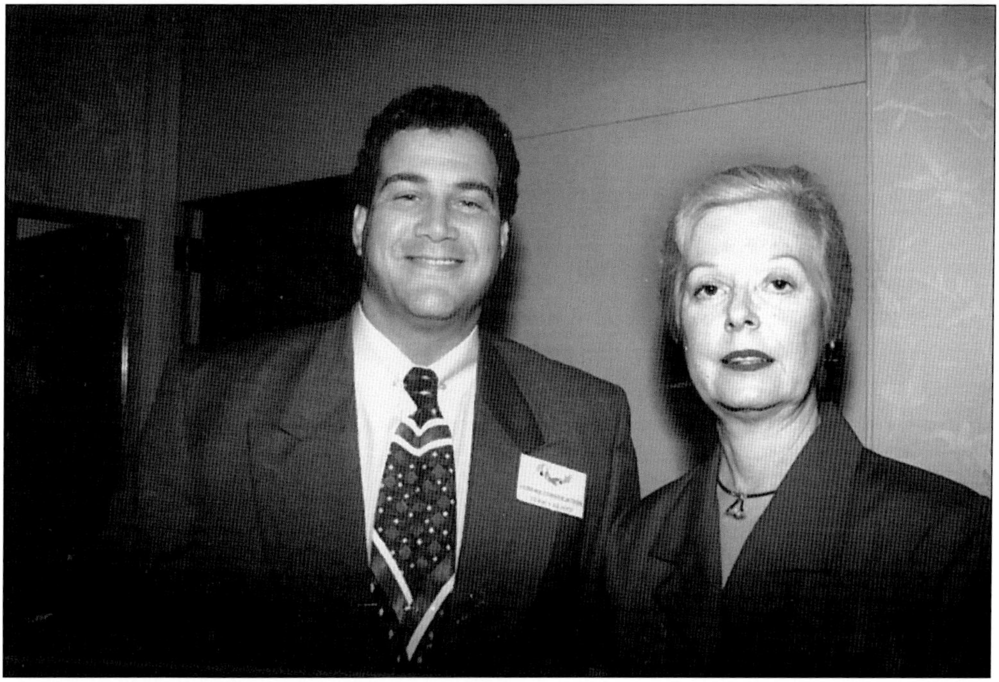

Electronic engineer Terry Glatt was awarded his Distinguished Alumni Award in 1996 by Dr. Jean Hunter, vice president for academic affairs.

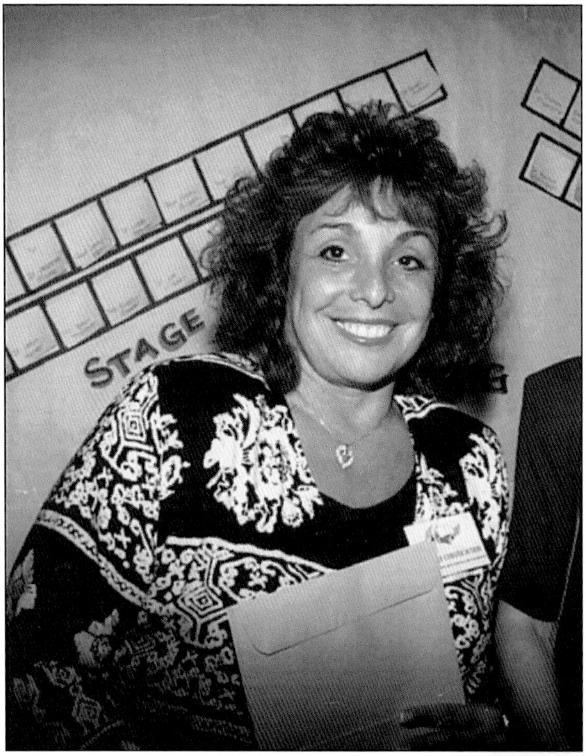


Some of BCC's best and brightest have returned to the college. Dr. Irmgard Bocchino, a Distinguished Alumni Award recipient in 1989, is now the director of the college's acclaimed Honors Institute.

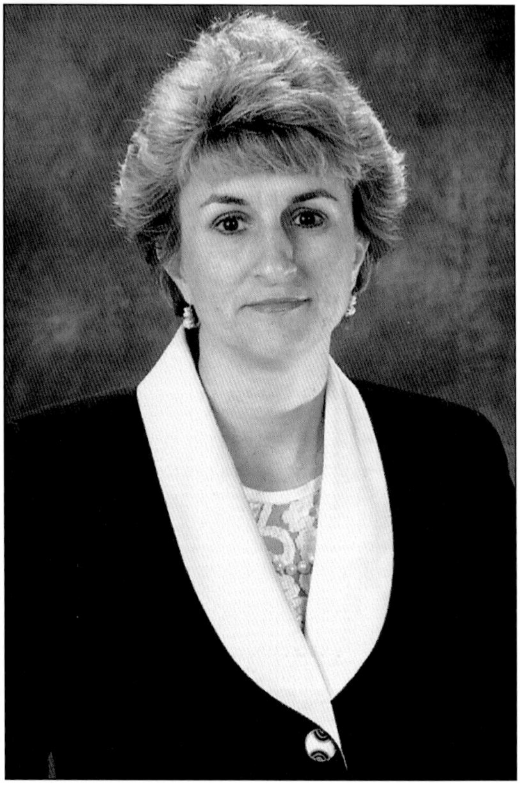

Dr. Deborah Sloan, a counselor at South Campus, became the first BCC graduate to be named recipient of an endowed teaching chair from the BCC Foundation in 1998.

Under the direction of Dr. William Greene, a BCC graduate and 1987 Distinguished Alumni Award recipient, the college's International Education Institute has established itself as one of the nation's most comprehensive programs.

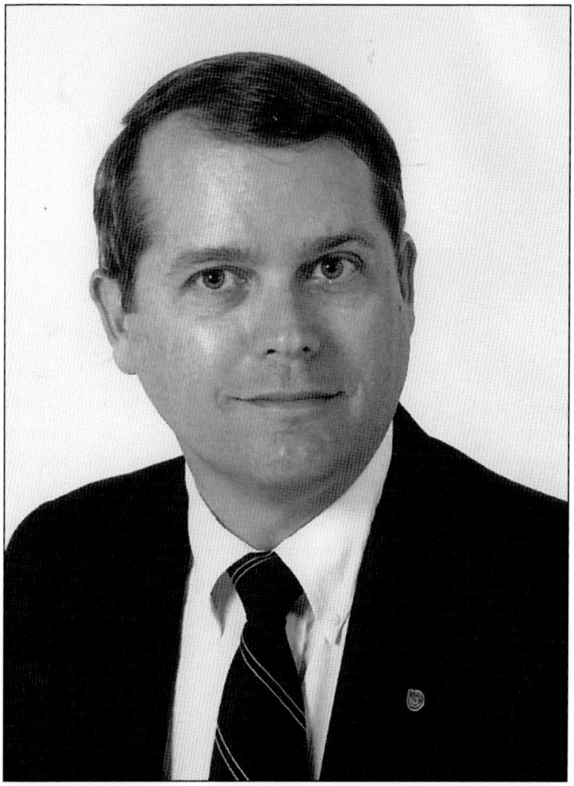

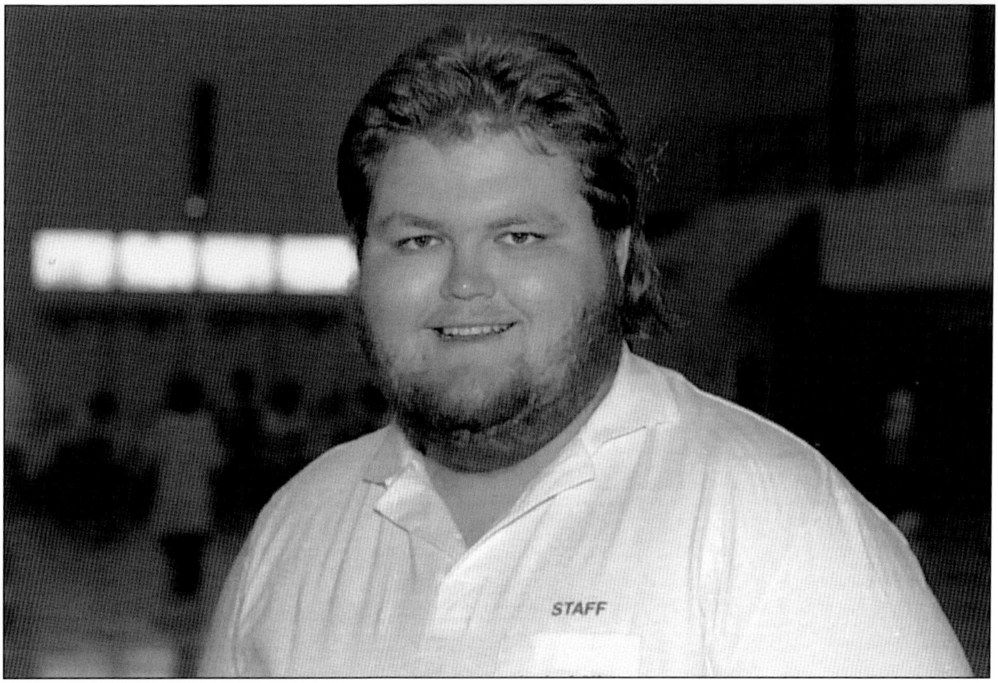


Charles Lyle, South Campus Student Life coordinator, is among the many BCC graduates who serve on the college staff with distinction.

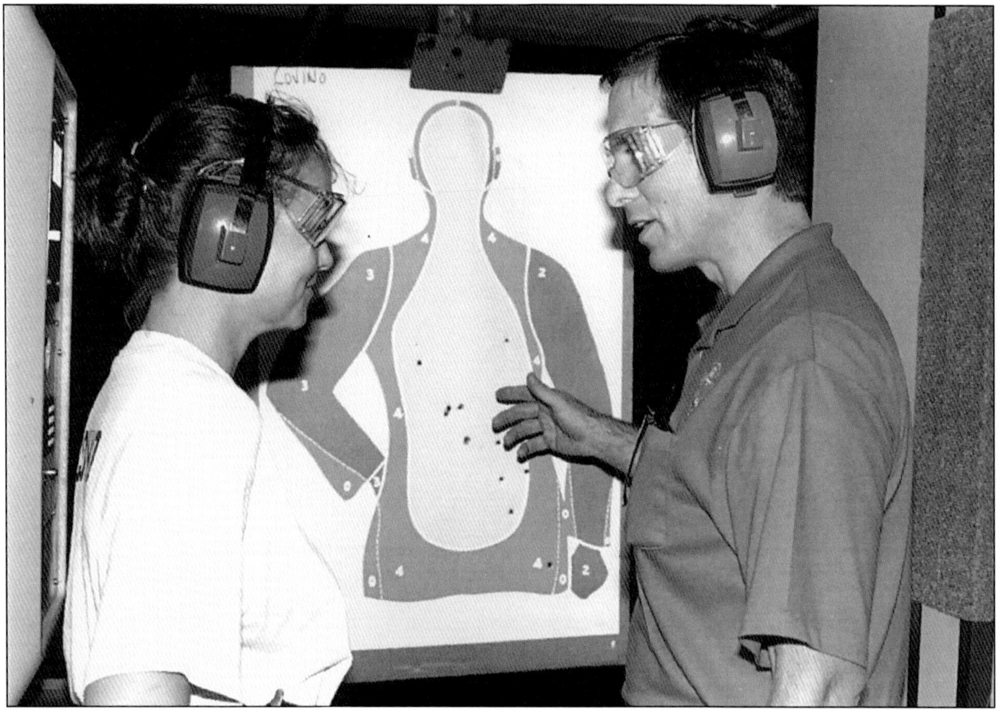

Whether back on campus or out in the community, BCC graduates distinguish themselves in many fields. One hundred percent of Broward County's law enforcement officers are trained at the college.

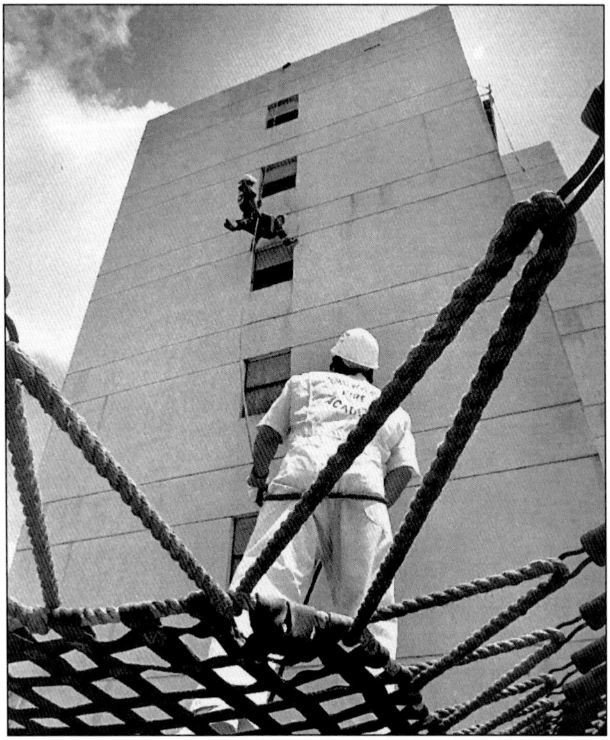

BCC also trains firefighters to protect property and save lives, and trains EMTs and paramedics to provide emergency care for the ill and injured.

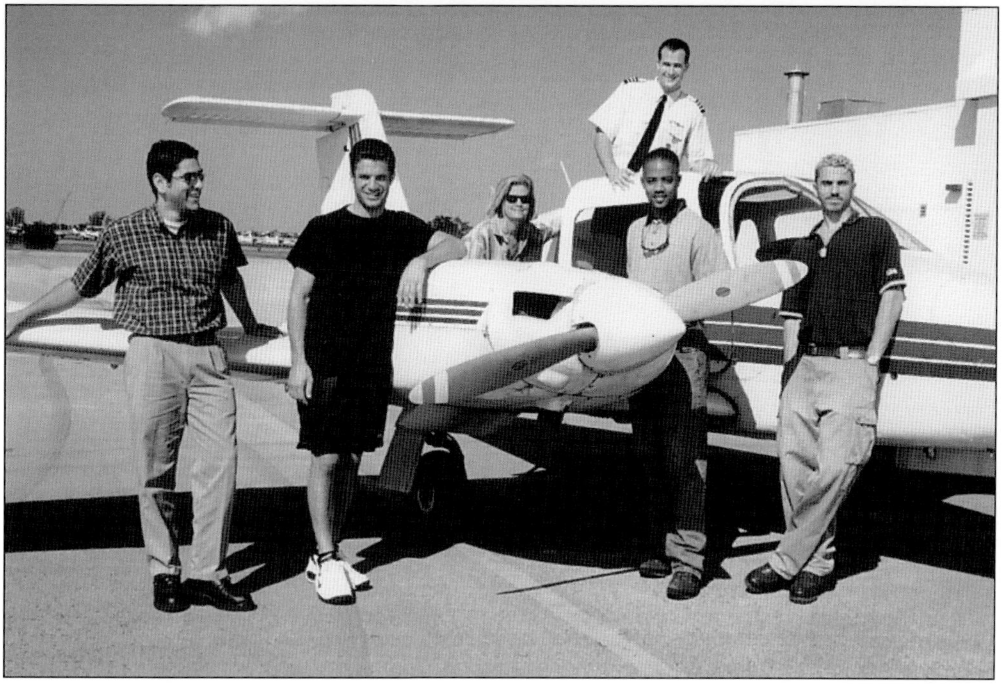

The Aviation Institute on South Campus offers the state's most comprehensive training center for students pursuing a career in aviation.

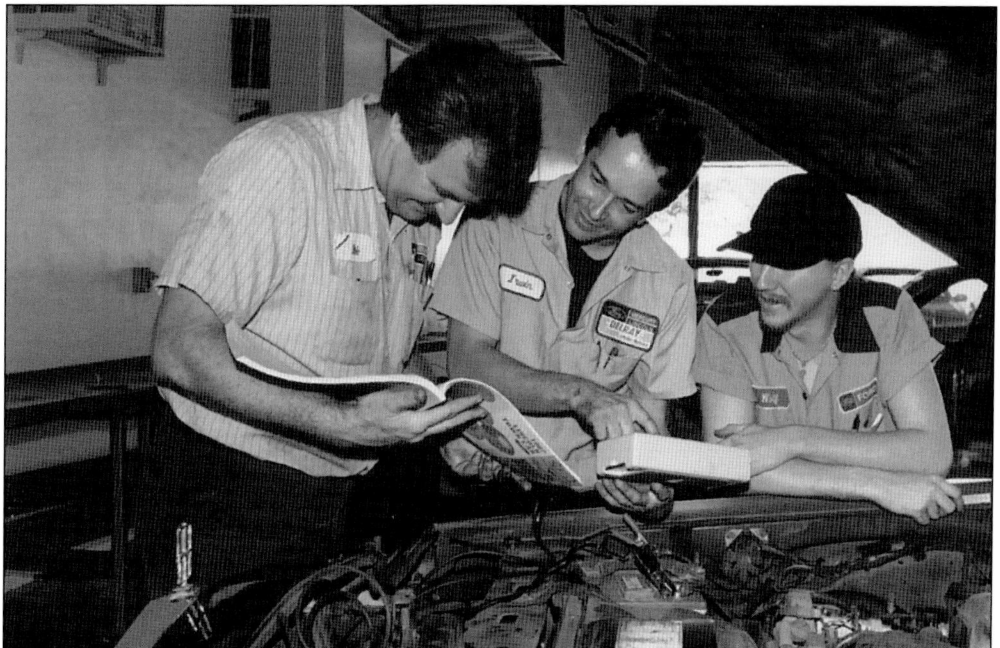

Today's automobiles require technicians with a strong knowledge of mechanics and computer technology. BCC's Miramar Center will become one of the nation's leaders and provide training of automotive technicians for all of South Florida.

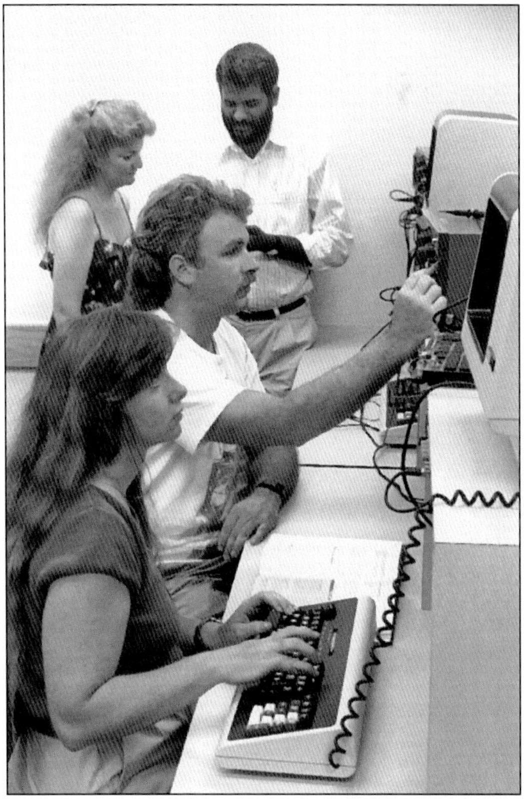

The Electronic Engineering Technology program on North Campus has been recognized as one of the nation's best and helps meet the needs of employers on South Florida's Silicon Beach. Technology has changed radically since 1992, when this picture was taken.

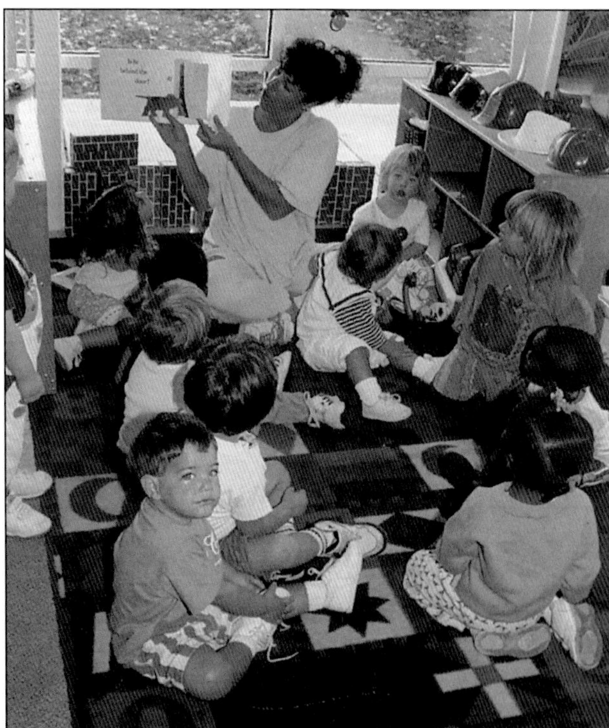

BCC offers childcare programs for the children of its students and staff and offers outstanding programs in Early Childhood Education. Programs in Continuing Education offer classes for daycare providers.

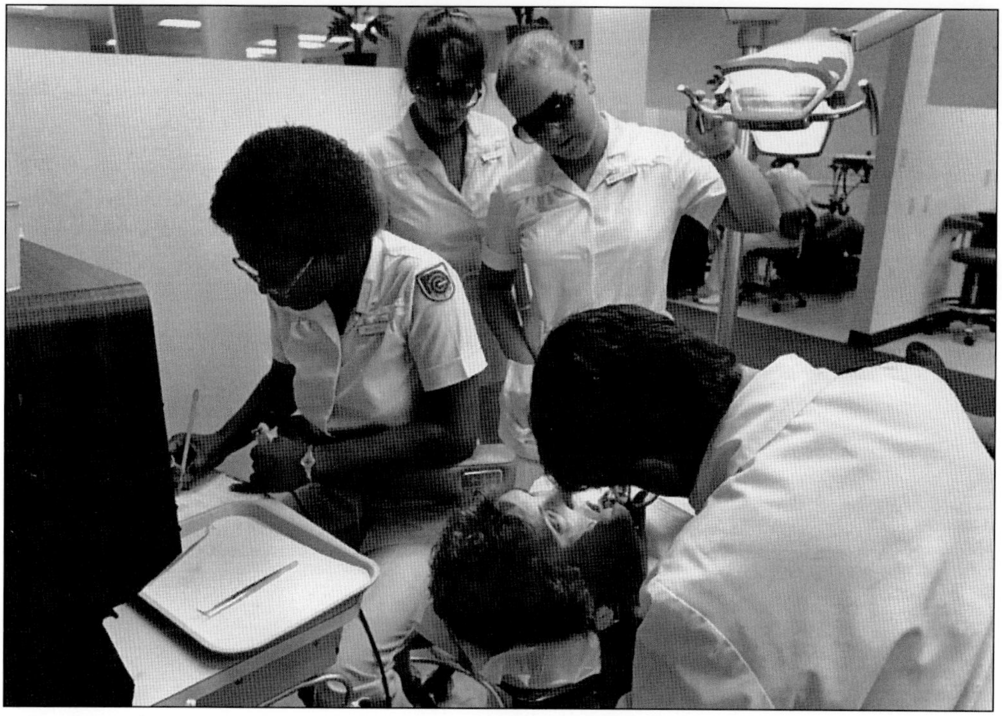

BCC trains about 80 percent of the allied health workers in Broward County, from dental assistants and hygienists to physical therapy assistants, massage therapists, and technicians in a variety of fields such as diagnostic sonography and radiography.

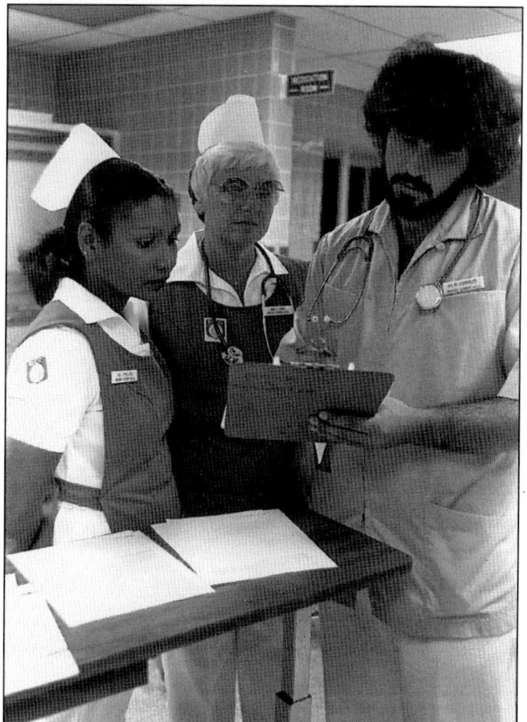

BCC and area healthcare providers have teamed up to offer full scholarships for nursing students and the promise of employment after graduation

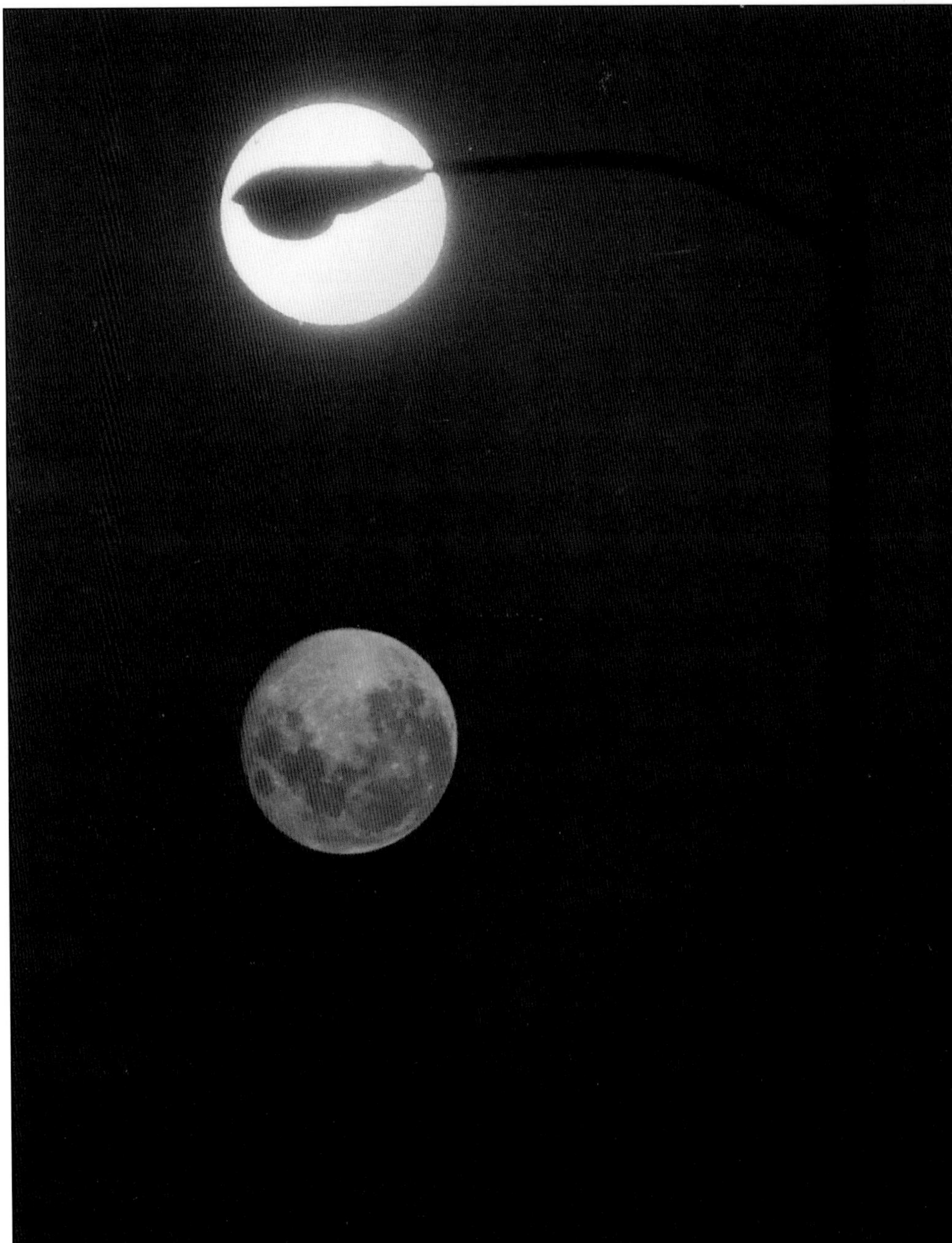

In its 40-plus years, BCC has positioned itself as one of America's finest community colleges, but as a relatively young institution of higher learning, the sky is still the limit.